AF707259

SOVEREIGNTY IN ACTION

Sovereignty in premodern times evoked the dynastic figure of the 'sovereign' or territorial monarch. In modern times it became a more abstract idea, referring to the power of the state, later of the people or 'the popular sovereign' as articulated and refined through constitutional arrangements. Today these inherited understandings of sovereignty confront various new challenges, including those of globalization, privatization of power and the rise of substate nationalism. An examination of key historical writers and trends from the seventeenth century onwards, including Hobbes, Bodin, Constant, Rousseau and Schmitt, brings out these developments and challenges. Sovereignty remains a malleable and 'active' feature of the global configuration of power. Will sovereignty become a redundant concept over time, or will it remain a key part of the grammar of modern politics?

BAS LEIJSSENAAR works at the Centre for Ethics, Social and Political Philosophy at KU Leuven. His research is focused on theories of sovereignty and constituent power in nineteenth-century and contemporary debates. The aim of his PhD project, funded by the Research Foundation Flanders (FWO), is to develop a pluralist conception of constituent power. He is one of four founding members of the Constituent Power Network, an international research network dedicated to the study of constituent power from interdisciplinary perspectives.

NEIL WALKER holds the Regius Chair of Public Law and the Law of Nature and Nations at the University of Edinburgh. His main area of expertise is constitutional theory. He has published extensively on the constitutional dimension of legal order at substate, state, supranational and global levels. He was Professor of European Law at the European University Institute in Florence (2000–2008) and has held various visiting appointments. His most recent books include *Intimations of Global Law* (2015) and *The Scottish Independence Referendum: Constitutional and Political Implications* (co-edited with Aileen McHarg, Tom Mullen and Alan Page, 2016).

SOVEREIGNTY IN ACTION

Edited by

BAS LEIJSSENAAR

KU Leuven

NEIL WALKER

University of Edinburgh

CAMBRIDGE
UNIVERSITY PRESS

CAMBRIDGE
UNIVERSITY PRESS

University Printing House, Cambridge CB2 8BS, United Kingdom

One Liberty Plaza, 20th Floor, New York, NY 10006, USA

477 Williamstown Road, Port Melbourne, VIC 3207, Australia

314-321, 3rd Floor, Plot 3, Splendor Forum, Jasola District Centre, New Delhi - 110025, India

79 Anson Road, #06-04/06, Singapore 079906

Cambridge University Press is part of the University of Cambridge.

It furthers the University's mission by disseminating knowledge in the pursuit of education, learning and research at the highest international levels of excellence.

www.cambridge.org
Information on this title: www.cambridge.org/9781108483513
DOI: 10.1017/9781108692502

© Cambridge University Press 2019

This publication is in copyright. Subject to statutory exception and to the provisions of relevant collective licensing agreements, no reproduction of any part may take place without the written permission of Cambridge University Press.

First published 2019

A catalogue record for this publication is available from the British Library

ISBN 978-1-108-48351-3 Hardback
ISBN 978-1-108-72876-8 Paperback

Cambridge University Press has no responsibility for the persistence or accuracy of URLs for external or third-party internet websites referred to in this publication, and does not guarantee that any content on such websites is, or will remain, accurate or appropriate.

CONTENTS

CONTRIBUTORS

OLGA BASHKINA is a researcher at the Institute of Philosophy, KU Leuven.

JASON FRANK is Robert J. Katz Chair of Government at Cornell University.

STEPHANIE FRANK is Associate Professor in Religion and Humanities in the Humanities, History, and Social Sciences Department at Columbia College, Chicago.

RAF GEENENS is Associate Professor in Ethics and Legal Philosophy at the Institute of Philosophy, KU Leuven.

DIETER GRIMM is Professor of Law at Humboldt University Berlin and former Justice of the Federal Constitutional Court of Germany.

BAS LEIJSSENAAR is a researcher at the Institute of Philosophy, KU Leuven.

PASQUALE PASQUINO is Distinguished Professor in Law and Politics at New York University and Research Professor at CRNS in Paris.

NORA TIMMERMANS is a researcher at the Institute of Philosophy, KU Leuven.

MIGUEL VATTER is Professor of Political Science in the College of Business, Government and Law at Flinders University.

NEIL WALKER is Regius Professor of Public Law and the Law of Nature and Nations at the University of Edinburgh.

PREFACE

This book emerged from discussions during the international conference 'Images of Sovereignty', held at KU Leuven in June 2017, where each of the contributors to this volume presented a version of their chapter. The conference, organized in the context of the research project 'Sovereignty in the Belgian Constitution: Its 1831 Meaning and Its Implications for Citizen Participation Today', was generously sponsored by the Research Foundation Flanders (FWO) and KU Leuven's Institute of Philosophy, Centre for Ethics, Social and Political Philosophy and Doctoral School for the Humanities. One editor, Bas Leijssenaar, is a member of the 'Sovereignty in the Belgian Constitution' project, which is attached to the Leuven Institute of Philosophy. The other editor, Neil Walker, was based in the Institute throughout the Spring 2017 semester as the International Francqui Professor.

Thanks are due to a number of people for their help in bringing this collection to fruition. The preparation of the manuscript has benefited from the invaluable logistical support of Finola O'Sullivan, executive publisher of law at Cambridge University Press, and Marianne Nield, editorial assistant at Cambridge University Press. The project also received much initial stimulus from the contribution of the many other participants to the Leuven conference – both those who prepared their own research papers or focused comments on the papers of the contributors and the various other local faculty, students and international academic guests and visitors who engaged more informally. Last, but by no means least, we are grateful to Raf Geenens, who leads the 'Sovereignty in the Belgian Constitution Project'. He helped in many ways – not just as contributor, funder and supporter but also by suggesting the simple but effective form of words that supplies the title to our collection.

Bas Leijssenaar and Neil Walker

Introduction

Sovereignty in Action

BAS LEIJSSENAAR AND NEIL WALKER

1 Sovereignty (Re)activated

Sovereignty is the 'boomerang' concept of Western legal and political thought. For all the best efforts of scholars, politicians, lawyers and citizens to consign it to oblivion, sovereignty always returns, typically with a vengeance. The more its normative and explanatory force and its political valence are challenged, the more ubiquitous the concept of sovereignty seems to become. Unsurprisingly then, despite the recent intensification of supranational and transnational patterns of legal and political authority, once believed to be one more – and perhaps final – nail in sovereignty's coffin, we stand today at yet another critical juncture, with sovereignty flying back in our faces.

Sovereignty's tendency to 'stir' whenever its demise is threatened seems significant, but it is not immediately clear why. Does sovereignty's apparent inescapability suggest something about the deep and resilient institutional structure of Western societies, or does its resonance have cultural roots – speaking to an understandable but problematic longing for a past that never was, a 'golden era' of unchallenged, autonomous statehood? Or does it perhaps indicate sovereignty's propensity to adjust and reconstruct itself under new conditions and in response to new sets of problems?

Whatever account we give of the pressure that sovereignty is under today, and however we understand or envisage the response to that pressure, there is widespread agreement in most of the recent literature that sovereignty – particularly the modern tradition of popular sovereignty – *is* under pressure. Some writers have declared the concept at odds with the fragmented, multipolar and multi-layered integration and development of European and other international and transnational political and legal systems. They have pointed out that the spread of governance technologies to which democratic input becomes increasingly remote has altered the political architecture in ways that challenge the centrality – and perhaps even the continuing relevance – of popular sovereignty. And it is also hard to ignore the increasing number of transnational political and legal projects that seek to overcome the sharp edges of the modern Westphalian system by reducing the scope of state sovereignty and enacting non-sovereign authoritative frameworks. Theoretically and practically then, the consensus seems to be that sovereignty – at least in its high modern, state-centred modality – can no longer provide an adequate framework for the explanation, justification and organisation of legal and political authority. In this vein, scholars have either rejected sovereignty as a concept no longer able to make sense of emerging patterns of political and legal authority,[1] or they have tried to modify or weaken the concept by means of its 'fragmenting',[2] 'layering',[3] 'pooling'[4] or 'mixing'[5]. Hence, the ubiquitous claims of sovereignty's 'conflict',[6] 'transition',[7] 'slipping' and the proclamation of periods of 'competitive', 'cooperative', 'late-'[8] or 'post-'sovereignty. Even recent attempts to re-assert sovereignty's status as a fundamental legal and political category depict the sovereign as an inactive, 'sleeping' force.[9]

And yet, sovereignty is making a comeback. Most clearly so in the realm of political practice. Here, we witness populist movements and

[1] Joan Cocks, *On Sovereignty and Other Political Delusions* (Bloomsbury, 2014).

[2] Hent Kalmo and Quentin Skinner, *Sovereignty in Fragments: The Past, Present and Future of a Contested Concept* (Cambridge University Press, 2011).

[3] Thomas Ilgen, *Reconfigured Sovereignty: Multi-Layered Governance in the Global Age* (Aldershot: Ashgate, 2003).

[4] Bruno De Witte, 'Sovereignty and European Integration: The Weight of Legal Tradition', in: Anne Marie Slaughter, Alec Stone Sweet, & Joseph H. Weiler (eds.), *The European Courts and National Courts* (Hart, 1998).

[5] Richard Bellamy, *Sovereignty, Post-Sovereignty and Pre-Sovereignty: Three Models of the State, Democracy and Rights within the EU*, in: Neil Walker (ed.), *Sovereignty in Transition* (Hart, 2003).

[6] Samantha Besson, 'Sovereignty in Conflict', in: S. Tierney & C. Warbricks (eds.), *Towards an International Legal Community? The Sovereignty of States and the Sovereignty of International Law* (British Institute and Comparative Law, 2006).

[7] Neil Walker (ed.), *Sovereignty in Transition* (Hart, 2003).

[8] Neil Walker, 'Late Sovereignty in the European Union', in: *Sovereignty in Transition* (Hart, 2003).

[9] Richard Tuck, *The Sleeping Sovereign* (Cambridge University Press, 2016).

parties, sub-state groups vying for independence and illiberal, authoritarian governments alike relying on the language of (national) sovereignty to assert their autonomy against larger, encompassing legal and political structures. But sovereignty has also returned in the theoretical domain. Although its status as the 'master concept' of Western legal and political thought may never be fully restored, several scholars have sought to reinstate sovereignty as central to an emancipatory politics. Some have delved deep into the concept's chequered history and found, in the shadows of the dominant tradition of sovereignty as command, a democratic store of sovereign thinking revolving around the notion of constituent power. Antonio Negri, for example, argues that 'to speak of constituent power is to speak of democracy'.[10] Similarly, Andreas Kalyvas writes that constituent power is 'attuned to the emancipatory promises of popular sovereignty'.[11] For their part, legal scholars, and in particular constitutional lawyers with their longstanding preoccupation with the formal pedigree of political authority,[12] have renewed their insistence on the importance of (national) sovereignty as an anchor of democratic self-rule and a bulwark of effective citizen participation against the encroachment of higher-level governance and the forces of global capital.

Clearly then, the proliferation of legal and political orders beyond the state leads not only to a challenging of old sovereign (state) claims but also to the emergence of new claims to sovereignty at a variety of (state, non-state and post-state) sites. Sovereignty today, in other words, is a concept 'in action', whether that involves *re*action to its many threats and provocations or new forms of *pro*active practice under its expanding umbrella. Its enduring legacy in a not yet transcended Westphalian imaginary fuels increasingly frequent re-assertive claims of traditional state sovereignty. At the same time, it is used to frame claims to legal and political authority of sub-state (e.g. new nationalist movements) and supra-state (e.g. the EU) polities. Protest movements more generally, whether nationally embedded or border-crossing transnational movements, also increasingly tap into an imaginary of sovereignty or constituent power to substantiate their claims in the face of already constituted powers.

10 Antonio Negri, *Insurgencies* (University of Minnesota Press, 1999) 1.

11 Andreas Kalyvas, 'Popular Sovereignty, Democracy, and the Constituent Power', *Constellations* 12 (2) 2005, 225.

12 See, for example, the essays collected in Walker, *Sovereignty in Transition*.

Sovereign practices are thus undergoing a renaissance of sorts. Sometimes insidious, as witnessed in the recent rise of authoritarian, illiberal states framing their claims and actions in terms of nationalistic sovereign statehood. Sometimes farcical yet destabilising, as in the overblown 'America first' rhetoric (and selective practice) of Donald Trump. Sometimes dubious and deeply contentious, as in recent attempts of nation-states reasserting and demarcating their national sovereignty in the face of secessionist claims (e.g. Catalonia & Spain) or reclaiming sovereignty from more cooperative models of sovereignty (e.g. how Brexit was sold to the British electorate in terms of reclaiming national sovereignty). But in other cases, these new sovereign practices involve more rounded attempts to reclaim and renew the modern tradition of sovereignty as a model of popular self-government of a community of free and equal persons. Consider, for example, attempts to create a new sovereign authority based on a foundational collective commitment by plural *demoi* in (previously) fractured states such as South Africa.[13] Or consider the European Union's attempts to 'soften' the mutual exclusivity of Westphalian sovereignty by 'rationing' the sovereignty of its member states, or its attempts to accommodate in its multi-layered polity some version of the awakening sovereign self-consciousness among sub-state communities such as Scotland, Catalonia and Flanders. For all the difficulties of these developments, and their darker slipstreams, they also intimate a creative reconfiguration of legal and political arrangements stimulated by the activity of newly self-asserting sovereign actors.

Despite growing recognition that the concept of sovereignty remains an enduring – and variable – staple of political thought and reality, there are currently no collective studies dedicated to what we are calling 'sovereignty in action'. And so it is this headline that supplies the title, and the flagship theme, of the current volume. It is a theme that embraces the dynamic relationship between sovereignty and constituent power in the generation of old and new (*re*active and *pro*active) frames, claims and guides for collective action within, beneath and beyond the state. The chapters presented in this volume seek to illuminate various aspects of such sovereign activity. They situate sovereignty's political dimension in balance with its legal dimension. The historical dimension plays an especially important role in capturing the diachronies of sovereignty in

[13] Andrew Arato, *Adventures of the Constituent Power* (Cambridge University Press, 2017); G. O'Donnell and P. Schmitter, *Transitions from Authoritarian Rule: Tentative Conclusions About Uncertain Democracies* (Baltimore and London: Johns Hopkins University Press, 1986).

action. It does so whether as a means of identifying key crossroads within the long development of the concept across political modernity, or of illuminating tensions within more recent debate, or of understanding the roots of interventions aimed at articulating newly 'active' components within contemporary sovereigntist politics.

More generally, instead of focusing on the constancy of sovereignty's role as a core concept in the international order of states, the chapters in this volume emphasise sovereignty's iterative remodelling and resurgence as a bottom-up notion and its theoretical and practical role as an imaginative framework for collective action. Against the grain of that seam of contemporary scholarship that portrays a redundant or reduced role for sovereignty in the near future, or argues that sovereignty can only be maintained as an important legal and political concept at the state level, the present collection seeks to characterise sovereignty as an important and resilient legal and political action-framing concept in *and* beyond the state. Going beyond claims of sovereignty's 'waning'[14] and such like adjectives signalling its reduced significance, and, in a different register, the claim that the popular sovereign is largely dormant,[15] our authors take issue with the literature that all too easily declares sovereignty's demise and argue that the awakening and re-assertion of popular sovereignty can be considered in more flexible and adaptable terms. They discuss the prospects and pitfalls for sovereignty's (re-)activation and focus on the manifold ways in which sovereignty can be, has been and continues to become active through the constitutive work of social, legal and political actors and institutions.

In differing measures, all of the chapters in this volume combine theoretical analysis and commentary on sovereignty's institutional history and contemporary direction. They seek to understand pivotal political events as framed and shaped by emergent theoretical understanding of sovereignty, just as they trace the challenges to and refinements of sovereignty theory to the history of political events and the debates surrounding these events. Sovereignty in action – these chapters therefore instruct us – is both about situating history in its formative ideational and theoretical context and, reciprocally, about situating theory in its formative historical context. These complementary focal points of inquiry – historical events and patterns emerging from (and reacting upon) ideas, and ideas emerging from (and reacting upon) history – provide the volume with its organising logic. The

[14] Wendy Brown, *Walled States, Waning Sovereignty* (MIT Press, 2014).
[15] Tuck, *The Sleeping Sovereign.*

volume's early chapters – attentive to the long evolution of ideas about sovereignty in the history of political modernity (Part I – *Theory in History*) – return to hitherto understudied yet fundamental debates constitutive of sovereignty's meaning and use. And in their broad sweep they revisit a number of key points of conceptual innovation, including the so-called *Sattelzeit* of the late eighteenth and early nineteenth centuries, during which newly imagined and intensely theorised calls for (popular) sovereignty were the driving force for legal and political transformations in the American and French Revolutions. The volume's more focused historical-theoretical chapters (Part II – *History of Theory*) consider, in different ways, how variations in our deep conceptual frames reflect and capture the context-specific aesthetic, representational and institutional issues and dilemmas accompanying sovereignty's iterative manifestations. Across both parts of the book, however, there is a common general purpose. Each of the authors makes a concerted effort to connect the vital early modern events and debates on sovereignty with the developments and problems of today. Or, to put it in terms of our guiding 'action' theme, the authors are each, in their quite distinct approaches, interested in examining how the ways in which the sovereignty frame 'acts upon' events and 'is acted upon' by events today are intimately connected to the ways in which that frame 'acted upon' events and 'was acted upon' by events in the key formative period of political modernity.

2 An Outline of the Chapters

The chapters in the first section of the volume, *Theory in History*, provide a variety of reflections on the immediate and enduring relevance and influence of the sovereignty idea. Taken together, these offer a long historical perspective on the concept. They canvas sovereignty's gradual development in relation to a fluctuating set of conditions of possibility. Moreover, they provide a synoptic overview of the manifold ways in which sovereignty is in the process of adjusting itself to contemporary conditions. Although the authors in this section differ in the way they approach sovereignty, they converge on the idea that today's sovereignty discourse remains an active influence over our shifting legal and political constellation.

In his characteristically lucid style, *Dieter Grimm* declares the claim that we have now entered a post-sovereign era to be premature. Through a careful consideration of changes in the historical conditions under which sovereignty once emerged and how these changes affected it as a concept and as a practice, Grimm shows that we live in an unprecedented world in which public power is divided between national and supranational entities. Historically, the identity between public power and state power was the nexus that tied together differing conceptions of sovereignty. In this light, the ongoing transfer of sovereign rights and competences from states to supranational institutions poses a fundamental challenge to sovereignty's viability as the organising axiom of Western legal and political thought. Public power now also exists outside the state. Yet, as Grimm shows, the concept's history is one of regular adjustment between theory and practice. Since the advent of the modern constitutional state, sovereignty has been progressively 'tamed', both internally and, with some delay, externally. The division of public powers between national and supranational powers is just another phase in that process. It does not follow, Grimm argues, that sovereignty is now divided, abolished, or transferred to supranational institutions. Sovereignty is merely *limited* by international law. Supranational bodies do not have state-like self-determination regarding their existence and competences, and they have seldom if ever claimed sovereignty. The key to understanding our current predicament, therefore, is to distinguish between public powers and sovereignty. Public powers can be transferred while sovereignty is retained. States have not yet thinned down their set of competencies to such a degree that they can no longer reasonably claim to be sovereign. Crucially, rather than declaring sovereignty obsolete, Grimm argues that it is worthy of defence. Now tamed, sovereignty can no longer justify wars of aggression, nor can it be relied on to systematically violate human rights. But importantly, contemporary sovereignty still leaves space for – even protects – democratic self-determination, which for the time being still depends on a bounded citizenry that shares a political identity and is capable of collective action. These conditions are presently much stronger in states than in supranational organisations. Rather than a post-sovereign era, Grimm concludes, ours is one in which sovereignty can be a haven of democracy against the encroachment of international authorities.

Whereas Dieter Grimm approaches the present state of sovereignty from a deep historical perspective, *Neil Walker*, while also grounding his study in the historical origins of modern sovereignty, takes a more contemporary approach in order to probe the limitations and indispensability of a sovereignty-centred approach. He aims to overcome, or at least challenge, the reductive logic of the recently revived Hobbesian metaphor of a 'sleeping sovereign'[16] – a dormant underlying power only

[16] Tuck, *The Sleeping Sovereign.*

occasionally roused to action – by inviting us to consider instead the adjusted figure of the 'stirring sovereign'. The Hobbesian imaginary, Walker writes, leads to settlement bias and precludes or marginalises the activities of putative sovereigns who seek to rouse themselves within and beyond the boundaries of existing political communities. The universality of form, comprehensiveness of authority, and mutual exclusivity of claims of Hobbes's paradigmatic state-sovereigntist figure fits uneasily with today's highly differentiated mosaic of legal and political entities. The image of sovereign stirrings, Walker claims, provides a better grip on the increasingly complex and interlocking patterns of authority and contestation that have emerged in the global political sphere. The stirring metaphor helps us escape the binary understanding of sovereignty, shifting our focus to the multiplicity of actors, activities, factors and processes involved in the emergence of sovereigntist actors and claims. Walker identifies four 'stirring tendencies': the *reassembling* of sovereignty in more elaborate and inclusive democratic procedures; the *raising* of sovereignty through territorial claims that challenge or reassert the present pattern of sovereign authority; the *rationing* of sovereignty by supranational or transnational bodies to overcome the omnipotence of sovereign entities by distributing sovereignty over a set of overlapping and interacting bodies; and the more reactionary *reassertion* or reaffirmation of (national) sovereignty in response to challenges associated with reassembling, raising and rationing. Unlike the image of a sleeping sovereign, these modes of sovereign stirring allow us to make sense of the patterns of innovation in sovereigntist claims-making and politics, while reminding us of certain timeless framing patterns and associated limitations inherent in the deep structure of the sovereign imaginary.

Wary of recent attempts to theorise the people as an abstract legal entity and bring popular constituent power into the fold of liberal constitutionalism, *Jason Frank* draws our attention to an issue largely neglected by democratic theorists: popular manifestation. Rather than treating such manifestation as a measure of collective identity or a source of legitimacy, this aesthetic-political inquiry into forms of public political display is concerned with the varied detail of how 'the people out of doors' appear, self-present and act. In his unique brand of historically inflected political theory, Frank shows the importance of the various modes of popular assembly outside established legal authority and authorised procedures. Popular manifestation played a crucial role in the development of the democratic idea that collectives can act deliberately, that the people can manifest itself as a collective actor capable of facilitating political change. Thus, Frank argues, democratic theorists should not approach popular constituent power as a juridical problem, or at least should not do so exclusively, but as a complex and dynamic political process that is mobilised and enacted in a range of ways. The problem of accommodating popular manifestation within a sovereigntist politics was recognised by major writers such as Carl Schmitt, Giorgio Agamben and Claude Lefort, but, as Frank shows, their emphasis on incarnation, incorporation and identity rather than appearance and collective enactment caused them to misrecognise its singular importance. Their otherwise divergent interpretations of popular manifestations coalesce in the more familiar framework of political theology, and so in a tendency to relate and reduce such manifestations to a sacralised (con)figuration of authority. Frank's contribution instead clears the ground for a fuller articulation of a theory of popular manifestation as part and parcel of a contested politics of democratic representation.

Raf Geenens returns to some of the issues that exercised Dieter Grimm in the opening chapter. He stands against a trend in the recent literature that, in response to cumulative challenges to the pre-eminence of a robust state-centred conception of political authority, holds that the concept of sovereignty has become conceptually incoherent and empirically redundant. He argues that we must rescue sovereignty because it might be our last vestige of resistance against the encroachment of global capitalism upon structures of democratic self-government. Geenens proceeds to defend a downsized but not emaciated conception of sovereignty as autonomy. Stripping the concept to its essentials, he contends that sovereignty's core purpose concerns the very possibility of consciously steering society. Rid of connotations of supreme and undivided power, sovereignty refers to the perspective a community adopts when it sees itself as collectively autonomous. Sovereignty therefore plays out at the level of our collective 'self-image'. It allows citizens to adopt a perspective from which they see themselves as a collective agent capable of autonomously choosing its own course.

The idea of sovereignty in action also guides the reflections in the second part of this volume, *History of Theory*. Its chapters focus on key moments or trends in sovereignty's history in which new manifestations of political power, critical junctures of political authority or shifting conditions of political possibility have led to innovations not only in practice but also in the theoretical conceptualisation of sovereignty, with its attendant aesthetic, representational and institutional dimensions.

Miguel Vatter argues that instead of constitutionally separating sovereignty and government, liberal constitutional thinking under the sign of contemporary 'public law' tends to turn sovereignty into the instrument of government. Rather than limiting government, Vatter claims, a constitutionalism based on the public law idea of a 'sleeping sovereign' produces a discourse that undoes any limitations on government. Vatter's chapter is distinctive in how it ties together debates on sovereignty, constitutionalism, neoliberalism and republicanism. Yet its core innovation consists of a novel interpretation of Ernst Kantorowicz's classic *The King's Two Bodies*. Overlooked in the recent recovery of 'public law' by scholars such as Martin Loughlin, Richard Tuck, Dieter Grimm and Quentin Skinner, Kantorowicz developed an innovative theory of political theology which he brought to bear on the origins of modern constitutionalism. Through his engagement with Kantorowicz, Vatter tells a cautionary story, criticising the dominant contemporary public law conception of sovereignty, according to which state sovereignty employs constitutionalism to limit government. Under the metapolitical narrative often associated with this conception, neoliberalism has emerged as a threat against which state sovereignty must be protected. But according to Vatter, the public law-centred conception of sovereignty, with its historically rooted suspicion of the unbridled sovereign, *in fact* leads to government assuming constituent power and employing constitutionalism in order to limit the political life of citizens. In Vatter's perspective, then, a public law conception of sovereignty, rather than a protection from or counterpoint to neoliberalism, is the condition of possibility for neoliberal governmentality to emerge. If sovereignty is to remain a viable concept to counteract the ongoing symbiosis between neoliberalism and global constitutionalism, Vatter concludes, we need instead an alert republican sovereign, not a sleeping one.

Pasquale Pasquino explores the double role of the people as both constituent and constituted power in our constitutional imaginary. These 'two bodies' of the people reflect the complex genealogy of constitutional thought. Not until Sieyès and his efforts both to justify and set limits on the prerogatives of the monarchical sovereignty of the early modern French state, did we acquire the basic distinction between constituent and constituted power, and so the conceptual means for the double invocation of the people. Pasquino's reflections dwell on the modern, post-Sieyès concept of popular sovereignty as constituent power. He shows that the constituent power of the people is the foundational principle of the contemporary constitutional state's framework of limited power. Although fully sovereign during the foundational moment, the people's constituent power is neither fully maintained nor fully exhausted within the constitutional framework it establishes. Rather, the people reappear within their constitutional order as one of several constituted powers. The *undivided* power of the constituent people, in other words, is the condition sine qua non of the constituted system of *divided* governmental powers, in which the people figure once more, but as only one component.

In her chapter, *Olga Bashkina* raises and addresses sovereignty's most urgent contemporary question through a recovery of sovereignty's revolutionary origins. With the emergence of a post-national cosmopolitan order subdued if not halted in its tracks by the political resurgence of national sovereignty claims and actions, she claims, liberal theory must re-engage with the discourse of sovereignty. By stripping sovereignty of its connotations of domination and presenting it as a principle representing the symbolic unity and unified authority of legal orders, Bashkina argues, liberal theory's attempts to rehabilitate the concept and reassert its centrality have also effaced or 'legalised' the dimension of subjectivity at the core sovereignty's historical meaning. Bashkina problematises liberalism's neutral understanding of sovereignty and its collective subject through recourse to the distinctions between 'people' and 'nation' and between 'popular' and 'national' sovereignty – contrasts deeply embedded in the French experience of revolutionary constitutionalism and theoretically developed by the early twentieth-century French legal positivist Raymond Carré de Malberg. This allows her to show that the conceptual neutralisation of sovereign subjecthood helps legitimise the suppression of political difference, which can in turn, as recent evidence indicates, feed a populist backlash.

Nora Timmermans' contribution is concerned with some of the same pressing contemporary issues, and with certain of the historical turnings that have brought us to this juncture. She points to the dangers involved in premising sovereign action on a unified collective subject. She does this by indicating a fundamental flaw in liberal democracy's theoretical underpinnings that renders it permanently vulnerable to populist stirrings. Looking at the genesis of today's mainstream 'liberal democratic' conception of sovereignty, she finds a leading culprit in Marcel Gauchet's influential 'Lefortian' appropriation of Benjamin Constant. Gauchet turned to Constant, such a key figure in revolutionary France's original liberal countercurrent, to find an alternative to the holistic and essentially conservative conceptions of sovereignty at the root of authoritarian and elitist regimes. Unfortunately, the liberal democratic conception that Gauchet approvingly ascribed to Constant does not escape the 'positive' logic of these conceptions, to adopt Timmermans' terminology, but only inverts it. Instead of positing a collective subject that stands in a direct, constitutive relation to its legal and political institutions, liberal democracy posits a legal and political sphere that stands in a constitutive relation to the – now denaturalised and contestable – collective identity of its people. Although this is in an improvement in view of the priority it accords to the constitutional order, the populism-inviting constitutive relation between a collective identity and a political sphere remains present. By freeing Constant's work from Gauchet's interpretation, however, Timmermans shows that his insights might yet be of use in a modern defence of liberal democracy. She finds an intriguing alternative in Constant's gestures towards a 'negative' conception of popular sovereignty, which does away with the demand of a collective subject altogether.

Stephanie Frank's concluding chapter returns to seventeenth- and eighteenth-century French debates over representation in order to challenge the plausibility of Carl Schmitt's famous dictum that 'All the concepts of the modern theory of the state are secularised theological concepts' and the homology between theology and politics that supported it. She shows that Schmitt was a rather unfaithful reader of Sieyès, to whom he ascribed a voluntaristic model of political sovereignty. Yet, Frank explains, the idiosyncrasies in Sieyès' thought that Schmitt misreads must be understood in relation to arguments espoused by Malebranche a century earlier. And once we see this, we understand that Sieyès and Malebranche held theological (or divine) sovereignty and political sovereignty to be different concepts, each with a different but overlapping referential domain. Schmitt's preferred model of sovereignty, with a sovereign who transcends the entire system and can suspend it at will, however, rests instead on a 'rearticulation' of theological sovereignty in a political register. That is, it posits a political sovereign completely detached from theology. In Frank's words, Schmitt's thinking on sovereignty constitutes a political *a*theology or *idolatry* rather than a political theology. These insights allow Frank to revisit critically the relation between the two core claims of Schmitt's *Political Theology* – the intellectual-historical claim about the theological derivation of the major concepts of the theory of the state, and the definitional claim about sovereignty according to which 'Sovereign is he who decides on the exception'.

In their very different ways, therefore, our various authors endorse the 'boomerang' effect. Understood both as an imaginary frame shaping key legal and political events and trends, and as an adaptive reaction to these events and trends, sovereignty has always possessed and today retains an active influence over the global constellation of authority. Sovereignty allows us to imagine and enact a wide array of governing arrangements, including some which, on account of their populist claims, their authoritarian tendencies, their centralising impulses, their state-centred myopia or their facilitation of a neoliberal economic regime, we might wish to refuse or modify. But without sovereignty, and absent the forms of agency it invokes, it remains difficult – arguably impossible – to imagine *any* plausible planetary architecture of legal and political authority.

PART I

Theory in History

1

Post-Sovereignty?

DIETER GRIMM

1 The Development of Sovereignty

"Sovereignty" was not always there. What is called "sovereignty" today emerged under certain historical conditions at a certain time and in a certain place, and it can disappear or lose its meaning if the conditions change. Some authors assume that this has already happened so that we find ourselves in a post-sovereign era. The best way to ascertain whether they are right seems to be a reconstruction of the conditions under which sovereignty originally emerged, followed by an analysis as to whether the conditions have changed in the meantime, and, if so, how the changes affect sovereignty. Without such a historical assessment it is difficult to understand the present situation.[1]

The origins of "sovereignty" are marked by the religious civil wars of the sixteenth and seventeenth centuries. Luther's Reformation had undermined the medieval world order. This order had been regarded as based on divine revelation and thus exempted from man's disposition. As such it could exist only as long as its transcendental basis remained uncontested. It was just this precondition that lost its basis through the Reformation. To be sure, the Reformation did not question that God's will was the source of the worldly order. But it destroyed the unanimity about what God's will actually was. The dispute about the divine revelation concerned a question of eternal truths and was thus fought unforgivingly. It is not without reason that we speak of religious wars.

In this situation of existential threat, a group of French theoreticians deemed it necessary to give security priority over truth in order to end the civil war and enable peaceful coexistence of people with different

[1] For a fuller historical assessment, see D. Grimm, *Sovereignty: The Origin and Future of a Political and Legal Concept* (New York: Columbia University Press, 2015).

religious beliefs. They opted for a political solution of the problem and were therefore pejoratively called *les politiques* by their contemporaries. The outstanding figure among these theoreticians was Jean Bodin, himself almost a victim of the civil war. In his book *Six livres de la République* of 1576 he was the first to develop a systematic theory of sovereignty. "Sovereignty" was his answer to the challenge of the traditional social order produced by religious antagonism.

Bodin started from the assumption that the civil wars could only be put to an end and that internal peace could only be restored if a superior power was established that succeeded in disarming the parties to the civil war. The precondition was that this power claimed for itself all the prerogatives until then dispersed among many independent holders, assembled them in one hand, and concentrated them into the public power in the singular. Thus equipped with the monopoly of legitimate force, the new power would be able to subject the religious parties to a new order that was independent of the contested religious truths. This presupposed, however, an equally novel power, namely the power to make law for society without being bound by higher law. These two elements combined, the monopoly of public authority and an original power to create law, were what Bodin called "sovereignty."

Under the prevailing circumstances the holder of this power could only be the monarch who, standing on top of the feudal pyramid, already possessed the majority of prerogatives. It is true that Bodin could build on earlier attempts of the French kings to enlarge their power and to become independent of the estates. However, one would not do justice to Bodin if one were to characterize his idea as a mere theoretical description of what had already developed in reality. Rather, his theory went far beyond reality in that it offered a coherent concept of a new system of political rule for which no example existed in the political reality of the time.

The notion of "sovereignty" thereby changed its meaning. The word "sovereignty" was not invented by Bodin; it had been in use in the French language long before he began to develop his theory. Yet it designated something quite different, as a concentrated public power did not exist at that time. Public authority was rather dispersed among many independent holders of various prerogatives. These prerogatives did not apply to a territory but to people, and they were not exercised as an autonomous political function but as an appendix of other legal positions, mostly that of the landowner. What we distinguish today as public and private was still inextricably intermingled.

Reflecting this situation, the word "sovereignty" described every power that was highest in relation to someone subjected to it. It was thus possible that many sovereigns existed upon one and the same territory, and a person could be subjected to different sovereigns, yet to everyone only in one or another aspect and to no one totally. Since one could be sovereign only with regard to certain prerogatives, it was not unusual that a person who was sovereign in one relationship was subject to a sovereign in another. The unity of this order was derived from God's will that assigned everybody his position and function in society and vis-à-vis which nobody was free.

Bodin retained the concept of highest authority but changed all the rest. The dispersed prerogatives were concentrated into a uniform public power that was more than a bundle of individual prerogatives and whose exercise was not subject to any external bond. This power was attributed to a single person, the ruler, who, as a consequence, became the only sovereign. Several sovereigns on one territory were no longer conceivable. Sovereignty was indivisible. This did not exclude other persons from being authorized to exercise public power, but only in the form of a mandate from the ruler and within the limits set by him. Vis-à-vis the sovereign, all others were subjects.

Bodin's theory did not only find academic interest. Rather, it became extremely attractive inside and outside France, as can be seen from the many editions and translations of his work within a very short period of time. Beginning with French King Henry IV, many princes set out to transform Bodin's program into reality by extending the monarchical position at the expense of the intermediate powers, freeing themselves from the codetermination of the estates, and developing an independent power basis in the form of a bureaucracy, a standing army, and a taxing authority.

Where these attempts were successful, a new form of political rule emerged for which a new term soon appeared, namely "state."[2] "State" was derived from the Latin word *status* that did not stand for itself but needed an object: the state *of* something. Now the term could be used independently of an object, just as politics had emancipated itself with the emergence of the modern territorial and monarchical rule. State and sovereignty figured as mutual conditions: Where a ruler succeeded in becoming sovereign, the territory was transformed into a state; when the attempt failed or was not undertaken at all (as in the Holy Roman

[2] See P. L. Weinacht, *Staat* (Berlin: Duncker & Humblot, 1968).

Empire) the premodern order survived, albeit sometimes behind a statist façade.

However, the emergence of sovereign rule and its transformation into a state should not be regarded as an event. Rather, it took place in a long process that was by no means linear. It resulted in different forms, varying from country to country, and was nowhere completed before the French Revolution. Sovereignty was a goal, one towards which certain political projects aimed and which could be reached more or less. The common denominator was the concentrated public power, necessary to overcome the civil wars. Sometimes it led to an identification of the state with one of the competing religious beliefs, while the other one was extinguished. Sometimes it led to mutual tolerance together with neutrality of the state in religious matters.

The immense attraction of this program becomes apparent through the fact that all sorts of political regimes began to describe themselves in terms of sovereignty or were described as sovereign in academic writing, even if the preconditions of sovereignty in Bodin's sense did not exist. This could, however, not happen without a number of adaptations. Consequently a uniform notion of sovereignty never existed. There were only versions that gained temporary predominance. Whereas Bodin could conceive of sovereignty only as indivisible and complete supreme power, soon notions of sovereignty emerged for which it sufficed that someone was highest in his field of competence or that the highest power was shared by several holders.

This shows that "sovereignty" as conceived by Bodin was originally a concept for the internal organization of a political entity. Its historical function was to enable a peaceful coexistence of people with different beliefs, which could only be achieved by a concentration of power in one ruler. Since the new unified entities emerged as territorial states, the sovereign was functionally unlimited (*legibus solutus*) but limited in terms of space. Every sovereign was sovereign in his territory. Outside the territory there were other sovereigns who claimed the same absolute power with regard to their territory. Under these circumstances the internal sovereignty could only be maintained if it went along with external sovereignty, which required independence from other sovereigns regarding the internal affairs of the state. Sovereignty meant to be highest in two respects: externally independent and internally self-determinate.

The coexistence of various sovereign states required legal regulation. But in view of the predominant concept of sovereignty, their relationship could only be regulated in the form of coordination, not in the form of subordination as within the state. Since all rulers were legally equal, the legal relations among states consisted in mutual self-limitations or treaties. There was but one legal precept that had to be generally valid regardless of the consent of particular parties if the system were not to collapse, namely the rule *pacta sunt servanda.* However, as no superior enforcement mechanism for treaty obligations existed, international law allowed what was forbidden within the state, namely self-help. War as a means of enforcing one's rights could not be excluded but only tamed.

The absolute monarchical state was abolished by the French Revolution. However, the revolution did not abolish either the state itself or its key property, sovereignty. To the contrary, state and sovereignty were completed by the revolution. In spite of its claim to absolute rule the monarch had not succeeded in disempowering all holders of prerogatives, especially the nobility, and in concentrating all public authority in his own hands. In many respects he had to content himself with the claim that the non-state holders of powers exercised them on his behalf, which they of course denied. The complete fulfillment of sovereignty claims was reached only with the abolition of all intermediate powers in the revolution.

As far as sovereignty is concerned, the revolutionary aspect of the revolution is thus the exchange of the subject of sovereignty. Following natural law theory, the revolutionaries assumed that legitimate rule must emanate from a consensus of all. Consequently, sovereignty belonged no longer to the monarch but to the people. However, the people was not able to govern. It needed agents for this purpose that acted on its behalf. The danger of an estrangement of the agents from the principal was met by the constitution. The constitution regulated the principal–agent relationship. It was the document in which the sovereign formulated the conditions under which the agents were authorized to exercise public power.

These conditions also had been developed in natural law theory. According to this theory, the purpose of rule was no longer the enforcement of a certain concept of the common good but securing the equal liberty of the subjects. The common good was regarded as the automatic product of societal self-regulation by way of contract. In order to guarantee individual freedom, fundamental rights limited the government and separation of powers prevented the abuse of power. However, fundamental rights and separation of powers did not limit or divide sovereignty. They gained their place below sovereignty. They were the product of a sovereign decision of the people, which found expression in the act of constitution-making. Sovereignty thus retreated into the constituent power of the people. Within the constitutional state no sovereign existed but only limited competencies. The rulers held only *constituted* power.

How does Germany fit into this picture? In Germany the French Revolution was received with sympathy, but a German revolution did not come about in the same era. And when Germany finally attempted to establish political rule on the basis of popular sovereignty in 1848, the revolution failed. Nonetheless, there were constitutions in Germany, but they owed their existence to a decision of the monarch who was willing to give up the absolute character of rule.[3] Does this mean that he gave up his sovereignty? The monarchs themselves did not think so. The Final Act of the Vienna Congress explicitly confirmed their unabridged sovereignty. The defense of monarchical sovereignty was the main reason for the German Federation, founded in Vienna in 1815.

However, it was difficult to overlook that, after having granted constitutions, the monarchs were no longer *legibus solutus*. They tried to bridge this difference by distinguishing between possessing and exercising power: The monarch was the exclusive holder of sovereignty, but on the level of exercising it he bound himself voluntarily to the provisions of the constitution. This was no longer sovereignty in the sense of Bodin. Yet, there could be no doubt either that sovereignty had not been transmitted to the people like in France. The location of sovereignty in monarchical constitutionalism was a constant topic of German public lawyers. Finally, agreement was reached on the position that sovereignty belonged to the state as such whereas the monarch was but an organ of the state, albeit the most important one.

Another challenge for the concept of sovereignty consisted in political entities composed of states. The founders of the theory of sovereignty were not concerned with this question because they had a unitary state in mind when they developed their ideas. Where, then, was sovereignty located in federal entities? With the member states, with the central state, or with all of them together? This was an issue not only in Germany but in all federal states of that time, so too in Switzerland and the United States, where it needed a civil war finally to decide the question. Yet, in contrast to Germany in the nineteenth century, these two states were (and still are) able to imagine sovereignty as divided.

[3] See D. Grimm, *Deutsche Verfassungsgeschichte* (Berlin: Suhrkamp, 4th edn., 2015).

Irrespective of the answer to the question as to who was sovereign in a federal state, Bodin's concept of sovereignty could not be maintained in federal units. On the one hand, those who assumed that sovereignty was located within one part of the state, either the member states or the central state, were forced to give up the principle of indivisibility of state and sovereignty. Rather, it became possible to conceive of a form of state that was not sovereign. This immediately entailed the question of the true location of sovereignty. The answer was again heavily contested. The dispute could finally be settled by the assumption that sovereignty was vested in the entity that disposed of the *Kompetenz-Kompetenz*, i.e. the power to allocate competences. On the other hand, those who thought that sovereignty was shared by the central state and the member states had to waive the indivisibility of sovereignty. It was then possible to be sovereign without possessing the entire public authority.

External sovereignty remained unaffected by these controversies. In international relations sovereignty belongs to the state as such, irrespective of who is sovereign within the state. Likewise, public international law was not interested in the rights that the state claimed or exercised vis-à-vis its citizens. Public international law remained thus unaffected by changes regarding internal sovereignty. Its scope was limited to the relation among the states and consequently stopped at the borders of the state. It recognized the equal legal sovereignty of states just by closing its eyes before the internal situations of states. The only limitations of external sovereignty were those that the states had voluntarily accepted in treaties. Self-limitation was not regarded as compromising sovereignty.

2 Sovereignty Today

Today the discussion about sovereignty is no longer limited to the question of who is sovereign and what it means to be sovereign. Rather, the more radical question comes to the fore as to whether it is still appropriate to think in categories of sovereignty and to act based on sovereignty claims.[4] Behind these questions appears the experience of two devastating world wars and numerous violations of elementary human rights that were committed under the umbrella of sovereignty. They have led to a rapid development of public international law and international relations. This has had consequences for external sovereignty and also affects internal sovereignty, which, in turn, can only exist

[4] See N. MacCormick, *Questioning Sovereignty* (Oxford University Press, 1999).

to the extent that external sovereignty protects it against interventions from outside.

The attempt to construct a more effective protection of peace started already after World War I with the founding of the League of Nations. Yet, the League of Nations did not exceed the limits of traditional public international law as it was not endowed with the means to enforce treaty obligations vis-à-vis the member states. This changed after World War II with the founding of the United Nations (hereafter UN). Different from the League of Nations, the member states of the UN did not only renounce their right to use force in cases of conflict. In addition, the UN was authorized to enforce the treaty obligations, if necessary with military force, against which the states could no longer invoke their sovereignty. Sovereignty continued to exist in the horizontal dimension vis-à-vis other states, but it became permeable in the vertical dimension, i.e. vis-à-vis the UN.

The characteristic weakness of public international law, which flowed from the predominant understanding of sovereignty, was thereby overcome. The sources of public international law were no longer limited to treaties and customary law. International legislative acts with binding force independently of state consent became possible. Obligations under international law could be enforced against reluctant states. War was no longer a legitimate means to assert one's rights. The use of military force was limited to fighting military aggression. War was legitimate only for purposes of self-defense, not for purposes of aggression. Measures of the UN required unanimity in the Security Council but not the consent of the states affected by these measures.

The development that started with the founding of the UN has made further progress in the course of time, at an accelerated tempo after the end of the East–West divide in 1989/90.[5] New supranational organizations were established and endowed with public power by the states. They were authorized to exercise their powers more or less independently of the states, and they do so frequently, even against the will of the states from whom these powers have been transferred. A considerable number of international courts have been established, many of whom have jurisdiction to act without prior consent of the states.[6] Their judgments are binding for the states. Within public international law a *ius cogens* has

[5] See A. L. Paulus, *Die internationale Gemeinschaft im Völkerrecht: Eine Untersuchung zur Entwicklung des Völkerrechts im Zeitalter der Globalisierung* (München: C.H. Beck, 2001).

[6] See the comprehensive survey in K. J. Alter, *The New Terrain of International Law: Courts, Politics, Rights* (Princeton University Press, 2014).

emerged that claims legal force independently of state recognition and is binding for the states when they conclude treaties.

A special feature of the new public international law is the emergence of international human rights protection. While no binding legal force was accorded to the Universal Declaration of Human Rights of 1948, the two international covenants of 1966 – on Civil and Political Rights and on Social, Economic, and Cultural Rights – are binding for the signatory states, even if they still lack effective enforcement mechanisms. Special covenants prohibit genocide, torture, and race discrimination. The most recent developments have produced a second ground for UN interventions next to peace keeping: humanitarian intervention and even a "responsibility to protect" if states commit systematic violations of human rights vis-à-vis groups of the population or if they allow violations to be committed by others. Today we talk of a "humanization of public international law."[7]

However, nowhere has the progress been greater than in Europe. It began in 1951 with the founding of the Council of Europe and the enactment of the European Convention on Human Rights (ECHR). The purpose of the ECHR is to guarantee a minimum standard of fundamental rights protection to the (currently) forty-seven member states. Enforcement of the Convention was placed in the hands of the European Court of Human Rights. The Convention partly remains within the framework of traditional international law, as the European Court is not authorized to annul national acts that violate the Convention. The states are merely obliged under international law to eliminate the violation. Partly however, the Convention transcends traditional international law because individuals have the right to sue member states for acts of their organs violating the Convention. If a violation has been found, the victims are entitled to a remedy.

More far-reaching than the Council of Europe is the European Union (hereafter EU), founded in 1957 as the European Economic Community and presently comprising twenty-eight member states. It is a unique political entity, somewhere between a supranational organization and a federal state but closer to the latter than the former. It is true that the EU, unlike the UN, lacks the power to employ compulsory means vis-à-vis the member states. Yet, the use of compulsory means by the UN is permitted only in

[7] Regarding the humanization of international law, see, e.g., A. Peters, "Humanity as the A and O of Sovereignty," *European Journal of International Law*, 20 (2009), p. 513; see also J. Klabbers, A. Peters and G. Ulfstein, *The Constitutionalization of International Law* (Oxford University Press, 2009).

exceptional cases and occurs rarely because the vast majority of states do not pose problems that would justify a UN intervention or because they possess veto power in the Security Council. This is why most of the states have never been an object of UN interventions.

The member states of the EU, to the contrary, are constantly affected by acts of the Union. These acts claim direct and superior validity within the member states and supplant national law that contradicts EU law. Any law of a member state that is found to be in contradiction to European law automatically loses its applicability – with no involvement of the member state itself required. An explicit provision to this effect is missing from the EU's founding treaties. But the European Court of Justice derived it from the purpose of European integration, and the judgments have found acceptance in the member states.[8] The activity of the EU extends to all branches of government, legislative, executive, and judicial and has consequences for almost all fields of politics. The EU thus offers the greatest challenge to the modern concept of sovereignty.

What then is the state of sovereignty after all these changes? One statement can be made with certainty: He who identifies sovereignty with the classical concept of Bodin must conclude that sovereignty has disappeared. The identity between public power and state power that persisted for 300 years no longer exists. There is now also public power beyond the state. Because of this development no state is sovereign any longer, in the sense that states could still be sovereign in the first half of the twentieth century. Bodin's notion of sovereignty no longer corresponds closely with reality. Therefore, many assume that the concept of sovereignty is useful only to describe the past but is no longer able to explain the present situation.

However, before drawing this conclusion one should remember that Bodin's concept of sovereignty was never universally accepted. There were always competing notions, which, in spite of their differences, converged insofar as they lowered the rigidity of Bodin's concept. But also in political reality sovereignty à la Bodin could hardly be observed in unmoderated form. The absolute state that emerged in reaction to religious wars was certainly not as absolute as it might seem. Even where the monarchs of modern territorial states had no superior above them, they found a number of holders of public powers around them, which limited

[8] See the two groundbreaking judgments of the European Court of Justice *Van Gend & Loos* v. *Netherlands*, [1963] ECR 1 and *Costa* v. *ENEL*, [1964] ECR 585.

their power. In Germany, in addition, the Holy Roman Empire was a barrier against full development of monarchical absolutism.

When after 200 years the modern constitutional state replaced the absolute state, the highest degree of approximation to Bodin's concept of sovereignty was reached, yet only by conceding that internal sovereignty largely exhausted itself in the act of constitution-making, and thereafter remained latent within the state. Here, in the constitutionally developed architecture of the state, only legally created and limited competencies existed, whose holders were not regarded as sovereign. In cases of federal states, none of their components enjoyed the full possession of public power, with the consequence that sovereignty could only refer to the general competence to determine the allocation of powers. Here, the central state and the member states had to share public powers.

External sovereignty was left unaffected by this development. The states remained legally independent of other states or superior political entities and enjoyed self-determination with regard to their internal affairs. Sovereignty was therefore not questioned in international law. But even this is no longer the case after the changes that occurred in the second half of the twentieth century. Unlimited self-determination no longer exists. Self-determination is valid only within the limits of international law. These limits may differ in degree, depending on the supranational organizations to which a state belongs. They are particularly narrow in the EU. Here, even the constituent power of the member states is subject to certain European restraints.[9]

On the other hand, sovereignty has not passed to supranational organizations. No supranational organization has emerged through a process or act of *self*-constitution like a state. All are creations of states and received their basic legal order from states, just as states retain the power to alter or abolish the order. Furthermore, no supranational organization has received the plenitude of public power; all have but limited tasks, and only those public powers that they need in order to fulfill these tasks. Finally, no state has given up the monopoly of legitimate physical force in favor of a supranational organization. If enforcing decisions of supranational organizations requires physical force, they have to borrow it from the states.

[9] See D. Grimm, "The Significance of National Constitutions in a United Europe" in D. Grimm, *The Constitution of European Democracy* (Oxford University Press, 2017), 131.

However, the fact that supranational organizations have not acquired sovereignty does not mean that it still lies with the states.[10] Sovereignty is not a necessity. Just as it was lacking before Bodin, it may disappear after Bodin. Are we then already in a pre-Bodinian state? This is not the case either. The pre-Bodinian state was a state without States, so to speak. States emerged together with sovereignty. And states continue to exist, regardless of the developments that have occurred in the last sixty years, albeit not unchanged.[11] States continue to form the basic units of the international order. This order has been created by states and is based on the existence of states. The states do not possess only scattered prerogatives but a general public power.

The division of public power between national and supranational units is new. Nevertheless, the states are still dominant. They possess the plenitude of public powers, diminished by the portion that has been transferred to supranational organizations, whereas these organizations have no more than their specifically transferred powers. Their scope varies from organization to organization. The EU has without doubt the highest number of public powers of all supranational organizations. But even here the principle of conferral is in force, and in a number of member states the national constitution contains limits to the further transfers of powers.

However, the division of public power between supranational organizations and their member states might suggest that sovereignty, too, is divided or shared. Many authors think that this is so.[12] But one should not overlook one significant difference: The self-determination of states regarding their internal affairs may be limited by international law, but it is not abolished. Supranational organizations, to the contrary, have no self-determination regarding their existence, purpose, organization, competencies, and means. Concerning all these questions they are hetero-determined. This is even the case with the EU. Should one really call a supranational organization sovereign whose existence and legal foundations depend on the decision of third parties?

[10] See D. Grimm, "Sovereignty in Europe" in D. Grimm, *The Constitution of European Democracy* (fn. 9), 39.

[11] See S. Leibfried, E. Huber, M. Lange, J. D. Levy and J. D. Stephens (eds.), *The Oxford Handbook of Transformation of the State* (Oxford University Press, 2015).

[12] See N. Walker, "Late Sovereignty in the European Union" in N. Walker (ed.), *Sovereignty in Transition* (Oxford University Press, 2003), 14; U. Haltern, *Was bedeutet Souveränität?* (Tübingen: Mohr Siebeck, 2007), 22.

Rather, one has to distinguish between sovereignty and public powers. The Federal Constitutional Court of Germany insists on this difference when it reminds us that article 23(1) of the Basic Law authorizes parliament to transfer public powers but not to relinquish sovereignty.[13] However, it seems not impossible that states transfer so many public powers that the rest no longer deserves the name "sovereignty." But, this situation has not yet arrived, even in the EU. Public powers are undoubtedly divided between supranational organizations and their member states; sovereignty is not divided.

Furthermore, it seems insufficient to consider only the vertical dimension of sovereignty, namely the relationship between states and supranational organizations. Since the new world order presupposes the existence of states, the horizontal dimension, namely the relationship among states, has not disappeared. Here sovereignty continues to exist with almost no change. State boundaries are not obsolete.[14] Outside the highly aggregated EU, sovereignty is still a clearly evident phenomenon. But even the boundaries between the member states of the EU have not disappeared. They still divide legal orders. The Schengen system means that one can pass national borders without control. It does not mean that one can take one's national laws along.

Moreover, sovereignty is still omnipresent in current political imagination as well as in political reality. No supranational organization claims sovereignty, states do, often at highlighted places in their national constitutions. Supranational organizations treat states as sovereign, just as states treat each other as sovereign. Legal claims are raised or rejected with reference to sovereignty. National and international courts render judgments based on the principle of sovereignty. Irrespective of all theoretical assertions that sovereignty has disappeared, it is still present as a social fact. One does not escape sovereignty even if one takes it for obsolete.

But is it necessary to take it for obsolete? Self-determination of political entities concerning their internal affairs and their corresponding independence from external forces is still the property of sovereignty, albeit no longer unlimited. Sovereignty neither justifies aggressive wars nor a systematic disregard of human rights. Inasmuch as the fight against sovereignty is conducted because it is the supposed enemy of human

[13] BVerfGE 123, 267 (2009) – *Lisbon Treaty.*

[14] See U. Di Fabio, *Der Verfassungsstaat in der Weltgesellschaft* (Tübingen: Mohr Siebeck, 2001).

rights, it goes astray. Sovereignty and rights, statism and internationalism, are no longer antagonisms.[15] There are new limits, but these limits do not go so far as to throttle sovereignty. They leave sufficient space for national self-determination.

This space deserves preservation. It is true that self-determination is not the same as democracy. But democracy has become the usual form of self-determination. The people shall decide about its order and its political leaders, rather than the rulers deciding for the people. For the time being, democratic self-determination remains bound to a citizenry conscious of its identity and capable of conducting its own affairs. The preconditions for self-determination are still much better in states than in supranational organizations. It follows that sovereignty functions today also as a protection of democracy against the attempts of international authorities to constantly expand their scope of action, even though their democratic legitimacy and accountability remain feeble.

[15] See, e.g., M. Risse, *On Global Justice* (Princeton University Press, 2012), 42 ss.

2

When Sovereigns Stir

NEIL WALKER

1 The Hobbesian Legacy

Richard Tuck's recent book-length study of Thomas Hobbes' depiction of the 'Sleeping Sovereign'[1] offers an eloquent reminder of the contribution of the great seventeenth-century English philosopher to the political imaginary within which our modern conception of constitutional democracy has emerged. Central to that imaginary is the retention of an evolved conception of sovereignty as the organizing device of political society, and, as one key facet of that evolution, the establishment of a fundamental distinction between sovereignty and government. Hobbes would not be the first to draw such a distinction – that prize belongs to Jean Bodin, writing in the previous century.[2] Yet it was Hobbes who developed this idea in ways that were to alter radically our understanding of the condition of the modern polity, and which still resonate today. As I will argue in this chapter, the theoretical lens and accompanying metaphorical language of Hobbes, suitably extended to cover the stirring of new forms of sovereigntist consciousness and practice, continues to offer a powerful perspective through which we can appreciate both the strengths and the limitations of a sovereignty-centred approach to the contemporary global political condition.

(a) *Of Sovereignty and Government*

Let us begin with the history of the sovereignty/government distinction and Hobbes' vital contribution to that history. Where sovereignty had

[1] R. Tuck, *The Sleeping Sovereign: The Invention of Modern Democracy* (Cambridge: Cambridge University Press, 2016).

[2] J. Bodin, *The Six Books of a Commonweale* (K. D. McRae (ed.), R. Knolles trans., Harvard: Harvard University Press, 1962) (1576). See further, Tuck, above n1, ch.1.

been personal and dynastic in the mediaeval age, the basic authority to rule over a territory on the one hand, and, on the other, the particular ruler's preeminence and control of a governing apparatus, were difficult to disentangle. But with the gradual emergence of an impersonal and abstract conception of sovereignty, involving the claim of a polity to political unity and to an autonomous and absolute authority to govern itself across an expanding and increasingly differentiated public domain, the separation between the general structure of authority and its specific articulation became clearer. As both Bodin and Hobbes recognized in contemplating the unfolding political landscape of modernity, while the rightful power of rule is one thing, and belongs to the state, the complex of offices and mechanisms through which that sovereign power is exercised is quite another.

Where Hobbes goes beyond Bodin, however, is in his understanding of the source and locus of the ultimate lawmaking power of the sovereign state. Bodin's principal aim was to defend the French monarchy against its enemies, although in so doing, despite what many of his critics have claimed, he did not advocate royal absolutism. Rather, while holding that fundamental sovereign power rested with the King, he also emphasized the importance of the French *Parlements* – judicial offices held independently of the King and responsive to local populations, as a legitimate if secondary level of government.[3] What is more, Bodin did not rule out other combinations of sovereignty and government, including those that would have seen the ultimate authority of the state reside with the aristocracy, or even with the majority of the whole community.[4] Yet it was Hobbes who undertook the first serious exploration of the possibilities of a modern democratic polity. More systematically than any of his predecessors, he sought to replace the late mediaeval sense of 'the people' as a natural entity, prior to and independent of the institutions of politics, with one in which peoplehood was a matter of design, something that could only be fashioned through a process of individual consent to collective self-rule. The people in other words should no longer be viewed as some kind of mystical pre-social essence, recognizable through the lens of sovereign authority only as a vaguely defined external consultee.[5] Rather, they should be understood as an artificial construct, self-formed

[3] Tuck, above n1, ch. 1, esp. 36–41.

[4] Bodin, above n2, 199–200, 249.

[5] See e.g. T. Hobbes, *On the Citizen* (R. Tuck and M. Silvethrorne eds. and trans., Cambridge: Cambridge University Press, 1998) (1642) 71–72; T. Hobbes, *Leviathan* (R. Tuck ed., Cambridge: Cambridge University Press, 1991) (1651) 9.

through a mutually binding social contract – a construct which could itself lay claim to the mantle of sovereignty.

But just as Bodin's defence of monarchical sovereignty did not make him a royal absolutist, Hobbes' exploration of the conditions of possibility of democratic sovereignty patently did not make him an advocate of a thoroughly democratic system of rule.[6] In both cases the sovereignty/government distinction allowed a clear differentiation between deep legitimating principle and quotidian practice. Democratic – or popular – sovereignty need not imply government by democratically responsive officials according to laws passed by democratically elected legislators, although in the twentieth and twenty-first century's 'age of democracy',[7] democratic sovereignty indeed has increasingly, if unevenly, gone hand-in-hand with an everyday framework of 'representative democracy'.[8] For Hobbes, however, and more emphatically for Rousseau writing a century later from a more committed standpoint,[9] the key point was that the fundamental contract of popular sovereignty could be seen as a second-order embodiment of the democratic principle regardless of the first-order system of government chosen by that popular sovereign. And through the making of that further claim, predicated on the new basic distinction between sovereignty and government, the democratic method could be rescued from the then prevalent view that, with the emergence of the large territorial polity, democracy had become an anachronism – only ever appropriate to the intimate environment of the city states of the classical period where it had served as a direct form of collective self-rule.[10]

Just as Hobbes was not much of a democrat by today's standards, nor was he much of a constitutionalist. As sponsor of the notorious figure of the all-powerful Leviathan,[11] Hobbes himself emphatically declined to imagine the 'government' side of the sovereignty/government distinction

[6] Hobbes became notably more critical of democracy over time, reflecting his experience of the English Revolution. In particular, he is less generous in his assessment of democracy in *Leviathan* (1651) than in *De Cive* (*On the Citizen)* (1642). See further Tuck, above n1, 96–107.

[7] J. K. Dubrow, *Political Inequality in an Age of Democracy* (London: Routledge, 2014).

[8] See e.g. N. Urbanati, 'Representative Democracy and Its Critics', in S. Alonso, J. Keane and W. Merkel (eds.) *The Future of Representative Democracy* (Cambridge: Cambridge University Press, 2012) 23–49.

[9] J. J. Rousseau, *The Social Contract and Discourses* (G. D. H. Cole trans, London: Dent & Son, 1923); see also Tuck, above n1, 121–145.

[10] Se e.g. Tuck, above n1, 1–9.

[11] Above n6.

in the kind of systematically rule-directed terms that were to become central to the political technology of statecraft following the great documentary constitutional initiatives of the late eighteenth century. Again, however, the importance of the Hobbesian legacy is undeniable. For it is clear how the very idea of the sovereignty/government distinction, and the attendant understanding that sovereignty can rest with the people, underwrites the architecture of modern constitutional government. The notion that the fundamental rules of the polity should have both a different (and, in the increasingly dominant late modern understanding, a more basically democratic) author and a higher authority than the practitioners and practices of the government established by these rules is a central premise of constitutionalism. Its efficacy, however, depends not just upon the successful implementation of the original compact through which 'We, the People' lay down our collective will but also upon the continuing capacity of that popular sovereign – or, in the later language of Sieyes, the *pouvoir constituant*[12] – to exercise its authority, even beyond the founding generation. It is here that the graphic image of the sleeping sovereign enters the picture. Once the power of the state has been assigned to government and divided amongst its various organs by the original settlement, the sovereign, *just in order to remain sovereign*, should not expire but should retain a slumbering presence, capable of waking from time to time as appropriate so as to reassert control.[13]

(b) *The Problem of Constitutional Authorship*

If Hobbes' suggestive metaphor anticipates – and makes vivid – a key question about the nature of political legitimacy in the presence of the constitutionalized forms of political order of the contemporary world, the device of the constitutional amendment might appear to provide an obvious answer to that question. For the constitutional amendment is the formally established means by which the sovereign people are permitted to act again, and in so doing issue new or modified instructions as regards the ground rules of the polity. It is, so to speak, the people's official alarm clock – their mechanized method of waking up to reconsider the terms of their collective self-rule. How the alarm should be triggered, whether by

[12] E. Sieyes, *Political Writings* (M. Sonenscher trans., London: Hackett Publishing, 2003) 136, See further Tuck, above n1, 163–169. See further the essays by Pasquale Pasquino, Olga Bashkina and Stephanie Frank in the present volume.

[13] For Hobbes' own elaboration of various scenarios in which a sovereign people may be considered to be asleep but still in charge, see *On The Citizen*, above n5, 98–100. For discussion, see Tuck, above n1, 86–95.

referendum or special assembly or some other typically super-majoritarian means, and what, if any, are the allowable limits of reconsideration of the basic compact once the sovereign is roused are all matters that are laid down in the original constitutional settlement. As a matter of democratic theory, therefore, the amendment procedure might seem to exhibit an impeccable and smoothly reflexive form of auto-legitimation. Only the democratic sovereign itself, speaking and acting through its promulgated Constitution, gets to decide when, and on what terms, it may rouse itself to speak and perform again.

Yet if we move beyond form to substance matters become more complicated and more controversial. There is a tension – perhaps even a paradox[14] – at the heart of popular sovereignty, one that the mechanism of constitutional amendment can only reflect rather than resolve. For the ideal of democratic sovereignty does not depend upon the refinement over time of one single value of collective self-determination but upon the joining and reconciliation of two quite distinct principles of political morality; namely 'popular authorship' and 'present consent'.[15] The 'people' must be the source of the overall framework of self-rule, but, beyond the act of original self-authorization, later iterations of the 'people' deserve an equivalent say over the terms of their self-government. The danger lies in either principle being given too much weight at the expense of the other. To focus too much on the first settlement, as so-called constitutional Originalists are inclined to do, is to sacrifice the will of subsequent generations to the dead hand of the founders. But to focus too much on the moving target of popular will, as so-called Living Constitutionalists tend to do, ignores or dilutes the special significance of the founding moment as the point at which the identity of the polity *qua* constitutional polity was settled, and without which the very idea of a particular people engaged in an ongoing and reflexive process of self-rule could not have got going in the first place.[16]

In the face of these dual and somewhat competing imperatives, all that a constitutional amendment rule, and its subsequent practice, can achieve is

[14] See e.g. M. Loughlin and N. Walker (eds.) *The Paradox of Constitutionalism: Constituent Power and Constitutional Form* (Oxford: Oxford University Press, 2007).

[15] For an elegant restatement of this argument in the context of a discussion of Tuck's assessment of Hobbes, see D. S. Grewal and J. Purdy. 'The Original Theory of Constitutionalism' 127 *Yale Law Journal* 664 (2018); see also M. Loughlin, 'Constitutional Theory: A 25th Anniversary Essay' 25 *Oxford Journal of Legal Studies* 183–202 (2005).

[16] Grewal and Purdy, above n15, 691–696.

to decide how these are to be accommodated in the particular case. But the solution struck does not reflect any kind of optimal balancing. It offers no supra-contextual working out of the ideal formula for continuous self-rule. Rather, as the wide variety of actual mechanisms and practices of constitutional amendment across different constitutional regimes worldwide makes clear, each solution is the product of its own highly particular circumstances, shaped by actors who are far from disinterested participants. In the first place, by dint of the very text-centred logic of constitutional rulership those asked to strike the formal textual balance between popular authorship and the consent of later generations can be none other than the original popular authors themselves. And in the second place, over time the actual practice and prospects of constitutional amendment will be affected by a range of other considerations. These include contingent and changeable features of the political settlement like the size and diversity of the polity, as such factors can influence the range and strength of amendment veto points. They also include the practical attitudes and agendas of later generation actors with their own stake in the constitutional present and future – in particular the judiciary, but also, to a lesser extent, members of other branches of government (who may, of course, be involved in the selection and tenure of the judiciary),[17] as regards both the appropriate degree of latitude in the interpretation of the unamended constitutional text and the precise meaning and extent of the amendment clause itself.

In sum, as eloquently expressed by the endless debate over the adequacy of the Article V amendment clause of the US Constitution – which has delivered only twenty-seven reforms in 230 years – in finding its own point of accommodation of original authorship and popular consent, any particular constitutional amendment rule and practice, even that of the world's most enduring constitutional settlement, will attract unceasing controversy. Ever since the Philadelphian initiative, and today spread across the global range of constitutional democracies, we see the emergence and pursuit of various points and lines of disagreement: between those endorsing differently nuanced philosophical understandings of the optimally balanced

[17] This may have abusive consequences. For example, many recent attempts to circumvent established constitutional doctrine or practice by populist governments, from Donald Trump in the USA to Viktor Orban in Hungary and the Law and Justice Party in Poland, have involved openly partisan approaches to the appointment and tenure of constitutional judges or to the restructuring of high appellate courts. On the recent Polish and Hungarian situation in the context of the EU's broader jurisdiction over the rule of law, see K. L Scheppele and L. Pech, 'Protecting the Rule of Law in the EU. Why Poland and not Hungary?' *Verfassungsblog* March 8, 2018, available at: https://verfassungsblog.de/why-poland-and-not-hungary/. See also Section 3(b) (iv) below.

meaning of democratic sovereignty, between those possessing different interests in the terms and unfolding outcomes of the constitutional settlement, and also, whatever their underlying motives, amongst those who have greater or lesser capacity to exert real influence over the evolving meaning of that constitutional settlement.[18]

2 Sovereign Reductions

Like all good metaphors, the more we probe Hobbes' image of the sleeping sovereign, the more we learn. Deeper investigation reveals that, in a number of different ways, the sleeping sovereign offers a highly *reductive* picture of legal and political authority. As we shall see, this is true of the two parts of the metaphor – both the emphasis on dormant power and, more basically, the very focus on a single 'sovereign' entity as the seat of that power. And, I contend in the present section, it is precisely the reductive quality in Hobbes' portrayal that helps expose, and to explain, some of the wider difficulties associated with the modern constitutionalized form of sovereignty for which it provided an early conceptual framework. More specifically, its reductive quality is significant in two closely related and mutually reinforcing respects. In the first place, and most obviously, the metaphor has a *descriptive* significance. It is richly evocative of some of the objective limitations and restrictions attendant on a sovereignty-based practice of legal and political authority. In the second place, however, the metaphor also has a *performative* significance. For Hobbes' way of thinking about sovereignty is not just a mirror on political reality. It also helped set the very tone in which and through which sovereigntist discourse has come to impose itself on the modern political imaginary. In particular, Hobbes' metaphorical language expresses and thereby underlines the propensity of the sovereigntist mindset to assume and assert its own dominant centrality to our political way of being. In so doing – in striking this attitude – it tends only to reinforce the objective tendency of sovereignty-based practice to preclude or marginalize political forms that do not fit its frame of action.[19]

Following on from these critical reflections, in the remainder of the chapter the idea of the sovereign *stirring* is proposed and explored as

[18] See e.g. Grewal and Purdy, above n15, 683–705.

[19] For an interesting recent account of (and plea for) the performative dimension in political and constitutional theory, organized around the idea of the 'theorist-imaginer' or 'conjuror of peoplehood', see Z. Oklopcic, *Beyond the People: Social Imaginary and Constituent Imagination* (Oxford: Oxford University Press, 2018).

a fruitful extension of the Hobbesian metaphor – one that, through striking a somewhat different attitude, helps see beyond some of the rigidities in sovereigntist thinking. This more expansive image, I argue, is particularly useful as a vehicle for investigating and illuminating sovereignty's contemporary innovative edges and appreciating the positions and counter-positions associated with these innovative edges. Yet, in stretching our understanding of sovereignty, the extended metaphor also brings the deep structure and the outer boundaries of sovereigntist thought and action into clearer focus. And in so doing it demonstrates the ineradicable limits of the very notion of a sovereignty-centred political imaginary and practice in *any* world – past, present or future.

(a) The Limits of Binary Vision

In what ways, then, is the image of the sleeping sovereign reductive? To begin with, there are a number of more or less immediate and more or less specific ways in which the image encourages a narrowly binary approach to the question of political authority. First, and most immediately, there is the implicitly binary framing of its subject's range of consciousness. The sovereign is reduced to one of two states, either asleep or awake, but with the stress on the former. This sends two messages. It accurately describes the constitutional orthodoxy according to which, following the initial sovereign act, the continuing dimension of sovereign power is merely latent and residual. That is to say, continuing sovereignty is normally passive rather than active, its contribution occasional and atypical. Additionally, in what it stresses, and also in what it chooses *not* to stress, the binary approach has a performative dimension. It turns our attention away from what might lie between sleeping and waking. It suggests that what matters is the long silence and the occasional burst of sound, as well as the contrast between the two. With the development of modern constitutional mechanics, the sovereign's waking process is governed by the formal and precise device of the amendment trigger – the setting and ringing of the constitutional alarm clock; and, under the binary approach, what precedes or accompanies this mechanical procedure is relegated to the background, its only relevance as instrumental to the achievement of the distinct state of full sovereign alertness.

In the second place, not only does the metaphor of the sleeping sovereign reduce the process of constitutional amendment to a binary yes/no of realization or non-realization – success or failure – but it is also restrictive in the more general sense of its reduction of the dynamic process of constitutional authorization and re-authorization to the narrow vehicle of the constitutional amendment in the first place. That is to say, it assumes a wider binary distinction between that which pertains to the domain of formal authorization, and so should be recognized, and that which falls outside that domain. This certainly succeeds in drawing attention to the objective significance of that narrow amendment vehicle, but to make this the sole focus can also be distorting. It leaves out of consideration the ways in which significant constitutional influence over the overall direction of the polity, perhaps equivalent or even greater in impact than a formal constitutional amendment or renewal, may be exerted by other actors and other means. These other methods may take the form, already noted, of creative judicial interpretation of the existing constitutional text. Or significant constitutional influence may be exerted through important sub-constitutional rule-making by the legislature, or the use of prerogative or other special powers by the political executive, or the actions of broader currents within civil society that prevent, influence or accelerate changes in constitutional or other high legislative text, interpretation or practice.

In the third place, and more broadly still, the insistence on the figure of the sovereign, whether asleep or awake, as *the* image of authority within the polity – the single and comprehensive source of political power – speaks to a more basic set of exclusions and to the reductive understandings associated with these exclusions. For such a particularized and personalized conception of rulership – even if the personality in question becomes the corporate personality of the people – reflects and reinforces a significant settlement bias in favour of the existing sovereign. Again, we see a binary opposition in play, in this case through a categorical distinction between the existing sovereign and all other putative authorities. It was noted above that the continuing power of the sovereign to modify the settlement may be modest, both largely passive and dependent on the original author. But it is, nevertheless, the continuing sovereign *alone* who possesses any such modificatory power. No claim to sovereignty other than that whose pedigree is that of the first sovereign can speak authoritatively within the sovereign register. Sovereignty may be reflexively adaptable, but this self-referentiality precludes or marginalizes any alternative or additional authorial source. The message, in a nutshell, is that other aspiring sovereigns to the whole or even to any insular or overlapping part of the jurisdiction in question can have no legitimate claim to the title and so need not apply.

(b) The Deep Structure of Sovereignty

If we continue to dig deeper into the sovereigntist imagery, we discover that the sense of exclusion which favours the existing sovereign extends to a second and more abstract level. For not only does the settlement bias preclude or marginalize the claims of other putative sovereigns who may seek to rouse themselves, it simply does not allow the basis and basic efficacy of political authority and power – both *potestas* and *potentia* – to be conceived of other than in and through the singularity of the (more or less alert) sovereign. In other words, the very existence of the monopolistic figure of the sovereign – even in its constitutionalized form – not only rules out rival sovereigns but also precludes any kind of political ontology other than that centred upon sovereignty. Here, then, we reach the most fundamental level of reduction associated with the language and practice of sovereignty, a structural baseline which shapes and informs all the other reductive features considered above, and the binary logic of inclusion and exclusion through which they operate. The pros and cons of this most significant form of reduction, therefore, demand a more detailed exploration.

Defenders of the modern constitutionalized version of sovereignty might consider its monopoly to be a good thing. Certainly, this version of sovereignty has decided advantages over its predecessors – both the medieval personalized version and the more abstract but still pre-constitutional version articulated by Hobbes himself. Unlike its predecessors, modern constitutionalism's default is not to defer to its normative past – and 'to the sanctity of immemorial traditions'.[20] Instead of reifying its pre-constitutional heritage, or even freezing its original settlement, as we have seen modern constitutionalism attempts to use the legacy of community and its founding commitments as a justificatory and motivational platform for an aspirational and adjustable project of collective self-rule. Unlike its predecessors, modern constitutionalized sovereignty is not tied to a particular and parochial vision of political authority owing little to the active authorship of its subjects. Instead, as an ordered form of collective self-rule oriented towards the common interest, it seeks to blend a distinctive expression of popular sovereignty with a framework of universal rule-based public reason born of general commitment to free and equal membership of a political community, and informed and encouraged by a growing bank of comparative examples of

[20] M. Weber, *Economy and Society: An Outline of Interpretive Sociology* (Berkley, CA: University of California Press, 1978) (1922) 215.

techniques of constitutional government.[21] Unlike its predecessors, modern constitutionalism is not weighted towards a form of governmental capacity, or *gubernaculum*, based on dynastic privilege. Instead, it treats an increasingly expansive and socially ambitious form of governmental authority and the principled, rule-based, limitation of government in the name of its free and equal subjects – its *iurisdictio* – as two sides of the same enterprise. And unlike its predecessors, modern constitutionalism does not see governmental authority as indistinct from sovereignty, and so as a necessarily unitary structure, but, as we will explore in greater depth later,[22] at least in some instances as reflecting and responding to a plurality of founding constituencies.

We may observe, therefore, how modern constitutionalism is distinctive in its embrace and negotiation of various antinomies at the heart of collective self-rule, not only the elementary trade-off between past and future – founding authority and continuing consent, but also the particular and the universal, collective and individual, unity and plurality.[23] Yet in the dominance of the state constitutional method we can also see dangers and drawbacks. For it remains vulnerable inasmuch as, inevitably, it fails to resolve fully the resulting tensions. The modern constitutional appeal to the abstract normative text as the mature expression of popular sovereignty, complemented and corroborated by certain universal standards, carefully balancing governmental authority and constraint, reconciling the need for a unitary structure of governance with the accommodation of group differences, and all sustained by a narrative that treats the documentary or other fundamental source as a reflexive framework of development, has always been a fragile accomplishment. The emphasis on an abstract normative framework incorporating a mechanism for occasional amendment may be constitutionalism's paradigmatic, if – as we have noted, far from perfect, method of recognizing popular sovereignty as extensive over time, yet that method cannot avoid and, indeed, may help foster other tensions and produce further dilemmas. If unduly deferential to universal standards and to the strict terms and close constraints of a canonical text, this can lead to a deracinated political culture in which popular sovereignty is either sidelined or its achievements fossilized. Alternatively, in the name of

[21] See e.g. D. Armitage, *The Declaration of Independence: A Global History* (Harvard: Harvard University Press, 2007).

[22] Section 3(b)(ii) below.

[23] N. Walker, 'The Antinomies of Constitutional Authority' in M Del Mar and R. Cotterrell (eds.), *Authority in Transnational Legal Theory* (London: Edward Elgar, 2016) 125–150.

constitutional populism – of which we will have more to say later – only lip service might be paid to the universal, and insufficient attention to the textually abstract and the jurisdictionally constraining aspects of the constitutional settlement. In the former case, the fear is of capture of the constitutional high ground by narrow interests presenting themselves in universal terms, or of a political system gripped by inter-institutional gridlock and undermined by a too thinly spread culture of common commitment. In the latter case, the danger is that the constitution becomes the vehicle for a narrow and chauvinistic nativism.[24]

These vulnerable tendencies towards elite capture, towards stasis or towards parochial nationalism may be more or less pronounced and more or less combined. No mature constitutional system ever escapes the attendant tensions. Even in the most robust and most widely endorsed constitutional settlements there is endless debate not only over the rigidity of the forms of constitutional amendment but also over the merits of strong constitutional review of legislation, over the range and depth of inter-institutional checks and balances, over the justification of constitutional exceptionalism and, more generally, over whether constitutionalism is better understood as the governing legal code of the national democratic project or as its instrument.[25] But often constitutional failure, and even state failure, ensues where the contradictions attendant upon our constitutional antinomies become too pronounced.[26] In turn, this highlights the deeper burden and a more pronounced weakness of state-centred constitutionalized sovereignty. For precisely because its approach *is* holistic, announcing and seeking to secure the comprehensive self-containment of the political sphere, constitutionalized sovereignty purports to monopolize all available resources of legal authority and political imagination. To the extent that state constitutionalism is the 'only game in town' that both intensifies the competition to influence its terms of application and amplifies the consequences of its failure.

This trend towards monopolization is reinforced by the global systemic effects of sovereignty's deep structure. The high modern world of

[24] See e.g. N. Walker, 'Beyond the Holistic Constitution?' in P. Dobner and M. Loughlin (eds.) *The Twilight of Constitutionalism?* (Oxford: Oxford University Press, 2010) 291–308.

[25] See e.g. N. Walker, 'Constitutionalism and the Incompleteness of Democracy: An Iterative Relationship' 3 *Rechtsfilosofie &Rechtstheorie* (2010) 206–233.

[26] Z. Elkins, T. Ginsburg and J. Melton, *The Endurance of National Constitutions* (Cambridge: Cambridge University Press, 2009) chs. 6–8.

constitutionalized sovereignty is one in which individual sovereignties are sustained by the overall framework of relations between sovereigns. The state is the only polity form recognized as sovereign, so supplying a universal template. That universal template is one that treats sovereignty as a comprehensive title to internal authority. And, in turn, these two features of universality of form and comprehensiveness of authority complement, and are complemented by, the relational principle of mutual exclusivity of sovereign claims. Otherwise put, the principle of *mutual* exclusivity of sovereign claims considered together is both cause and consequence of the exclusivity of each formally identical sovereign claim considered independently.[27]

But the monopolizing impulse, as well as emphasizing the vulnerabilities of the state constitutionalist template as a vehicle for framing and resolving underlying antinomies, also discriminates against approaches to political authority and community that do not fit its self-reinforcing systemic logic. Take, first, the question of empire and its legacy. The relationship between constitutionalism, sovereignty and the history of modern imperialism is complex. It is undoubtedly the case that, even with the advent of the constitutional age, a resiliently expansive conception of *external* sovereignty as a force outstripping those constraints of constitutionalism that had begun from the late eighteenth century to attach to the domestic realm of *internal* sovereignty for long permitted the kind of constitutional 'double think' that enabled the unchecked power of colonialism.[28] Moreover, even as the process of decolonization has gradually unfolded, one protracted consequence of the growing dominance of the state-centred constitutional form has been the imposition of 'low intensity'[29] constitutional democratization on indigenous and other non-Western peoples with insufficient regard either to their initial political consent or to their ongoing participation. Here again, we see how the modern template of constitutionalized sovereignty may be harmful not just because of the objective conditions of its application and reception but also because of the limitations inherent in its vision of authority. For the deep Western tradition, centred on the very idea of sovereignty as an active, agency-based concept, has shaped and sustained

[27] See e.g. N. Walker, 'Sovereignty and Beyond: The Double Edge of External Constitutionalism' 57 *Virginia Journal of International Law* (2018) 799–820.

[28] See e.g. J. Pitts, *Boundaries of the International: Law and Empire* (Harvard: Harvard University Press, 2018).

[29] J. Tully, 'The Imperialism of Modern Constitutional Democracy' in M. Loughlin and N. Walker (eds.) *The Paradox of Constitutionalism* (2007) 315–338, 333.

a particular understanding of what counts as polity-generative, allowing the move from premodern to modern to be comprehended in initiative-centred terms. In this perspective, the establishment of modern political community involves an unprecedented act of collective agency, one typically ceremonialized as a revolutionary break from the premodern and preindustrial past. And however limited this is as a self-description of Western political method, it may be even more inappropriate to the more continuous conceptions of consent and more fluid sense of the organization of self-rule that we find within other political traditions.[30]

If the age of empire was one in which sovereign self-determination remained a rare prize, monopolized or controlled by the imperial powers themselves, the postcolonial age, particularly since the end of the Second World War and the advent of the United Nations, has been one in which the systemic logic of state sovereignty has been more fully exploited and rolled out on a global scale. And yet this formal generalization and equalization of sovereign authority has also generated irritants within the system. In becoming more widely available, the privileges of sovereignty are also subject to greater competition from those who want to join the club or who seek new forms of supervening authority to deal with the 'anarchy'[31] or supplement the fragmented influence of a world of sovereign monads. That leads us to a second and more immediate misfit between the template of constitutionalized state sovereignty and certain deep trends of political authority. In a nutshell, this concerns the contemporary tendency towards the transnational and subnational extension of political authority and the uneven accompaniment of this rescaling by new forms of constitutional discourse and treatment.

Palpably, the new horizon of possibility offered by transnationalization fails to match the systemic logic of state constitutionalism. Monopolistic state constitutionalism can accommodate only a thin sense of the transnational, conceived of as the narrowly *inter*-national – a sphere of limited relations between mutually exclusive and compartmentalized state sovereigns. Yet in a world of ever increasing economic, military and technological externalities that escape the material capacity and political authority of any individual state, and of communities of attachment or purpose that straddle national boundaries, a narrow insistence on the state as the only or primary political form may leave the domain of

[30] See e.g. J. Tully, *Strange Multiplicity: Constitutionalism in an Age of Diversity* (Cambridge: Cambridge University Press, 1996).

[31] H. Bull, *The Anarchical Society* (New York: Columbia University Press, 1967).

transnational regulation in some respects under-recognized and underpowered, and in other respects significantly empowered and enabled without appropriately inclusive forms of voice or accountability.[32] These concerns – that transnational law is either inadequately or excessively empowered in the face of new global challenges – crystallize in the ongoing constitutional controversy surrounding the development of social and economic regulatory orders such as the European Union – the thickest global experiment in transnational polity to date – the United Nations, the World Trade Organization, the World Bank, the global climate change regime and the International Criminal Court. Compounding the controversy, while the spread of sovereignty has undoubtedly increased the influence of the global South, all such entities were crafted and continue to be disproportionately influenced by the traditional Western powers.

Alongside these global and transnational tendencies, other disturbances to the authority of the state emanate from below. Ironically, the seeds of this challenge to the modern state-centred constitutional system were sown in the foundational American settlement. As well as the first modern state, the United States was also the first mature federation. For in seeking to bring together a range of prior political communities – the former British colonies – into one, it generated one of the key antinomies of modern constitutionalism, namely the opposition between unity and plurality – the people conceived of as a politico-cultural singularity and the *peoples* understood as a combination of groups, joined together in a web of mutual interests. The federal solution was to give novel constitutional form to the accommodation of this tension through the idea of territorially distributed power *within* the polity. This involved a clear division between the two levels of authority and their respective policy spheres, a relatively high degree of ethnic or cultural homogeneity between the different state units, and uniform and symmetrical legal and institutional treatment of these units.[33]

32 The key literature on these questions includes: A. Paulus, 'The International Legal System as a Constitution' in J. L. Dunoff and J. P. Trachtman (eds.) *Ruling the World? Constitutionalism, International Law and Global Governance* (Cambridge: Cambridge University Press, 2009) 69–112; A. Peters, 'Membership in the Global Constitutional Community' in J. Klabbers, A. Peters and G Ulfstein (eds.) *The Constitutionalization of International Law* (Oxford: Oxford University Press, 2009) 153–262; M. Kumm, 'The Best of Times and the Worst of Times: Between Constitutional Triumphalism and Nostalgia' in P. Dobner and M. Loughlin (eds.) *The Twilight of Constitutionalism?* (Oxford: Oxford University Press, 2010) 201–220.

33 The classic English language analysis is still that of K. C. Wheare, *Federal Government* (Oxford: Oxford University Press, 1964, 4th edn.).

Contemporary federalisms and quasi-federalisms have gradually departed from that classical norm. Most newer federations, such as Germany, are 'co-operative' rather than 'dual' arrangements, involving a significant degree of policy overlap and institutional interlocking between central and local levels. Many, such as Canada, Spain or Belgium, as well as the quasi-federal or 'Union State'[34] UK, are also multinational or multi-ethnic rather than merely territorial compacts, with some constituencies retaining aspirations towards stronger forms of constitutional recognition. And these multinational or multi-ethnic federations tend, in addition, towards uneven or asymmetrical treatment of their provinces; those with the clearest or most longstanding traditions of distinctiveness, or the strongest claim to national identity, are accorded more ample recognition of cultural goods such as language or religion, greater regional governmental autonomy or disproportionate influence at the federal centre. All these factors combine to create a looser and more fluid political form, challenging the earlier conception of the federal state as a mere variation of the sovereigntist ideal of a well-ordered and permanently settled unity.[35]

So when considering the overall contemporary challenge to the state sovereigntist template we must look to both flanks – to pressures from the sub-state interior as well as from the transnational beyond. Furthermore, the two dynamics feed off one another. Claims to sub-state national recognition or protection are powerfully sponsored through global mechanisms for the promotion of individual or collective rights, while supranational institutions such as the EU provide a scale of policy and economic support that makes the ambition of greater regional autonomy within existing states more viable. By the same token, just because existing states have gradually ceded authority and capacity upwards to other territorial or functional institutions, they may become less attractive magnets for sub-state nations and less well equipped to maintain their sovereign integrity.[36]

Taken together, these shifts do more than simply challenge the position of individual sovereigns or the centrality of the conventional constitutional method through which they act. If the high modern world ushered in by the new constitutionalized sovereignty emphasized universality of form,

34 See e.g. C. Kidd, *Union and Unionisms* (Cambridge: Cambridge University Press, 2010).

35 See e.g. M. Keating, *Plurinational Democracy: Stateless Nations in a Postnational Era* (Oxford: Oxford University Press, 2005).

36 See e.g. S. Tierney, *Constitutional Law and National Pluralism* (Oxford: Oxford University Press, 2005) ch. 4.

comprehensiveness of authority and mutual exclusivity of claims, the late modern world of today disturbs that systemic logic. While the state remains the focus of political organization, it is now merely first amongst equals. In place of a universal and uniform template of sovereign statehood we have a highly differentiated global mosaic of legal and political capacities. In place of internal sovereignty as comprehensive, final authority is sometimes partial – distributed between various political sites and levels, states and otherwise. And in place of mutual exclusivity as the default condition of external sovereignty, we have an increasing incidence of overlap, interlock and mutual interference.

3 Sovereignty's New Stirrings

(a) Extending the Metaphor

If the metaphor of the sleeping sovereign has a reductive quality, both describing the objective limitations of a sovereignty-centred political practice and contributing to the very political imaginary in which such a practice and its limitations appear as natural and dominant features of the political landscape, what value lies in introducing the idea of a *stirring* sovereign? How, if at all, does it help us in thinking beyond the binary logic of the dominant sovereigntist vision and in addressing the vexed question of fit between new patterns of authority and state sovereignty's deep and systemically reinforced structure?

There is, of course, something obviously 'in-between' about the image of stirring. The stirring sovereign is on the cusp of wakefulness. The stirring sovereign may be anticipating the ringing of the alarm clock, preparing to wake up at a predetermined time, or struggling awake to deal with unanticipated developments, perhaps disturbed by the clamour outside. The stirring sovereign may also have devised or negotiated a new and more or less elaborate procedure for coming to full consciousness. Extending the metaphor further, we may liken this procedure to hitting the 'snooze' button on the alarm one or more times to delay rousing, or to the opening of the bedroom curtains and gradual exposure to the natural light of the external environment, or to responding to a distant phone call. The stirring sovereign may, alternatively, suffer from insomnia, and go through phases where sleep is shallow and fitful, and consciousness is never far off. The stirring sovereign may, by contrast, fail to wake up. The alarm or wake-up call may be slept through, the clamour pass unheard. The sleeping sovereign may be too tired to wake up, exhausted by recent or repeated activity. Or too ill, perhaps, even comatose. And, most tellingly, the image of stirring, unlike full sovereign alertness, may encourage us to look beyond the present incumbent. There may be adjacent rooms where other prospective sovereigns are trying to rouse themselves for the first time, whether newcomers stirring themselves towards new and perhaps altered states of sovereign consciousness or old sovereigns, thought dead or moribund, showing fresh signs of life.

We can multiply the imagery, but the basic idea is the same; that the stirring metaphor helps us move beyond a binary understanding of the practice of sovereignty. It allows us to contemplate what factors bear upon and what processes lead to the achievement of full sovereign alertness. It focuses our interest on what happens beyond and before the activation of the constitutional renewal or amendment procedure, and which may or may not affect that procedure. It allows us to ask why sovereign activity in some circumstances fails to progress to actual constitutional change. And it alerts us to the possibility that there may be multiple candidates, with overlapping or competing plans, seeking to achieve and act upon some measure of sovereign standing at one and the same time.

Can this extended metaphor of the stirring metaphor point us towards and allow us to articulate a recent pattern of innovative or intensified developments within sovereigntist politics? I will argue that it can, but that the message to be drawn from this is double-edged. As emerged in the previous section, today there are various constitutional stirrings that can be understood as a challenge and response to the limitations of the deep structure of sovereignty. Yet, crucially, all such stirrings, however non-binary in intention or design, continue to take place *within* the deep structure of sovereignty, and so continue to be informed by the limits of that deep structure. And, indeed, some of the new stirrings, at least in part, involve a reaction to and against the challenge to the deep structure offered by other new stirrings.

(b) The Four 'R's

We can illustrate these stirring tendencies, and how they relate to each other, by reference to the four Rs. The *Reassembling* of sovereignty refers to the ways in which more elaborate and inclusive procedures that go beyond the normal menu of constitutional amendment techniques are being used to bring about constitutional settlement or galvanize constitutional change. The *Raising* of sovereignty refers to the making of new claims or the resurrection of old claims by those who dispute the present pattern of sovereign authority. The *Rationing* of sovereignty refers, most radically, to the process by which certain entities seek to split the sovereignty atom. Sovereignty is understood as something to be shared and balanced out, and so as involving a moderated capacity and altered perspective on the part of still autonomous but now overlapping and interacting and so no longer omnicompetent entities. Finally, the *Reassertion* of sovereignty involves the restatement and reaffirmation of an existing sovereign claim, often in response to the challenges associated with reassembling, raising and rationing. Let us now look at each of these trends in greater detail.

(i) Reassembling

The *reassembling* of sovereignty responds to secular trends in global attitudes to democratic self-government. In the post–Second World War years, while there have been repeated waves and troughs of democratic initiative and consolidation, the overall tendency has been sharply towards the championing of democracy as a 'universal commitment',[37] and so as the normal template of government. The proto-democratic impulse in the original modernist endorsement of constitutionalism as an act of collective self-authorship, which was expressed in the work of Hobbes and Rousseau, has matured into a more general attachment to democratic method in matters of governance. And alongside that trend, and indeed as one particular manifestation of it, the sustaining of political society is today more than ever concerned with the negotiation and reconciliation of the differences in self-understanding and world-view between different self-identifying groups who live together in physical and practical proximity.[38] These two tendencies have fed new concerns over the appropriateness of the classical means both of founding and formulating constitutional authorship and of establishing and maintaining continuing consent, and also over how to accommodate the resilient tension between these values. And it is in response to these

[37] A. Sen, 'Democracy as a Universal Value' 10 *Journal of Democracy* 3–17 (1999). In 1941 only 13 countries could meet the most basic criteria of democratic self-government, but by the end of the century as many as 119 out of 192 countries could be described as electoral democracies – a figure that has stayed fairly constant since; see Freedom House Report, *Democracy's Century: A Survey of Global Political Change in the 20th Century* (1999).

[38] See e.g. S. Chambers, 'Democracy, Popular Sovereignty and Democratic Legitimacy' 11 *Constellations* 153–173 (2004).

concerns that we can see the development of new methods of constitutional initiative and reform that involve some measure of reassembling of sovereignty.

At the point of constitutional initiative, various contemporary authors have drawn attention to the growing significance of so-called 'pacted transitions'.[39] The trend here identified is one of movement beyond 'the old antinomy of reform and revolution'[40] and the devices normally associated with these. Where a revolutionary rupture in both legitimacy and legality has taken place, the Constituent Assembly has typically been favoured, as, for example, in the French Revolutionary period of 1789–1795, the Weimar Constitution of 1919 or the Indian Independence Constitution of 1948–1950. Where the general legitimacy of a system of government continues, but there is a rupture in constitutional legality, the Constitutional Convention has instead been the typical tool of initiative, as, for example, with the American federal Convention of 1787, the Argentinian Constitution of 1949 or the Russian Constitution of 1993. Under the pacted transition, by contrast, the emphasis is upon the establishment of new grounds of legitimacy within a framework of legal continuity. The focal case is one of the assembling or reassembling of a corporate sense of peoplehood from varied sources, and often, too, a highly conflicted prehistory. Constitution-making in this context no longer presupposes a monolithic people but acknowledges the plurality and diversity of the constituencies from which new or renewed constitutional demos will be constructed.

There is no single procedural pathway along which all pacted transitions travel. Instead, we can identify a range of mechanisms that tend to be present.[41] Round table type negotiations between representatives of different constituencies provide a frequent starting point in lieu of the unitarian decision-making structure of the Constituent Assembly or Convention. The development of an interim constitutional settlement by the Parliament of the existing regime, but guided by the round table conclusions, may follow. Next in sequence are free PR-based elections for

[39] G. O'Donnell and P. Schmitter, *Transitions from Authoritarian Rule: Tentative Conclusions About Uncertain Democracies* (Baltimore and London: Johns Hopkins University Press, 1986).

[40] A. Arato, *Post Sovereign Constitution Making: Learning and Legitimacy* (Oxford: Oxford University Press, 2016) 10.

[41] *Ibid.* chs 2–3. Arato does not use the language of 'pacted transitions'. He prefers to talk of the 'round table paradigm', but the phenomenon he identifies, and of which he offers a useful and subtle 'thick description', is essentially the same.

a new assembly, which then seeks to develop a final constitutional settlement – whose conformity with the diversity-respecting guiding principles of the interim constitution may be subject to judicial scrutiny and ratification. Post-apartheid South Africa is perhaps the best-known example of the successful achievement of this type of constitutional transition, and post-Franco Spain displays similar attributes. Other recent examples, exhibiting varying degrees of success, include Poland, Bulgaria, Czechoslovakia, Hungary, Iraq and Nepal. What these cases have in common are an emphasis upon legal continuity, publicity of proceedings, electoral accountability, the negotiation of a pluralist consensus and a commitment to constitutional learning manifest both in the passage from interim to full constitution and in a preparedness to learn from the experience of similar processes worldwide.[42]

Just as there is a stress on continuity even at the initiative stage, many new constitutional arrangements of recent years, in pacted transitions but also more generally, incorporate or come to endorse highly inclusive, public and deliberative procedures for constitutional amendment. Examples range from National Forums, Citizen's Assemblies and wider digital methods of crowdsourcing[43] to deliberative forms of referenda.[44] Just as new beginnings are increasingly framed in a relatively non-discontinuous way, it appears that subsequent constitutional reforms are increasingly treated as self-standing events and processes that are held to a high independent standard of legitimacy. The very distinction between original and ongoing consent, therefore, and so between constituent and constituted power, becomes blurred because of convergent movement from both ends; initiative is approached *less* as a fundamentally constitutive event, while amendment is treated rather *more* like a rebooting moment in its own right. And so, the old tension between founding authority and continuing consent is increasingly accommodated by the introduction of a suite of mechanisms that tend to treat them as of similar import.

One of the leading chroniclers of these new methods of constitutional reassembling has explicitly labelled them as 'post sovereign' types of stirrings.[45] The stress upon the diversity of the parties to renewed

[42] *Ibid.* esp. 100–118.

[43] See e.g. S. Suteu, 'Constitutional Conventions in the Digital Era: Lessons from Iceland and Ireland', 38 *Boston College Int'l & Comp. L. Rev.* 251 (2015).

[44] See e.g. S. Tierney, Constitutional Referendums; The Theory and Practice of Republican Deliberation (2012).

[45] Arato, n40 above.

constitutional agreement and upon a form of legal continuity stretching back to an increasingly remote original authority feeds the suggestion that this type of activity has somehow escaped the frame of unitary sovereignty. Yet such language threatens to overstate what is involved. In terms of a conventional sovereigntist logic, the new forms of assembling are better seen as *pre*-sovereign, or perhaps even as reiteratively sovereign. They are part of an exercise of constitutional construction intended *not* to move beyond sovereign authority but rather to remake sovereign authority from more plural and inclusive materials. If these stirrings are successful, they lead to the articulation of a new sovereign authority. If unsuccessful, there will be reversion to an old form of sovereign authority or to a power vacuum which different potential sovereigns will vie to fill. Whichever way, sovereignty, whether present or temporarily absent, remains the master category.

(ii) Raising

The trend towards the affirmation of a wider range of political identities is also at the heart of the new type of sovereignty stirring involved in the *raising* of new sovereign claims below the state. Constitutional engineering has become increasingly adept at developing markers of group recognition within the existing state sovereign framework. These markers include language and other group-based cultural rights (education, etc.) organized around 'personal' jurisdiction (e.g. Belgium's Communities and Language Areas, as distinct from its territorial regions), forms of symbolic recognition (e.g. recognition of Catalonia and other historical territories as distinct 'nationalities' in the Spanish Constitution), forms of distinct representation within central institutions (e.g. weighted representation in federal second chambers, rights of representation and veto in consociational governing arrangements), as well as the institutions of territorial self-government we noted in our earlier discussion of the development of federal and quasi-federal states. Yet the rolling out of these various forms of recognition is far from a universal trend. In some cases the dominance of an integrationist or even an assimilationist approach[46] within the domestic constitutional culture militates against accommodation.[47] And

[46] See e.g. J. McQuarrie, B. O'Leary and R. Simeon, 'Integration or Accommodation? The Enduring Debate in Conflict Regulation' in S. Choudhry (ed.) *Constitutional Design for Divided Societies: Integration or Accommodation?* (Oxford: Oxford University Press, 2008) 41–88.

[47] And as we shall see, some reassertions of a more monocultural approach can be seen as a conscious reaction against pluralist tendencies; see Section 3(b)(iv) below.

even where measures of accommodation are in place, this may not satisfy the constitutional aspirations of those whose collective identities do not map easily onto the prevailing settlement of sovereign constitutional space. It is in these circumstances that we encounter the stirrings of new claims of sovereignty from below.

As already noted, these new bottom-up aspirations are to some extent also nourished by top-down developments in the global configuration of authority. Sub-state entities gain legal, political and economic support and encouragement from planetary and regional institutions seeking to uphold universal standards of rights protection or to promote locally realizable aspect of global public goods in matters as diverse as language promotion and environmental protection. By acting as checks on state sovereigns and by providing a more favourable context for the pursuit of sub-state rights, an ever-denser framework of global and regional governance can help nurture the ambitions of sub-state national movements to be something more than the contained part of an established sovereign whole.

In the case of the EU, as the most fully developed supranational polity, the encouragement offered to sub-state national movements is arguably most pronounced. As discussed further below, the EU is engaged in its own type of sovereignty stirring. It can be persuasively understood as an explicit experiment in the *rationing* of the sovereignty of its member states. Not only do its institutional arrangements have significant material benefits for sub-state parties, permitting them through a raft of regulatory, redistributive and representative mechanisms to deal directly with the EU alongside the member states within a new '3D' quasi-federal arrangement.[48] In addition, the EU's very existence as an experimental polity of this sort may be seen as giving ideological support to a new type of post-national politics in which sub-state parties need not be limited to a subordinate role.

It is at least partly in response to its unsettling of the systemic logic of two-dimensional mutually exclusive sovereignty that there has been a significant recent shift in the domestic politics of the EU member states from 'teleological nationalism' – the conventional, traditionally sovereigntist form of sub-state nationalism – to what I have elsewhere described as 'reflexive nationalism'.[49] This reflexive orientation, which

[48] See N. Walker, 'Federalism in 3D: The Reimagination of Political Community in the European Union'. 1 *Catolica Law Review* 67–90 (2017).

[49] N. Walker, 'Teleological and Reflexive Nationalism in the New Europe' in J. Jordana, M. Keating, A. Marx and J. Wouters (eds.) *Changing Borders in Europe* (London: Routledge, 2018).

involves a less linear pattern of stirring towards full sovereign consciousness, has become prominent in Scotland, Ireland, Catalonia, the Basque Country, Flanders, Brittany and Northern Italy, amongst other venues of sub-state aspiration. Where teleological nationalism typically involves a set menu of goals, the ultimate dish being full sovereignty, reflexive nationalism, by contrast, involves a fluid relationship between a self-defining 'people' and the varied means of projection of its collective voice that are available in a multilevel polity. Here goals are cumulative rather than predetermined, relative rather than absolute. Instead of the pursuit of a predetermined state of affairs by a fixed subject, the project of reflexive nationalism involves a shifting nexus between a putative 'people' whose very membership and territorial extension is revisable and contestable – and an adjustable set of political institutions and objectives. Moreover, the reflexive approach is also sensitive to shifts in the relationship of its national 'people' to other intersubjective constructions of peoplehood (British and English as well as Scottish; Belgian and Wallonian as well as Flemish; Spanish and Castilian as well as Catalan) that attach themselves to overlapping territorial domains, and to the political institutions and goals associated with these constructions.

Reflexive nationalism, in consequence, emphasizes process over substance and output. The nationalist project does not, on this view, imply either a duty to pursue or a right to enjoy any particular outcome. Rather, it involves an entitlement to recognition and consideration of the nationalist claim as a resilient feature of the political landscape and, provided certain conditions of popular support and of respect for other identities are met, as something to be given procedural form. Crucially, therefore, reflexive nationalism claims a standing right to decide – a *sovereignty of choice* rather than teleological nationalism's *sovereignty of outcome*. In some cases, including the relatively stable democracies of Western Europe, these procedural claims to recognition and consideration will have – or at least be asserted by their proponents to have – an internal constitutional pedigree in the host state, however tenuous.[50] Alternatively, in more deeply and resiliently divided societies like Cyprus or Kosovo, such procedural claims and their institutional supports may depend entirely on international initiative.[51] Whatever the

[50] See e.g. C. Closa (ed.) *Secession from a Member State and Withdrawal from the European Union: Troubled Membership* (Cambridge: Cambridge University Press, 2017).

[51] In Cyprus, which joined the EU in 2004, there have been repeated rounds of (so far unsuccessful) talks organized through the offices of the United Nations between the Greek South and the Turkish North since the Turkish occupation in 1974. In Kosovo,

balance of internal and external support, just as outcomes favourable to the nationalist cause are not guaranteed, so, too, occasional failure or frustration of the nationalist project need not exhaust the underlying procedural claim.

Yet support for the distinctively reflexive sovereigntist politics of sub-state nationalisms in the European theatre extends only so far. The EU, as we have seen, gives both normative and material succour to those who would see the political constellation in multilevel and multipolar terms and who would seek to protect various projects of collective autonomy and the resilient aspirations associated with these. Yet for both ideological and strategic reasons, the EU cannot be an unequivocal champion of the rights of sub-state nations. Ideologically, while the EU supports a pluralist identity politics, precisely because it can be understood as an experiment in splitting the sovereignty atom and rationing its distribution it is bound to have reservations about any sub-state nationalist project being pursued in explicitly sovereigntist terms – however subtly qualified or deferred. Arguably, the aim of the EU should be to make sovereignty struggles between its different internal levels redundant – a gratuitous symbolic indulgence in the face of a new spread and coordination of authority, rather than to encourage their fuller articulation. And strategically, the EU remains, at least in pedigree terms, the creature of its member states, many of whom are jealous of the sovereigntist claims of their sub-state parts.[52]

It is not surprising, therefore, that the EU, despite providing background conditions conducive to the development of sub-state political identities, has been at best neutral and at worst unsupportive in its reaction to concrete manifestations of the sovereign stirrings of reflexive nationalist movements. In the case of the Scottish independence movement, the EU, having witnessed the unusual flexibility of the unwritten British constitution in allowing a secession referendum in 2014, remained non-committal on the politically vital question of how easily a sovereign Scotland might rejoin the EU.[53] And as Scottish nationalists,

the United Nations Interim Administration Mission in Kosovo (UNMIK) has been a key player in negotiating the internal and external relations of Kosovo before and after its unilateral declaration of independence from Serbia in 2008. The European Union Rule of Law Mission in Kosovo (EULEX) has also been actively involved since 2008 to ensure peace and continued external oversight and to prepare Kosovo for eventual accession to the EU.

[52] See e.g. J. H. H. Weiler, 'Secessionism and Its Discontents' in C. Closa (ed.) *Secession from a Member state and Withdrawal from the European Union* 12–31.

[53] See Walker, n49 above.

following a 'no' vote in the first instance, seek to reassert their 'sovereign' right to decide through a second referendum in the face of the changed circumstances brought about by Brexit, the voice of the EU remains muted. As regards the case of Catalonia, here the position of the EU is clearer, its implications more profound. Under the terms of its federal constitution the Spanish central government has remained resolutely opposed to the claim of the Catalan people to a right to decide on their own sovereign future. And when matters came to a head with the Spanish government's punitive reaction to a unilateral declaration of independence by the Catalan nationalist government following an unofficial referendum in the autumn of 2017, the EU supported the default right of the Spanish sovereign to enforce the *status quo ante*.[54]

In summary, Europe offers some level of support to the raising of the sovereign banner at the subnational level. Indeed, the new politics of reflexive nationalism – including the right to decide, or, at least, 'to be taken seriously'[55] as potential sovereigns also has resonance beyond Europe. Yet the use of a sovereigntist narrative to pursue aspirations below the level of the state, even one of the moderated varieties associated with reflexive nationalism, also has a downside. It both confines sub-state nationals within a normative framework which, at least in traditional understandings, view the prize in all-or-nothing terms that fail to reflect the complex distributions of multilevel governance, and it provokes defensive reactions from those who feel their existing sovereign prerogatives to be directly threatened.

(iii) Rationing

If we approach contemporary global politics from the perspective of regional and planetary institutions, then rather than the surfeit of sovereignty claims – state and sub-state – that we witness from a bottom-up perspective, we see instead a movement towards the *rationing* of sovereignty. Whether it be the jurisdiction of the International Criminal Court in respect of genocide, war crimes and crimes against humanity, or the United Nations and its various organs in respect of the maintenance of peace and the pursuit of human rights, or the World Trade Organization in respect of international trade, or the various regional organizations – most prominently the EU – as regards the creation and regulation of

[54] See e.g. BBC, October 13 2017; 'EU Spain: Juncker does not want Catalonian independence' www.bbc.co.uk/news/world-europe-41610863.

[55] J. Klabbers, 'The Right to be Taken Seriously: Self-Determination in International Law'. 28 *Human Rights Quarterly* 186–206 (2006).

common markets, what we see is a tendency towards the curtailment of the previously comprehensive sovereign authority of the states in the name of a larger collective goal.

The idea of *rationing* captures important features of this process. It conveys how each of these powerful transnational organizations has enacted a planned restrictive distribution of the scarce resource of sovereignty in order to protect or advance some other good valued by the relevant sovereign entities. It is, then, in the first place, an exercise in restriction, indeed in self-denial. It stipulates a reduction in the sovereignty of each in the interests of all. The initial net result appears to be one, therefore, of an overall depletion of sovereignty.

In a landmark case in the early years of European integration, the European Court of Justice famously talked of the 'permanent limitation of the sovereign rights'[56] of member states as a step voluntarily undertaken by the member states themselves. Here, in the world's more powerful supranational organization, we find a clear statement of the rationing rationale, explicitly couched in terms of an overall reduction of sovereignty. Yet the narrative of rationing does not end there. For the question increasingly arises for all powerful transnational organizations, but most pressingly for the EU, whether, reflecting their gradual widening and deepening of competence – in the case of the EU in areas of social, fiscal and security policy beyond the original economic core – their position has graduated from one in which they are a vehicle for the collective self-restriction of the sovereign powers of the states to one in which they have acquired or seek to acquire a self-standing title to some element of sovereign authority; where, so to speak, they are not simply the rationing agency but are themselves in receipt of sovereign 'rations'. We see this in the gradual development of language of the 'pooling' or 'sharing' of sovereignty rather than its mere restriction.[57] Or in the development of various sovereignty proxies in the narratives of integration, through the use of terms such as the 'supremacy' or 'primacy' of European law.[58]

What we see, then, is another form of sovereign stirring – one in which transnational organizations begin to claim for themselves some of the attributes or ambitions of sovereignty. And in so doing, they draw much from the tradition of constitutionalism, with its deep involvement in

[56] *Flaminio Costa v ENEL* case 6/64, [1964] ECR 585.

[57] See e.g. N. Walker, 'Late Sovereignty in the European Union' in N. Walker (ed.) *Sovereignty in Transition* (Oxford: Hart, 2003) 3–30.

[58] See e.g. M. Avbelj, 'Supremacy or Primacy of EU Law: (Why) does it Matter?' 17 *European Law Journal* 744–763 (2011).

forms of modern state sovereignty. Sometimes this is a matter of language, and here constitutional self-reference can function as another of the proxy languages of sovereignty – and so as part of a rhetoric of self-assertion.[59] But it can also be a matter of practice. The project to make a first written Constitution for the EU in 2003–2005 may have failed, but one of its legacies has been a gradual mainstreaming of a way of thinking about and seeking to reform the architecture of the EU in constitutional terms.[60] This covers typical constitutional subjects such as fundamental rights and questions of institutional balance. But also, and increasingly, it embraces the sovereignty-centred question of supranational Europe's own constituent power: whether it is possible to imagine a popular sovereign at the EU level to rival the national sovereigns, or perhaps a 'dual' system in which the sovereign authors of the EU are conceived as the citizens of two *demoi* – Europe and the member states?[61]

For all these developments, however, we can see two persistent objections, which mirror the objection to the raising of sub-state sovereign claims. The first concerns the appropriateness of the assumption of the language of sovereignty by supranational entities which were founded just in order to tame the excesses and overcome the disorder of the existing system of sovereignty. The second concerns the reaction that the pursuit of supranational sovereigntist ambitions might invite from state sovereigns.

(iv) Reassertion

And so, finally, we return to the response of a certain type of state sovereigntist orientation to the various stirrings of these various new sovereign sensibilities. Here, it is useful to distinguish two types – or levels – of stirring, although the distinction between them often becomes blurred.

In the first place, there is a basic defensive type of response, one that involves familiar institutions of state government developing strategies

[59] See e.g. M. Maduro, 'The Importance of being called a Constitution; Constitutional Authority and the Authority of Constitutionalism' 3 *International Journal of Constitutional Law* 332–356 (2005).

[60] See e.g. N. Walker, 'The Legacy of the Lost EU Constitution' Edinburgh School of Law Working Papers, 2018/22: available at: https://papers.ssrn.com/sol3/papers.cfm?abstract_id=3188090.

[61] See e.g. M. Patberg, 'Challenging the Masters of the Treaties: Emerging Narratives of Constituent Power in the European Union' 7 *Global Constitutionalism* 263–293 (2018); see also D. Grimm, *The Constitution of European Democracy* (J. Collings trans. Oxford: Oxford University Press, 2017).

that seek to preserve a traditional understanding of constitutionalism's systemic pattern. This takes shape through the development of an intense form of 'demarcation sovereignty',[62] concerned with the staking and maintaining of boundaries deemed necessary to ensure the continuing basic integrity of the state sovereign unit. These boundaries run on either side, erected against the encroachment of sub-state aspirations and of transnational claims alike. They involve longstop protection of the domestic sovereign's control over both domestic and international affairs. Rules securing the federal system and preventing or restricting secession guard the inner boundary.[63] Often the power of these protections remains latent, but as we have seen with recent European sub-state independence movements, especially in the case of Catalonia, national sovereigns can be stirred towards very active forms of defence of the basic federal pact.

At the outer boundary, the demarcation strategy is typically more elaborate. One line of defence is to ensure that, notwithstanding membership of an increasing range of transnational organizations, an independent capacity to act as sovereign in external affairs is retained or is capable of being recovered. Quite apart from the power to withdraw from or denounce treaties, this may involve explicit constitutional provisions forbidding adherence to international agreements that would breach constitutional standards,[64] or requiring prior constitutional amendment before entering into treaties at variance with existing constitutional standards.[65] Another line of defence is the safeguarding of certain core features of the sovereign's constitutionally shaped expression – or what is sometime called its 'constitutional identity'[66] – from threat by transnational organizations.

[62] Walker, above n25, 815–820.

[63] Few contemporary state constitutions, federal or otherwise, explicitly permit secession – only Ethiopia, St Kitts and Nevis, and Liechtenstein, or even indirectly countenance its prospect – only Austria and Singapore. In all cases the procedural route is formidable. A far greater number of constitutions adopt the opposite posture, enshrining ideas, such as state 'indivisibility', 'national unity', and 'territorial integrity', which are more or less emphatically inconsistent with secession.

[64] See e.g. Constitution of the Democratic Socialist Republic of Sri Lanka, 1978 Article 33(f): German Basic Law, 1949 Article 23(1).

[65] See e.g. Constitution of the Fifth French Republic 1958, Article 54.

[66] See e.g. G.J. Jacobsohn, *Constitutional Identity* (Harvard: Harvard University Press, 2010); M. Rosenfeld, *The Identity of the Constitutional Subject: Selfhood, Citizenship, Culture, and Community* (London: Routledge, 2010).

As we have seen most intensely with regard to the EU, there is a growing body of constitutional jurisprudence in this area. This amounts to the active stirring of the national judiciary in response to those moves of the EU, or of its high judiciary, that are seen as violating certain fundamental normative standards or claiming control over competences deemed to be indispensable elements of the constitutional independence of the member states.[67] The new defensive jurisprudence often relies on explicit constitutional provisions but national constitutional or supreme courts have also become more prepared to discover unalterable or irreducible constitutional cores on the basis of a broader interpretation of the structural integrity and underlying ethos of the constitution.[68] In these types of situations, constitutional judges have been increasingly minded to oppose, write down or qualify external authority in matters as diverse as nationally affirmed human rights standards, the maintenance of the basic integrity of the state as a self-governing representative democracy, and national direction and control over core policy issues of national security and 'monetary sovereignty'.[69]

But if we look beyond these defensive strategies, the reassertive stirrings of national sovereigns can also take a more proactive and much less conservative form – one that, for shorthand, we can identify under the label of populism. Earlier we noted that populism was one response to the tensions built into the foundations of modern constitutionalized sovereignty, and so a recurring phenomenon of the constitutional age. But in the era of Trump, Erdogan, Orban, Maduro and many others, we are today confronted with a particularly high tide of populist governments and movements – one, moreover, that is strengthened by a measure of transnational support and coordination amongst the various nationalist tribes.[70] Again, in an age of enhanced Euroscepticism, with Brexit opening up a new horizon of revanchist possibility for nativist parties across

[67] See e.g. N. Walker, 'Constitutional Pluralism Revisited' 23 *European Law Journal* 333–355 (2016).

[68] See e.g. Y. Roznai, *Unconstitutional Constitutional Amendments: The Limits of Amendment Powers* (Oxford: Oxford University Press, 2017) esp. ch.3.

[69] Again, the European Union has provided a fertile context for the development of this type of defensive jurisprudence, in particular through the influential judgments of the German Constitutional Court. See e.g. M. Claes, 'The Validity and Primacy of EU Law and the "Cooperative Relationship" between National Constitutional Courts and the European Court of Justice' 23 *Maastricht Journal of International and Comparative Law* 151 (2016).

[70] See N. Walker, 'Populism and Constitutional Tension' 17(2) *International Journal of Constitutional Law* (2019).

the continent, and the governments of Poland and Hungary emerging as powerful nationalist critics inside the tent of European integration, the EU is an important centre of activity and collaboration,[71] but the populist strain of sovereignty reassertion is clearly also a wider global trend.

The intense contemporary variant of populism has been well described as involving 'a particular *moralistic imagination of politics*, a way of perceiving the political world that sets a morally pure and unified – but . . . ultimately fictional – people against elites who are deemed corrupt or in some other way morally inferior'.[72] But if the political arena is viewed as one involving a binary opposition between 'two homogenous and antagonistic camps',[73] then it is not clear whether constitutionalism has *any* significant role to play in the populist version of sovereignty. Populist regimes, armed with such a Manichean word view, are inherently sceptical towards all forms of intermediation between the exercise of power and their conception of a pure and unified popular will. And this scepticism will often register as hostility or 'resentment'[74] towards constitutional structures and rules that provide for the pluralist distribution of power, especially prominent in support of sub-state national movements, against its unitary articulation; or that supply individual protections, often used by powerful interests opposed to the regime, against the collective will; or that brook interference in their particular populist vision by reference to transnational or other supposedly universal or non-native norms.

Yet, crucially, it is by running these various scepticisms together that populism can find a voice *within* and not simply against the discourse of constitutionalized sovereignty. For the populist critique speaks precisely to how the deep tensions or antinomies within constitutionalism noted earlier – between plurality, individualism and universalism on the one side, and, on the other side, unity, collectivism, and particularism – can be seen to provide a mutually reinforcing set of 'nested oppositions',[75] with the populists defining themselves on the side of that great divide that

[71] See e.g. J. Schultes, 'The Complacency of Legality: Constitutionalist Vulnerabilities to the populist conception of constituent power' EUI Working Papers, LAW 2018/07 available at: http://cadmus.eui.eu/bitstream/handle/1814/51724/LAW_2018_07.pdf?sequence=1.

[72] Jan-Werner Muller, *What Is Populism?* (Philadelphia: University of Pennsylvania Press, 2016) 19–20.

[73] C. Mudde and C. R. Kaltwasser, *Populism: A Very Short Introduction* (Oxford: Oxford University Press, 2017) 5.

[74] P. Blokker, 'Populist Constitutionalism' *I-Connect/Verfassungsblog* May 4, 2017; available at: www.iconnectblog.com/2017/05/populist-constitutionalism.

[75] J. Balkin, 'Nested Oppositions' 99 *Yale Law Journal* 1699 (1990).

stands for the supposedly neglected *unitary collective particular*. In this perspective, the grievance of today's populist can be construed as but the latest instalment, amplified by a sense of increased threat from the sovereign stirrings of elite or other alien sources, in a familiar repetitive syndrome of constitutional action and reaction, protestation and redress, balance and counter-balance. In this conflict, the populists style themselves as the 'true' democrats, pitting themselves against the forces of a common enemy which goes under many names, perhaps most notably that of 'liberal constitutionalism'.[76]

In so doing, populists are not merely critics of the constitutional balance but are stirred into action to redress that balance. The practical constitutional strategies of populists range from the 'circumvention' of existing rules and procedures deemed to present a skewed inheritance to the broader 'commandeering' of the general process of constitutional revision and renewal in name of their own unimpeachable vision.[77] And in justifying and mobilizing support for these measures, populists also tap into that part of the modern constitutional imaginary, and its accompanying jurisgenerative method, that speaks to the most basic opposition between founding authority and continuing consent. Where, as we have seen, those engaged in reassembling try to resolve the tension by reducing the difference in constitutional gravity and method between different phases of popular sovereignty – treating both origins and contemporary moments as worthy of wide involvement and broad reflection – the populist simply refuses to acknowledge any such tension. The people as a moral unity are portrayed as timeless – neither 'then' nor 'now', neither original nor present, but always. They are reified – taken outside of and placed above history. That is why, indeed, constitutional populism can be both nostalgic and prophetic. It often involves a claimed redemption of a broken promise of original collective intent; but in conjunction with this, the constitutional politics will be forward-looking, the replacement of constitutional text and refashioning of constitutional institutions pursued not just as a commandeering strategy but also in symbolic affirmation of the renewal of a lost political unity.[78]

That is also why populists today tend to be supportive not just of large-scale constitutional change or regime succession but also of all the paraphernalia of constitutional events and moments – including

[76] See e.g. Muller, above n72; Blokker, above n74.

[77] Walker, above n70, 6–9.

[78] On these two sides of Trump's populism, see, for example, Michael Kazin, 'Trump and American Populism: Old Whine, New Bottles' 95(6) *Foreign Affairs* October 6 (2016).

referendums, constituent assemblies and other ceremonies of endorsement. The agenda of these demotic constitutional events is one of recovery.[79] Their content and direction have typically been preempted and prefixed by the populist insurgency, and even as it is fundamental to the populist credo that they take 'the people' seriously as a concrete sociopolitical entity against the false representativeness of elites or the stirrings of other local or cosmopolitan claims, because the interests of 'the people' are deemed to be self-evident and unchanging, there is scant recognition of the dangers of freezing this particular expression of popular sovereignty against later reconsideration.

4 Conclusion

Whenever and wherever sovereigns stir today, whether with a view to reassembling a scheme of foundational collective commitment, or to raising new and rival claims, or to rationing and redistributing existing claims, or to reasserting old claims and certain primitive sensibilities behind these claims, they remind us both of the limitations of a sovereignty-centred perspective and of the indispensability of that perspective to our modern political imaginary. We may have required Hobbes' genius to glimpse the outline of modern democracy and of modern constitutionalism, but the vital ingredient feeding Hobbes' imagination was the idea of sovereignty itself, and the ways in which it was being gradually recast for the modern age.

From Hobbes onwards, sovereignty has supplied 'a basic element of the grammar of politics',[80] and so it is no exaggeration to say that the political vocabulary of modernity would literally be meaningless in its absence. Yet as well as being epistemically vital, sovereignty is also materially and symbolically central.[81] It remains the top prize in the geopolitical game. As such, it is the vital means by which power and identity can be mobilized together to achieve our best collective ends. Yet it can also be a ruthlessly sought and jealously guarded asset, the reifying

[79] Jan Werner Muller, 'Populist Constitutions: A Contradiction in Terms' *Verfassungsblog* April 23 (2017) available at: https://verfassungsblog.de/populist-constitutions-a-contradiction-in-terms/

[80] R. Jackson, 'Sovereignty in World Politics: A Glance at the Conceptual and Historical Landscape' 43 *Political Studies* (1999) 431–456, 431.

[81] See e.g. N. Walker, 'The Variety of Sovereignty' in R. Adler-Nissen and T. Gammeltoft-Hansen (eds.) *Sovereignty Games: Instrumentalizimg State Sovereignty in Europe and Beyond* (London: Macmillan, 2008) 21–32.

support of the nation state, an impediment to transnationally coordinated action, the consolidator and exaggerator of political and cultural difference, a zero-sum calculator and the disappointer of diverse political expectations. Epistemic indispensability, material incentive and symbolic allure, and the wide variety of motives and predispositions associated with these are all mixed together in the various contemporary stirrings on which we have focused. As has ever been so of the modern age, it is at these places where the sleep of the sovereign is most profoundly disturbed that we witness both the vitality and the intransigence of the global political order.

3

The People as Popular Manifestation

JASON FRANK

Popular constituent power, once a concept closely associated with radical critiques of liberal constitutionalism on the left and the right, and with the investigations of such "Continental" topics as political theology, insurgent partisanship, and the sovereign state of exception, has recently become a key concern of Anglo-American democratic and constitutional theorists. As the concept has moved to the center of scholarly debates, it has also become more respectable, the subject of increasingly elaborate attempts to bring it within the fold of liberal constitutionalism itself: popular constituent power has become an important test of liberal constitutionalism's democratic capaciousness. This has had significant consequences for how its central concept – the constituent people – has been theorized. "As an actor," Andrew Arato writes, "the people are fictional unless they are redefined in legal terms as the collectivity of citizens or the electorate in which case they become an entity produced by law, rather than the ultimate source of law."[1] Viewing the people first and foremost as a legal entity rather than exploring their "fictional" status as "an actor" has been a hallmark of much of the recent scholarship on the popular constituent power.

Lost in these efforts to convert the people into an abstract legitimating norm and to ensure their enclosure within constitutional courts, conventions, and parliamentary proceedings is any sustained attention to what Joel Colón-Ríos has called the "informal practices" of the constituent people's "initiating powers": acts of civil disobedience, street assemblies, mass protests, insurgencies, and revolutionary upheaval.[2] Popular constituent power

[1] Andrew Arato, *The Adventures of the Constituent Power: Beyond Revolutions?* (Cambridge: Cambridge University Press, 2017), 28.

[2] Joel Colón-Ríos, *Weak Constitutionalism: Democratic Legitimacy and the Question of Constituent Power* (New York: Routledge, 2012), 178–182. See also Andreas Kalyvas, "Popular Sovereignty, Democracy, and Constituent Power," *Constellations* 12:2 (June 2005), 223–244, 230.

should bring these forms of extraparliamentary and insurgent politics into view because the people it envisions is irreducible to a legally authorized or institutionally articulated collective. The people of popular constituent power is always, at least in part, "the people out of doors." As such, the people of popular constituent power is poorly understood if it is reduced to the executive status of a constitutional author – "We the People" – and neglected as a dynamic, internally contested, and always provisional initiator of radical constitutional change. To dispel the "fiction" or the "myth" of the people as a collective actor is to neglect the dynamic generativity and concrete political productivity of these myths in contexts of radical democratic emergence and change. I will attempt to bring some of these neglected dimensions into view here by outlining a conception of the people as a problem of popular manifestation.

1 Constituent Power and the People Out of Doors

In a famous letter sent to James Madison in September of 1789, written from Paris in the midst of that summer's revolutionary upheaval, Thomas Jefferson elaborated on the principles of an inalienable and living popular sovereignty, wherein "the dead have no rights" and "no society" can legitimately "make a perpetual constitution, or even a perpetual law."[3] "The earth belongs always to the living generation," Jefferson proclaimed there, turning to the actuarial language of "generations" rather than "the people" to emphasize that the principles he invoked were not abstract principles of legitimation, so much as catalysts to the active and ongoing renewal of popular constituent power.[4] Every

[3] Thomas Jefferson, "Letter to James Madison, Paris, September 6, 1789," in Joyce Oldham Appleby and Terence Ball, eds. *Thomas Jefferson: Political Writings* (New York: Cambridge University Press, 1999), 593–8, 593.

[4] Jefferson, "Letter to James Madison, Paris, September 6, 1789," 596. See Mona Ozouf, "Regeneration," in François Furet and Mona Ozouf, eds. *A Critical Dictionary of the French Revolution* (Cambridge: Harvard University Press, 1989), 781–91. Herbert Sloan insightfully writes of this famous passage that "to speak of 'the people' is to speak abstractly . . . 'The people' never dies; it has the same corporate immortality and collective right of sovereignty that is attached to the king's political body in earlier theory. A 'generation,' on the other hand, and certainly a 'generation' as Jefferson defined it, is specific and identifiable. Unlike 'the people,' it has a limited duration, so there will be a time after which it no longer has rights. That limitation is critical, for it allows Jefferson to establish with precision who can exercise rights and when. With 'the people,' rights are, in effect, inchoate; with a 'generation,' we know exactly what we are dealing with." Sloan overstates the clarity and self-evidence of this knowledge and identifiability, but he is right to emphasize the importance of the contrast between abstract (if inchoate) principle and

nineteen years, Jefferson reasoned, the constitutional authority of the living generation "naturally expires" and must return to the reflection and choice of the people themselves. The recurrence to popular authorization could not be left up to the initiatives of reform movements of popular repeal, because "the people cannot assemble themselves . . . their representation is unequal and vicious."[5]

Jefferson's letter has been endlessly cited, parsed, and criticized by democratic and constitutional theorists interested in the political and legal dilemmas surrounding the concept of popular constituent power.[6] Alongside his equally famous comments on the value of insurrection – "a little rebellion now and then is a good thing, and as necessary in the political world as storms in the physical" – and even popular violence – "The tree of liberty must be refreshed from time to time with the blood of patriots and tyrants" – the 1789 letter to Madison is often cited as an example of Jefferson's dangerous political naivité, impracticality, and democratic romanticism.[7] Madison himself seems to have seen it in just this way, when, echoing arguments he had previously made in Federalist No. 49, he responded to Jefferson's letter with a set of "very powerful objections" to Jefferson's theoretical reasoning, most notably that Jefferson's schema would establish a government "too mutable to retain those prejudices in its favor which antiquity inspires" and which are "salutary to the most rational government in the most enlightened age."[8]

I turn to Jefferson's letter not to rehash familiar theoretical debates around the democratic legitimacy and practical viability of constituent power, constitutional precommitment, or popular constitutionalism. I am interested in the letter for what it more quietly suggests about Jefferson's understanding of the role of informal popular assemblies – crowds, mobs, gatherings of "the people out of doors" – in periods of

empirically existent collectivity. Jefferson implies that established procedures for assembling the living generation's constituent power will be in place to determine the authorized course of constitutional revision, which prevents an examination of the dynamics through which a people might be said to "assemble themselves." Herbert Sloan, "The Earth Belongs in Usufruct to the Living," in Peter Onuf, ed. *Jeffersonian Legacies* (Charlottesville: University of Virginia, 1993), 297.

5 Jefferson, "Letter to James Madison, Paris, September 6, 1789," 597.

6 See, for example, Stephen Holmes, *Passions and Constraint: On the Theory of Liberal Democracy* (Chicago: University of Chicago Press, 1995); Jed Rubenfeld, *Freedom and Time: A Theory of Constitutional Self-Government* (New Haven: Yale University Press, 2001).

7 Jefferson, *Political Writings*, 62, 110.

8 James Madison, "Letter to Thomas Jefferson, New York, February 4, 1790," in *Thomas Jefferson: Political Writings*, 606–9, 606.

revolutionary transition when constitutional authority does not "naturally expire" and where "unequal and vicious" representation has to be actively combatted and overcome by people who must precisely "assemble themselves" without relying on established legal authority or the authorized procedures of political will formation. Jefferson's famous letter, so thoroughly examined by contemporary democratic theorists interested in the problem of popular constituent power, indirectly points to another set of theoretical issues and problems that democratic theorists have generally avoided and that I am going to bring into focus through what I will call the problem of popular manifestation.

Jefferson's letters written from France during this period often returned to reflect on the mobs and crowds that propelled the Revolution forward, just as they had in the North American colonies a generation earlier. Already in 1774, Jefferson could write in his *Summary View of the Rights of British America* that "there are extraordinary situations which require extraordinary interposition. An exasperated people, who feel that they possess power, are not easily restrained within limits strictly regular."[9] Jefferson offered a conceptual contrast between "mobs" and "riots" that "seem to have no end in view but mischief and plunder," and those popular uprisings that intimate the very forms of popular democratic legitimacy described in his famous letter to Madison.[10] Jefferson distinguished, for example, between "mobs occasioned by want of bread in different parts of the kingdom" and those which have "connections generally with the constitutional revolution" underway.[11] Writing in the month after the fall of the Bastille, Jefferson concluded that "having observed the mobs with my own eyes in order to be satisfied of their objects, I saw so plainly the legitimacy of them."[12]

In the letters written from revolutionary France Jefferson tacks back and forth between what historians of contentious politics describe as

[9] Thomas Jefferson, *A Summary View of the Rights of British America* (The Avalon Project, Yale University Law School). http://avalon.law.yale.edu/18th_century/jeffsumm.asp2222

[10] Thomas Jefferson, "Letter to John Trumbull, June 29, 1789," in Julian P. Boyd, ed. *The Papers of Thomas Jefferson, Volume 15: March 1789–November 1789* (Princeton: Princeton University Press, 1958), 224. I am grateful to Angélica Bernal for drawing my attention to these letters. See her discussion in *Beyond Origins: Rethinking Founding in a Time of Constitutional Democracy* (New York: Oxford University Press, 2017), 159–92. See also Nicolaus Mills, "The Revolutionary Crowd of Adams and Jefferson," in *The Crowd in American Literature* (Baton Rouge: Louisiana State University Press, 1986), 18–40.

[11] Jefferson, *The Papers of Thomas Jefferson*, 121.

[12] Jefferson, "Letter to Diodati, August 3rd, 1789," in *The Papers of Thomas Jefferson*, 325.

"direct-action crowds" with immediate aims such as seizing grain supplies or publicly humiliating a deviant or criminal, and "symbolic crowds" invested with normative or legal authorization. During the late eighteenth century, the crowd went from being a localized collective seeking immediate redress of grievances – the direct action crowd acting only on the authority of those gathered and seeking redress from those immediately present – to a representative or symbolic crowd often seeking indirect redress of grievances and proclaiming to act on behalf of a larger symbolic entity: the people.[13] In Jefferson's view, the popular assemblies of Paris were an essential part of the project of total constitutional revision. "So strongly fortified was the despotism of this government by long possession, by the respect and fears of the people . . . the national assembly with all their good sense, could without mobs probably have only obtained a considerable improvement, not a total revision of it."[14] Far from being reduced to mere force, violence, or what Jürgen Habermas describes as the "pressure from the street," Jefferson approached "the ocular evidence" of revolutionary crowds and popular assemblies as signs of a formerly passive people emerging and taking form as a collective actor, a political collectivity giving tangible evidence of the people's existence and political capacity.[15]

Without offering a fully articulate theory of emergent popular assemblies, Jefferson's letters help us approach the revolutionary problem of popular manifestation, but he was hardly alone among prominent observers of the Revolution in identifying the formative role played by gatherings of the people out of doors – that is, the great *journees*, the popular insurrections and demonstrations, which broke out intermittently between 1789 and 1795 (one historian has counted 251 of them in Paris alone during these years) – in productively mediating the emergence of the people as a collective actor on the stage of history.[16] If democratic

[13] George Rudé, *The Crowd in History: A Study of Popular Disturbance in France and England, 1730–1848* (New York: Wiley and Sons, 1964).

[14] Jefferson, "Letter to Diodati, August 3rd, 1789," 325–26.

[15] "Laws passed under pressure of the street could hardly be understood any longer as embodying the reasonable consensus of publicly debating private persons." Jürgen Habermas, *The Structural Transformation of the Bourgeois Public Sphere: An Inquiry into a Category of Bourgeois Society* (Cambridge: MIT Press, 1992), 132; See Warren Montag, "The Pressure of the Street: Habermas's Fear of the Masses," in Mike Hill and Warren Montag, eds. *Masses, Classes, and the Public Sphere* (New York: Verso, 2000), 132–45.

[16] Micah Alpaugh, *Non-Violence and the French Revolution: Political Demonstrations in Paris, 1787–1795* (Cambridge: Cambridge University Press, 2014).

theorists, following Habermas's lead, have focused a great deal of attention on how a ratio-critical public emerged out of growing networks of print capitalism, coffee houses, reading publics, and so on, they have focused much less attention on how the proliferation of political crowds facilitated and gave tangibility to the people manifesting itself as a collective actor capable of facilitating dramatic political reforms and change. A century before Gustave Le Bon declared an "Age of Crowds" in 1895, there had been sustained attention paid to the significant role that informal popular assemblies played in mediating the transition from royal to popular sovereignty, and especially during the great democratic revolutions in America and France. "In political contexts animated by the emerging principle of popular sovereignty," Colin Lucas writes, "the physical display of the people as an embodiment of popular voice took on powerful new meaning."[17]

Revolutionary crowds like those that charged the Bastille intermingled with the emerging radical democratic idea – François Furet called it the "revolutionary catechism" – that collectives could act deliberately, indeed heroically, in taking their own political destiny into their hands.[18] This formative role of new collectivities was noted by some of the most influential and articulate observers of the Revolution, whether they were its passionate advocates or eloquent defenders of the *ancien régime*. Consider a familiar example. On October 5, 1789, a riot broke out in a central marketplace of Paris over the high price and the scarcity of bread. The riot was largely made up of women in the marketplace but it was soon joined by thousands of others who redirected the crowd's complaints beyond the price of bread to the larger political reforms being demanded by the National Assembly and the king's failure to respond effectively to the demands that had been mounting since earlier that summer. Over the course of the day the market women and their allies swelled into a crowd of thousands in front of the Hotel de Ville. Encouraged by revolutionary agitators, they ransacked the city armory for weapons and then marched the twelve or so miles to the royal palace at Versailles. Once there, the crowd besieged the palace, sent a delegation to meet the king, and finally the following morning broke into the palace itself, killed a few royal guards, and, in a dramatic confrontation that became the focus of many subsequent reports, compelled the king, the

[17] Colin Lucas, "The Crowd and Politics between 'Ancien Regime' and Revolution in France," *The Journal of Modern History* 60:3 (September 1988), 421–57, 434.

[18] François Furet, *Interpreting the French Revolution* (Cambridge: Cambridge University Press, 1981).

queen, their family, and members of Assembly to return with them to Paris.

This event was almost immediately mythologized as the Women's March on Versailles, and historians still debate the contours of what actually occurred. Along with the Reveillon Riots and the Bastille insurrection, it comprised one of the three great *journees* of 1789. According to George Rudé, the women's march "completed the Paris revolution of July, because so long as the King and Court remained at Versailles, power still remained divided between revolutionary citizens and the adherents of the *ancien régime*."[19] As the king and queen were compelled by the crowd to return to Paris against their will, many commentators identified a dramatic staging of the practical and symbolic transference of power from the crown to the people, here taking the form, in the words of Edmund Burke, of "the furies of hell in the abused shape of the vilest of women."[20]

Burke made this episode the centerpiece of his *Reflections on the Revolution in France*, the prism through which the revolutionary spectacle revealed its innermost essence as a brutal disenchantment of authority. It was a politics stripped of adornment and reduced to cold utility, "where laws are to be supported only by their own terrors," and where "at the end of every vista we see nothing but the gallows."[21] Burke's elaborate reflections on the world historical consequences of a crowd-ruined court and a violated queen had been provoked by a single line in Richard Price's political sermon "A Discourse on the Love of Our Country," which Price had delivered to London's Revolution Society in November of 1789 and then published in pamphlet form. For Price, the collective action of the October Days was nothing short of a sublime spectacle which condensed the broader revolutionary aspirations "of thirty millions of people, indignant and resolute, spurning at slavery, and demanding liberty with an irresistible voice, their king led in triumph, and an arbitrary monarch surrendering himself to his subjects."[22] Love it or loath it, Burke and Price agreed that the crowd played an essential role in the dynamic

[19] George Rudé, *The Crowd and the French Revolution* (Oxford: Oxford University Press, 1967), 61.

[20] Edmund Burke, *Reflections on the Revolution in France* (Indianapolis: Hackett Publishers, 1987).

[21] Burke, *Reflections on the Revolution in France*, 68.

[22] Richard Price, "A Discourse on the Love of Our Country," in D. O. Thomas, ed. *Price: Political Writings* (Cambridge: Cambridge University Press, 1992), 176–96, 195.

process of popular democratization that each identified with the unfolding Revolution itself.

For all of the attention contemporary observers and later historians placed on the emerging role of crowds and collectives in the dramatic events of the age, it is surprising they have received so little attention from democratic theorists, even those who have become centrally preoccupied with the politics of peoplehood and dilemmas associated with popular constituent power. Recent theoretical investigations into the politics of popular assembly – such as Judith Butler's performative theory of collective assembly or Jodi Dean's contrasting study of the disorganized desire of the crowd and the articulatory power of the vanguard party – are also largely disconnected from the history of these collective repertoires and their complicated entanglement with the history of popular sovereignty itself.[23]

The problem of popular manifestation emerges from this entanglement. It is related to, but conceptually distinct from, democratic theory's recent preoccupations with "the boundary problem" and the paradoxes of popular self-authorization, that is, the political and theoretical dilemmas that emerge from the fact that determining the identity of the sovereign people is an unavoidable democratic problem that is, nonetheless, not something that the people can themselves democratically decide: the very question subverts the premises of its resolution. In contrast to the dilemmas of legality, legitimacy, and authority posed by this "paradox of politics," the problem of popular manifestation might be more accurately described as an aesthetic problem.[24] It focuses instead on how this authorizing entity, the people, publicly appears, how it makes itself visible and tangible, how the people takes shape as a collective actor when no formal rules and procedures for identifying popular will exist, or when these rules and procedures are so deeply contested as to be effectively deauthorized.

The central question of popular manifestation is not primarily who the people are, in other words, but the related question of how the people appear and how they act. The problem of popular manifestation is not focused on the familiar question of the people as the legitimating source of public authority, but on the people as a collective actor pursuing a common set of goals. How to image and envision the people as a collective actor is an

[23] Judith Butler, *Notes Toward a Performative Theory of Assembly* (Cambridge: Harvard University Press, 2015); Jodi Dean, *Crowds and Party* (New York: Verso, 2016).

[24] Bonnie Honig, "Between Decision and Deliberation: Political Paradox in Democratic Theory," *American Political Science Review* 101:1 (February 2007), 1–17.

aesthetic-political problem that haunts modern democratic theory even though it is usually overshadowed by democratic theory's preoccupation with the principles, norms, and procedures legitimizing democratic rule. It is this aesthetic-political dimension of emergent popular sovereignty that the problem of popular manifestation helps bring into focus.

In his influential history of the emergence of popular sovereignty in Anglophone political discourses of the seventeenth and eighteenth centuries, Edmund Morgan offers a helpful indication of how the problem of popular manifestation appeared in the period of transition from royal to popular sovereignty. Morgan suggests that the replacement of the personal and external rule of the king with the impersonal and immanent self-rule of the people did not only pose representational difficulties of institutionalization and law but also of visualization and form. "The sovereignty of the people," Morgan writes, "is a much more complicated, one might say more fictional fiction than the divine right of kings. A king, however dubious his divinity might seem, did not have to be imagined. He was a visible presence, wearing his crown and carrying his scepter. The people, on the other hand, are never visible as such. Before we ascribe sovereignty to the people we have to imagine that there is such a thing, something we personify as though it were a single body, capable of thinking, of acting, of making decisions and carrying them out."[25]

Morgan's emphasis on the democratic imperatives of popular image and imagination is illuminating, although it is not a problem that he himself explores at any length. His point clearly resonates with Benedict Anderson's study of the discursive construction of "imagined communities," or Kevin Olson's more recent investigation of "imagined sovereignties."[26] However, this emphasis on imagination alone does not adequately engage how competing strategies of envisioning popular will were implicated in different conceptions of popular agency and power. Images of peoplehood mediate the people's relationship to their own political empowerment – how they understand themselves to be a part of and act *as* a people.[27] Making the people not only imaginable but

25 Edmund S. Morgan, *Inventing the People: The Rise of Popular Sovereignty in England and America* (New York: W.W. Norton, 1989), 153.

26 Benedict Anderson, *Imagined Communities: Reflections on the Origin and Spread of Nationalism* (New York: Verso, 1983); Kevin Olson, *Imagined Sovereignties: The Power of the People and Other Myths of the Modern Age* (New York: Cambridge University Press, 2016). See also Rogers M. Smith, *Stories of Peoplehood: The Politics and Morals of Political Membership* (Cambridge: Cambridge University Press, 2009).

27 Jason Frank, "The Living Image of the People," *Theory & Event* 18:1 (2015).

also tangible to the senses was a recurrent dilemma of the late eighteenth-century age of democratic revolutions.

These imperatives of collective tangibility and visualization were navigated in different ways and assumed different historical forms beyond crowds and popular assemblies. Miguel Abensour, for example, has examined how the transition from "the revolution of restoration to the revolution of the abyss" was mediated through the embodiment of the revolutionary hero – a Marat, a Robespierre, a Saint Just – who could "act without rules, without procedures or norms through a purely performative action."[28] In her classic study of the revolutionary culture of festival, Mona Ozouf has examined how the orchestrated popular festivals of the revolution sought to give expression to the sacred sublimity of the nation without artifice, how they sought to establish a "theatrical non-theatricality" to make the invisible constitution of the people present to themselves.[29] And many prominent historians, including Maurice Agulhon, Lynn Hunt, and Joan Landes, have examined the complex entanglement of political and aesthetic arguments surrounding the artistic depiction of the sovereign nation, from David's radical democratic proposals for a Hercules wielding his club to the allegorical depictions of Marianne.[30]

Crowds and informal assemblies, then, are only one constellation of practices for thinking about the problem of popular manifestation during periods of revolutionary transition, but they are a particularly important one for democratic theorists interested in the historical emergence of popular sovereignty and popular constituent power and the dilemmas it posed and continues to pose for our understanding of radical democratic politics. The idea that popular assemblies and crowds were manifestations of the popular will assumes a distinctly modern and democratic

[28] Miguel Abensour, "Saint Just and the Problem of Heroism in the French Revolution," in Ferenc Fehér, ed. *The French Revolution and the Birth of Modernity* (Berkeley: University of California Press, 1990), 133–48, 146–7.

[29] Mona Ozouf, *Festivals of the French Revolution* (Cambridge: Harvard University Press, 1991).

[30] Maurice Agulhon, "Politics, Images, and Symbols in Post-Revolutionary France," in Sean Wilentz, ed. *Rites of Power: Symbolism, Ritual, and Politics Since the Middle Ages* (Philadelphia: University of Pennsylvania Press, 1985), 177–205; Lynn A. Hunt, *Politics, Culture, and Class in the French Revolution* (Berkeley: University of California Press, 1984); Joan B. Landes, *Visualizing the Nation: Gender, Representation, and Revolution in Eighteenth-Century France* (Ithaca: Cornell University Press, 2003).

form in this period. William Sewell, for example, has argued that the French Revolution's "act of epoch-making cultural creativity occurred in a moment of ecstatic discovery: the taking of the Bastille, which had begun as an act of defense against the king's aggression, revealed itself in the days that followed as a concrete, unmediated, and sublime instance of the people expressing its sovereign will."[31] Popular constituent power should be approached by democratic theorists as a complex and dynamic political process, mobilized and enacted across multiple dimensions of political life, rather than viewed narrowly as a problem of juridical principles or constitutional norms.

This path has rarely been pursued and, when it has, it has been too quickly translated into other more familiar theoretical frameworks. One of the most influential of these has been political theology. In the remainder of this chapter, I will examine how the problem of popular manifestation I have just described has appeared, only to then be redirected, in the work of two influential theorists of democracy who have written extensively on the French Revolution: Carl Schmitt and Claude Lefort. Despite their very different interpretations of the French Revolution, their different theoretical preoccupations, and, most obviously, their very different political orientations, Schmitt and Lefort nonetheless exemplify how the problem of popular manifestation, when it has been recognized, has been translated into the political theological problem of incarnation. If the problem of popular manifestation is focused on appearance and collective enactment, incarnation is focused on incorporation and identity. I sketch here an encounter between Schmitt and Lefort on these questions, therefore, in order to illuminate the shared framework the opposition of their views sustains – that of political theology – and that has arguably prevented the distinctive problem of popular manifestation from coming into clearer view.

2 From Incarnation to Acclamation: Schmitt

Carl Schmitt is the most influential theorist of political theology and it is a problematic that animates his work well beyond his famous book on sovereignty which takes *Political Theology* as its title. The theological concept of incarnation is already central to Schmitt's early theory of

[31] William Sewell, "Historical Events as Transformations of Structures: Inventing Revolution at the Bastille," in *Logics of History: Social Theory and Social Transformation* (Chicago: University of Chicago Press, 2005), 225–70, 236.

political representation as elaborated in *Roman Catholicism and Political Form*. "To represent," he writes there, "means to make an invisible being visible and present through a publicly present being." Against the economic/materialist and individualist/private thinking of the modern age, an age defined by "the loss of the representative capacity," Schmitt asserts a Catholic political theology wherein the body of the church gives a visible and public form to "the reality of incarnation," representing "the civitas humana, the Person of Christ Himself. Through the church, God become man in historical reality."[32]

Schmitt's "political idea of Catholicism" is organized around its ability to incarnate "the great trinity of form: the aesthetic form of art; the juridical form of law, and the glorious achievement of a world-historical form of power."[33] Through the incarnational logic of the Church a worldly unity is realized out of contradictory proliferation of differences – what Schmitt calls the *complexio oppositorum* – and a political power is achieved that "rests neither on economic nor on military means but rather on the absolute realization of authority." For Schmitt, this idea of political representation as authoritative incarnation is so completely governed by conceptions of personal authority that to "represent in an eminent sense can only be done by a person," even though "'god' or 'the people' of democratic ideology," or even "abstract ideas like freedom and equality can all conceivably constitute a representation."[34]

Already in his early work on the political theology of representation, then, Schmitt raises the issue most relevant here, which is what he calls the modern and democratic "transposability" of God and people. Schmitt argues in *Roman Catholicism and Political Form* that nineteenth-century democratic parliamentarism itself initially "implied the idea of a *complexio oppositorum*, that is, the unity of the plurality of interests and parties," because "the whole of the people is only an idea ... not a material reality."[35] While already briefly indicated in this early work, Schmitt's thinking on the *democratic* iteration of the political theology of incarnation is much more clearly developed and historically elaborated in subsequent works, and especially in Schmitt's detailed historical account in *Dictatorship* of the shift that occurred during the French Revolution from the "commissarial dictatorship" of ancient republicanism, premised on preserving a legal continuity of state authority, to the

32 Carl Schmitt, *Roman Catholicism and Political Form* (New York: Praeger, 1996), 19.
33 *Ibid.*, 21.
34 *Ibid.*, 21.
35 *Ibid.*, 27.

"sovereign dictatorship" of popular constituent power, which heralds a revolutionary rupture with the existing legal order and the initiation of a new and unprecedented popular constitution-making power.[36]

"Sovereign dictatorship" is a concept Schmitt traces theoretically to the work of Sieyès and Rousseau, and beyond them to the halting and somewhat inarticulate emergence of the idea during the English Civil War. On his account, however, it is only practically enacted in October of 1793 when, responding to war abroad and counterrevolution at home, the Convention suspends the provisional government of France and becomes a sovereign dictatorship under Jacobin rule: Robespierre's initiation of "revolutionary government."[37] Popular constituent power comes to play an increasingly important role in Schmitt's work after the writing of *Dictatorship*, as his focus turns from the transcendent representational logic of incarnation to the dilemmas that inhabit the immanent logic of democratic identification.

Schmitt most succinctly developed this account of democracy built around mechanisms of identification in *The Crisis of Parliamentary Democracy*, and especially in the preface to its 1926 second edition. The "abstract logic" of democracy, Schmitt writes there, rests on "a series of identities" (between governors and governed, sovereign and subject, will and law, and so on).[38] However, all of these identities are not a "palpable reality" but solely the effect of "a *recognition* of the identity. It is not a matter of something actually equal legally, politically, or sociologically, but rather of identifications," and a "distance always remains between real equality and the results of identification . . . *Everything depends on how the will of the people is formed.*"[39]

For Schmitt, the "Jacobin logic" of democracy – the ability of a minority or even a single leader to speak on behalf of popular will – always exists as a democratic possibility because this symbolic identification is not encumbered by formal procedures, mediating institutions, or the tallying of votes but instead relies on a vital rearticulation of the qualitative identification with popular will on which all of these secondary quantitative mediations rest. It brings the otherwise latent or presumed reliance on popular constituent power into full articulation. As is well known, this Schmittian approach to democracy is directed against what he considers the false and deadening mediations of the constitutional state in favor of the existential

[36] Carl Schmitt, *Dictatorship* (New York: Polity, 2003).
[37] Schmitt, *Dictatorship*, 126–28.
[38] Carl Schmitt, *The Crisis of Parliamentary Democracy* (Cambridge: MIT Press, 1988), 26.
[39] Schmitt, *Crisis of Parliamentary Democracy*, 27. My emphasis.

immediacy of popular and oppositional identifications, or what he calls the "direct expression of democratic substance and power."[40]

The political and legal consequences of this transition from the transcendent logic of incarnation to the immanent logic of democratic identification are most precisely articulated in *Constitutional Theory*'s treatment of popular constituent power.[41] There, too, the French Revolutionary experience is a central part of Schmitt's argument, because it most clearly exemplifies a historical instance wherein "the people themselves determined the type and form of their own political existence." "With complete awareness," Schmitt writes, "a people took its destiny into its hands and reached a free decision on the style and form of its political existence."[42]

As "the formless form-giving power," an "inexhaustible source of all forms without taking form itself," Schmitt's theory of popular constituent power engages with the question, also crucial to a theory of popular manifestation, of how such "formlessness" assumes a visible worldly form, how the threshold of worldly tangibility, we might say, is crossed. Some have accused Schmitt of a "democratic mysticism" – the term is Stephen Holmes' – for affirming a constitution-making power wholly unbound by existing legal forms and procedures, and it is true that the discussion in *Constitutional Theory* raises a series of questions and problems that are not given wholly satisfying answers.[43]

The most relevant section of the book in this regard is the one dedicated to "the initiation of the constitution-making power." There Schmitt writes, "the people initiate their constitution-making power through some recognizable expression of their direct comprehensive will, which is targeted at a decision on the type and form of existence of the political unity." Many interesting questions are raised and then quickly passed over in Schmitt's invocation of "some recognizable expression of their direct comprehensive will." As Schmitt concedes, "special questions and difficulties stem from the distinctiveness of the subject of this constitution-making power." They stem, that is, from the fact that "the people as bearer of the constitution making power are not a stable, organized organ."[44] "The people in its essence," he clarifies later,

40 Schmitt, *Crisis of Parliamentary Democracy*, 17.

41 Carl Schmitt, *Constitutional Theory* (Durham, NC: Duke University Press, 2008), 266.

42 Schmitt, *Constitutional Theory*, 125.

43 Stephen Holmes, *The Anatomy of Antiliberalism* (Cambridge, MA: Harvard University Press, 1996), 8.

44 Schmitt, *Constitutional Theory*, 131.

"persists as an entity that is unorganized and unformed."[45] Schmitt considers this "the strength as well as the weakness of the people" as constituent power. It is a strength because it affirms the people's "superiority to every formation and normative framework"; it is a weakness because it demands "that the people should decide the basic questions of their political form and organization without themselves being formed and organized." This means that "their expressions of will are easily mistaken, misinterpreted and falsified."[46]

Schmitt's confident identification of the risks of such "mistaken" expressions hardly resolves the difficulties he himself raises and cannot mask the fact that he has denied the existence of any certain criteria for making such distinctions between the mistaken and the true, the falsified and the authentic expressions of popular constituent power (that a voting procedure, for example, would determine). Again: "everything depends on how the will of the people is formed." Schmitt relies here and elsewhere on the self-evidence of these "recognizable expressions." "The will of the people to provide themselves a constitution," he writes, "can only *be made evident through the act itself* and not through the observation of a normatively regulated process."[47] If popular manifestation is presented as a *problem* that initiates a scene of political contention, Schmitt's popular identification is evident and undeniable in its "recognizable expression."

The key question, then, is how Schmitt conceptualizes this self-evident act, this "recognizable expression of [the people's] direct comprehensive will." Here Schmitt turns to what he calls the "natural form of the direct expression of a people's will: the assembled multitude's declaration of their consent or disapproval, the acclamation."[48] In an essay titled "Referendum and Petition for a Referendum" published the year before *Constitutional Theory*, he is even more clear: "the real activity, capacity, and function of the people, the center of all popular expression, the original democratic phenomenon, what even Rousseau indicated as being a real democracy, is acclamation, the cry of approval or rejection from the united masses."[49]

[45] Schmitt, *Constitutional Theory*, 271.

[46] Schmitt, *Constitutional Theory*, 131.

[47] Schmitt, *Constitutional Theory*, 131. My emphasis.

[48] Schmitt, *Constitutional Theory*, 131.

[49] Cited in Giorgio Agamben, *The Kingdom and the Glory: For a Theological Genealogy of Economy and Government* (Palo Alto: Stanford University Press, 2011), 171.

The acclamation is clearly at the very heart of Schmitt's theory of popular constituent power, but, until recently, it has not received the sustained attention such centrality demands. Schmitt invokes the importance of acclamation to the formation of the people's constituent will already in the 1926 preface to *The Crisis of Parliamentary Democracy*, but it becomes increasingly significant as his work focuses more on popular constituent power and as he comes to present it as what he calls the "original democratic phenomena," a theatrical basis of a juridical structure.

Acclamation was opposed to the aggregation of individual votes in ancient Greek political thought. The *thorubos* (clamor or tumult) of the *ekklesia* (assembly) produced popular decisions that were based on the shouts and murmurs of the entire collective rather than disaggregated into a count of individual judgments and/or preferences that were taken to have a distinctive and intrinsic value. As Melissa Schwartzberg has recently written of the ancient Greek practice, what was most "salient is that these votes were heard or observed *qua* unified whole, rather than counted . . . acclamation holds that the body *as such* is the relevant agent of decision."[50]

Schmitt recovers and theoretically mobilizes this premodern practice of popular decision making, in part, to contrast it with the normative foundations of modern liberalism, with its prioritization of the individual and the private realm over the collective and the public. "Genuine popular assemblies and acclamations," Schmitt correctly writes, "are entirely unknown to the constitutional regime of contemporary bourgeois democracy."[51] As James Madison had written in Federalist No. 63, the "total exclusion of the people in their collective capacity" was essential to the system of political representation established by the US Constitution.[52] The acclamatory enactment of the collective people through "shouts and murmurs" provided Schmitt a way of conceptualizing collective decision beyond determinate formalized procedures while also emphasizing the theatrical self-evidence of the existence of the collectivity itself, so long as it appears as a "genuinely assembled people."[53]

[50] Melissa Schwartzberg, "Shouts, Murmurs, and Votes: Acclamation and Aggregation in Ancient Greece," *Journal of Political Philosophy* 18: 4 (2010), 448–68, 449.

[51] Schmitt, *Constitutional Theory*, 273.

[52] "Federalist, No. 63," in Jacob E. Cooke, ed. *The Federalist* (Middletown, CN: Wesleyan University Press, 1961).

[53] Schmitt, *Constitutional Theory*, 272.

While the example of the ancient decision procedure of acclamation provided important theoretical resources to Schmitt, it cannot be taken to be an unproblematic example of popular constituent power (as the very phrase "decision *procedure*" indicates). In addition to the ancient political practice of popular acclamation there exists a political theological dimension to acclamation that Schmitt refers to through his engagement with the work of the theologian Erik Peterson. This is the dimension of Schmitt's theory of acclamation that Giorgio Agamben has emphasized in *The Kingdom and The Glory*, where acclamation is presented as the vehicle for grasping "the liturgical sources of political history," or "the history of the ceremonial aspects of power and rights."[54] For Agamben, "acclamation is precisely the point at which [the juridical and the religious element] appear to coincide without remainder."[55] It "points toward a more archaic sphere . . . [of 'prelaw'] . . . in which terms that we customarily consider juridical appear to act in a magic-religious manner."[56] Acclamation is central to Schmitt's theory of popular constituent power on this account because it reveals the ceremonial or liturgical binds of "glory," which provides an "an immutable protocol" to bind power even in its most unconstrained, "efficacious," and sovereign form (even in its constituent form, in other words).[57] "If power is essentially force and efficacious action," Agamben writes, "why does it need to receive ritual acclamation and the hymns of praise, to wear cumbersome crowns and tiaras, to submit itself to an inaccessible ceremony and an immutable protocol – in a word, why does something that is essentially operativity and *oikonomia* need to become solemnly immobilized by glory?"[58]

Agamben's account insightfully amplifies the aesthetic and theatrical dimensions of Schmitt's account of acclamation that are at once central to his theory of popular constituent power and underelaborated by Schmitt himself. Agamben does not emphasize, however, how this "liturgical" dimension also manifests itself rhetorically in Schmitt's very text, and especially at the key moments where he engages directly with the popular and acclaiming assemblies that serve as the people's "natural form" of constituent power. For Schmitt, acclamation is the "natural form" through which popular constituent power becomes available to

[54] Agamben, *The Kingdom and the Glory*, 168–169.
[55] *Ibid.*, 188.
[56] *Ibid.*, 188.
[57] *Ibid.*, 188.
[58] *Ibid.*, 188.

the senses, but this does not in and of itself resolve "the special questions and difficulties" he identifies. How acclamation emerges as a "perceivable expression" of a "fundamental yes or no" when there is no prescribed "form of initiation" is left indeterminate, operating in his text and his constitutional theory as an uncertain but essential placeholder, a central spoke around which the theory turns.

Schmitt seems to at once address and evade the problem of "perceivable expression" by relying on a jargon of authenticity in these passages. "The distinctive meaning of the people," he writes for example, "reveals itself in the *genuine* presence of a publicly assembled people."[59] "In all the decisive moments in which the political meaning of a people can be affirmed," he elsewhere proclaims, "there first appear acclamations of approval or refusal that are independent of voting procedure, because through such a procedure their *genuineness* could be threatened, insofar as the immediacy of the people united, which defines this acclamation, is annulled by the isolation of the single voter and the secrecy of the ballot."[60] The "liturgical" or "magical" element emphasized by Agamben appears – and does its rhetorical work – in Schmitt's own texts via the unearned and unexplored appeal to the natural, the genuine, the authentic. Schmitt's repeated insistence on "genuine presence" and "genuine assemblies" enlists an underarticulated criterion of authenticity to assert the self-evidence in these moments of popular acclamation that is suspect at best. His invocations of "natural form" and "genuine assembly" work to rhetorically shore up the problems that the theory itself leaves uncertain and insecure. It raises the specter of indeterminacy or contestability around the initiation of popular constituent power that Schmitt does not consider in any depth, but that in the work of Claude Lefort, as we will now see, is not only openly acknowledged but elevated into the very ontology of democratic politics. Lefort's attempt to reveal the logic of incarnation as fundamentally incompatible with the symbolic transfiguration of modern democracy nonetheless remains, through its very opposition, invested in the political-theological framing he seeks to contest.

3 From Disincorporation to Democratic Terror: Lefort

Lefort is well known for approaching the political as a symbolic domain through which society represents its unity to itself. Following Ernst

[59] Schmitt, *Constitutional Theory*, 272. My emphasis.
[60] Cited in Agamben, *The Kingdom and the Glory*, 172.

Kantorowicz's *The King's Two Bodies*, and at least indirectly Schmitt's political theology, Lefort argues that the premodern doubling of the body of the king served as a necessary mediation between the visible realm of worldly power and the invisible realm of transcendental absolutes. This required incarnating these transcendental foundations, securely fixed in another realm, in the living body of the king, who thereby organizes the political by embodying a central locus of sovereign power.

The "democratic revolution" exemplified by revolutionary France, however, destroyed this symbolic unity and its transcendental anchoring, most obviously by destroying the body of the king. Lefort identifies democratic modernity itself with what he calls "the disincorporation of the political."[61] "When society," he writes, "can no longer be represented as a body and is no longer embodied in the figure of the prince, it is time that people and nation ... become the major poles by which social identity and social communality can be signified ... [But] this identity and this community remain indefinable."[62] "The people," as he more succinctly puts it elsewhere, "will be said to be sovereign ... but their identity will constantly be open to question, it will remain forever latent."[63] In modern democracy power cannot function as an incarnation.

The consequences of this historical shift in the organizing symbolism of power leads to Lefort's famous proclamation that in democracy the symbolic locus of power remains forever an "empty space," engendering the historical adventure of democratic politics, and "the dissolution of the markers of certainty," where no single group or individual can claim to wholly embody the people's power, but where the question of political legitimacy remains forever open and generates the irresolvable contestation and "radical indetermination" of democratic politics.

Does Lefort's democratic imaginary break with political theology? What is the answer to the question posed in the title of Lefort's famous and (famously obscure) essay "the Permanence of the Theologico-Political?" There is no space to go into the complexities of this essay here, but its primary aims are clear enough: to at once critique the transferential continuity of theology and politics affirmed by Schmitt and his followers, while also dismissing official liberal narratives of secular disenchantment incapable of recognizing the continuity between politics and religion in the realm of "the symbolic." Lefort accuses Jules

[61] Claude Lefort, *Democracy and Political Theory* (New York: Polity, 1991), 17.

[62] *Ibid.*, 18.

[63] Claude Lefort, *The Political Forms of Modern Society: Bureaucracy, Democracy, Totalitarianism* (Cambridge: MIT Press, 1986), 304.

Michelet of simply reversing a medieval political theology in his sacralization of the people and nation – "we find in Michelet's thought," Lefort writes, "the imprint of the theologico-political he is so determined to destroy" – but Lefort, too, even when emphasizing the unprecedented rupture of the symbolism of democratic power, is pulled by the political-theologico problematic toward thinking society as a structural totality, even if it is a structural totality sutured by an empty space of power at its center.

Nowhere is Lefort's continued investment in political theology more clear than when he deals with the reappearance of the logic of incarnation from within the democratic symbolism itself. Supplementing Kantorowicz with readings of Rousseau's unrepresentable general will and the democratic romanticism of Michelet, Lefort diagnoses how democracy engenders an internal imperative to incarnate the people as a collective body, in his words "to extract the People from within the people."[64] Lefort characterizes this as the dangerous fantasy of "the People as One."

For Lefort, the incarnational logic of this unitary "image of the People as One," this "phantasmagoria of popular power," already appears within the development of the democratic revolution itself, and it does so in the form of terror. Like Schmitt, Lefort identifies a "Jacobin logic" to democracy, but he understands it as a democratic pathology wherein the unified People, the source of all legitimacy, all truth, all virtue, instantiates itself against the empirical mass of aggregate individual people. "The People as One" can only be made visible and tangibly incarnate through terror. In this sense, terror should not be conceived as merely an instrument of the revolutionary people's power, a mere means to a political end, but rather its "constituent foundational act."[65] For Lefort, "the motive of the Terror was to make visible in the *real* that which can only exist in the *imaginary*," that is, to make visible in the real the unitary body of the emergent revolutionary people.[66] In a formulation that at once echoes and reorients Schmitt's concept of the political, the "People as One" becomes incarnated for Lefort through the identification and ultimately the physical and visible destruction of the people's enemies. "The image of society at one with itself," Lefort writes, "delivered from social division and conflict, can be grasped only during the purge, where there is

64 Lefort, *Democracy and Political Theory*, 88.
65 *Ibid.*, 84.
66 Bernard Flynn, *The Philosophy of Claude Lefort: Interpreting the Political* (Evanston: Northwestern University Press, 2005), 137.

a separation between the enemies of the people and the People; or better yet during the enemy's extermination."[67] The inner truth of Robespierre's famous proclamation that Louis must die, so that the nation can live, is revealed in the purge which was "motivated by the desire to furnish proof of the reality of the Revolution in the shape of the death of its enemies."[68]

In this, Lefort's account of revolutionary terror prefigures at the very emergence of modern democracy, "the image of the body in totalitarianism" that marks its twentieth-century collapse. Democratic terror and totalitarianism both aim to close democracy's irreducible gap between a society's image of unified collectivity and its actuality of social division. They aim to give society a body once more through state imperatives of incarnation, where the people are compelled to publicly appear in mass assemblies, party rallies, torch light parades, physical attacks on enemies, and, of course, through the ubiquitous circulation of movement symbols and the image and voice of "the egocrat," whose body becomes the living locus of the people's sovereign power and the unchecked instantiation of their own identity and will.[69]

Lefort's arguments about democracy's disincorporation of power and the continued dangers of incarnation initiated a tradition of theoretical reflection on these questions.[70] They echo in the anti-Marxist historiography of the French Revolution represented by François Furet and his followers and were extended by such theorists and former students of Lefort's as Miguel Abensour, Marcel Gauchet, and especially Pierre Rosanvallon, whose work has attended much more closely to the politics of crowds and popular assemblies emphasized here.

Rosanvallon followed Lefort in tracing in great historical detail "how the concept of the people struggled to incarnate itself in the revolutionary years."[71] The revolutionary conception of popular "representation as incarnation," Rosanvallon has argued, drove the dynamics of ever intensifying revolutionary radicalism. For Rosanvallon, "the challenge of

67 Lefort, *Democracy and Political Theory*, 84.

68 *Ibid.*, 83.

69 Lefort, *The Forms of Modern Society*, 306; For Carl Schmitt's attempt to offer a systematic theory of fascist identification, see *State, Movement, People*. See also Stefan Jonsson, *Crowds and Democracy: The Idea and Image of the Masses from Revolution to Fascism* (New York: Columbia University Press, 2013).

70 See Samuel Moyn, "The Intellectual Origins of François Furet's Masterpiece," The Tocqueville Review / *La Revue Tocqueville* 29:2 (2008), 59–78.

71 Pierre Rosanvallon, "Revolutionary Democracy," in Samuel Moyn, ed. *Democracy Past and Future* (New York: Columbia, 2006), 79–97, 81.

figuration," or the "founding aporias of representative government," emerged unavoidably for revolutionary actors at the very moment of popular sovereignty's accepted triumph. Once the people is affirmed as sovereign, he writes, "its face becomes problematic" and the "ambiguity and enigma of its constitution becomes most clearly tangible."[72]

For Rosanvallon, as for Lefort, this challenge of figuration emerges in modern democracies in the form of an irresolvable tension, gap, or contradiction between the idea, symbol, or representation of a unitary sovereign people and the messy and pluralistic empirical assemblage of individuals given in the social world it proclaims to represent. He refers to this as "the aporia of representation" which illuminates "the necessary distance between the figuration of reality and reality itself."[73] It is the basis of what Lisa Disch has described as his "constructivist" theory of political representation.[74]

Rosanvallon emphasizes that the appearance of this "aporia" of democratic representation engenders a felicitous appreciation of the necessary elisions and obfuscations of any and all authoritative claims of political representation.[75] The laudable political maturity and civic moderation Rosanvallon and so many others working within this tradition associate with accepting this invariable failure of incarnation or correspondence – keeping the "empty space" of power open, to use Lefort's language – is prevented or inhibited, however, by what he calls "the incandescence of the event."[76] If Lefort emphasized terror as the "constituent foundational act" of democratic incarnation, Rosanvallon invokes "the saving availability of the people as event" as a form of popular incarnation that seems to obviate, at least temporarily, the challenge of figuration as an irresolvable challenge that defines democracy. "The visibility of the people as actor," he writes, "whether in the tumult of the street or in the good behavior of the patriotic festivals . . . allowed the possibility of postponing the conceptual and practical difficulties posed by the distance between representatives and those they represented."[77]

72 Rosanvallon, "Revolutionary Democracy," 88.
73 *Ibid.*, 91.
74 See Lisa Disch, "The People as 'Presupposition' of Representative Democracy: An Essay on the Political Theory of Pierre Rosanvallon," *Redescriptions* 12 (2008): 47–71.
75 A similar argument is developed in Frank Ankersmit, *Political Representation* (Palo Alto: Stanford University Press, 2002); and Frank Ankersmit, *Aesthetic Politics: Political Philosophy Beyond Fact and Value* (Palo Alto: Stanford University Press, 1997).
76 Rosanvallon, "Revolutionary Democracy," 92.
77 *Ibid.*, 92.

It does so because as the people becomes manifest as a collective event it assumes a "recognizable face" and "gives itself an audible voice."[78] The evental availability of the people to the senses dangerously obscures, for Rosanvallon as it had for Lefort, the awareness of the people's fictive impossibility. "The people as event" sustains a dangerous political fantasy of overcoming the "challenge of figuration" altogether and ultimately terminates in the revolutionary "culture of insurrection" defined by a "permanent quest for an identity that cannot be satisfied."[79] It signals a degeneration of the democratic logic because it helps practically sustain the discredited metaphysics of the general will and "its mythology of a unified people as transcendental sovereign."[80] "The people as event" helps sustain the fantasy, in other words, of the "People as One."

While there is much to challenge in Rosanvallon's argument, and the broader discourse of "democratic totalitarianism" to which it is indebted, he does offer a compelling and historically detailed account of how the pressures of popular incarnation emerged in the revolutionary transition from royal to popular sovereignty.[81] The tradition of theoretical reflection on these issues that was inaugurated by Lefort, however, treats the problem of manifestation as a fetish, a democratic golden calf that irrationally seduces its citizens with the temptations of sense while undermining the political maturity and civil moderation of accepting democratic indeterminacy. It moves too quickly from the aesthetic-political problem of manifestation to the theological problem of incarnation.

4 Conclusion

The close association of democracy with popular disincorporation resonates in contemporary democratic theory well beyond the tradition of theoretical reflection initiated by Lefort. In her study of the American and French Revolutions, for example, Hannah Arendt anticipated Lefort's association of democracy with disincorporation as well as his diagnosis of the dangers of the drive to popular incarnation.[82] Arendt, too, sought to think the revolutionary emergence of the people beyond the purview of

[78] *Ibid.*, 97.
[79] *Ibid.*, 96.
[80] *Ibid.*, 92.
[81] See Kevin Duong, "'Does Democracy End in Terror?' Transformations in Antitotalitarianism in Postwar France," *Modern Intellectual History* 14:2 (2017), 537–63.
[82] Hannah Arendt, *On Revolution* (New York: Penguin, 1990), 50.

"a tradition which was partly founded on an event in which the 'word' had become flesh."[83] For Arendt, the growing demands of the poor over the course of the Revolution – the so-called social question – did not only overwhelm and destroy the "free space of appearances," as so many of her critics have emphasized. The emergence of the social demand also helped to sustain the political fantasy that she saw given clearest theoretical articulation in the work of Rousseau and brought to terrible realization in the Jacobin Terror: the fantasy that the people can appear and speak as a collective body capable of being incarnated as a unitary presence and a sovereign will. "What urged [the poor] on was the quest for bread," Arendt writes, "and the cry for bread will always be uttered with one voice. In so far as we all need bread, we are indeed all the same, and may as well unite into one body and act as though possessed by one will." For Arendt, the appearance of the social question in revolutionary France gave practical support to the political fantasy that the people were a collectivity whose virtuous will could be fully incarnated and made present in the unifying claim of the revolutionary crowd, the popular assembly, the revolutionary hero or the monstrous impersonation of the charismatic leader. Robespierre had, after all, likened the people to a sublime ocean to which the great lawgiver had to give form and bring into articulation. He inverted Louis XIV absolutist dictum "L'Etat Ces moi" into his own popular authorizing claim: "I am not the courtier, nor the moderator, nor the tribune nor the defender of the people, I am the people myself."[84]

Similarly, in his own writing on the French Revolution, Jürgen Habermas asked whether "the orienting power of the French Revolution is exhausted," and examined the extent to which "the shift in mentality that marks 1789 can still be a vital resource for our own needs of orientation."[85] Habermas's efforts to identify the living normative principle in the events of the Revolution led him to insist that we must first and foremost disenthrall ourselves from the idea "that the people from whom all governmental authority is supposed to derive . . . comprises a subject with will and consciousness."[86] It is

83 Arendt, *On Revolution*, 160.

84 Cited in Carol Blum, *Rousseau and the Republic of Virtue: The Language of Politics in the French Revolution* (Ithaca, NY: Cornell University Press, 1986), 160.

85 Jürgen Habermas, "Popular Sovereignty as Procedure," in *Between Facts and Norms: Contributions to a Discourse Theory of Law and Democracy* (Cambridge: MIT Press, 1998), 463–490, 464.

86 Habermas, "Popular Sovereignty as Procedure," 469.

only by renouncing "an overly concrete reading of popular sovereignty," Habermas argues, and accepting that it cannot reside in a "visible identifiable gathering of autonomous citizens" that the normative resources of the Revolution can be safely recovered for liberal constitutionalism. The collective manifestation of the people must be replaced by the indirect communicative rationality of the public. Only through a self-critical and dispersed conception of the public can we identify "the place to which the expectations of a sovereign self-organization of society has withdrawn." He describes this withdrawal as a process of disincarnation. "Even the notion that a network of associations could replace the dismissed body of the people – that it could occupy the vacant seat of the sovereign, so to speak – is too concrete. This fully dispersed sovereignty is not even embodied in the heads of the associated members. Rather if one can still speak of 'embodiment' at all, then sovereignty is found in those subjectless forms of communication that regulate the flow of discursive opinion and will formation in such a way that their fallible outcomes have the presumption of practical reason on their side. Subjectless and anonymous, an intersubjectively dissolved popular sovereignty withdraws into democratic procedures and the demanding communicative presuppositions of their implementation."[87]

It is arguably the weight of this common association of democracy with collective disincarnation, the conceptual flipside of Schmitt's political theology of democratic incarnation and popular identification, that has prevented investigation into the historical dynamics of popular manifestation I have proposed here. As popular constituent power has become a central preoccupation of democratic theorists, it has been approached primarily as a juridical problem or as a problem of philosophy or political theology. I have tried to instead see popular constituent power more broadly as a dynamic and deeply contested political process that mobilizes popular actors and brings improvised collectivities into being across different registers of political life. One of these registers which has been largely absent from the discussions in democratic theory is best characterized as aesthetic, and is captured by the idea of the people as a popular manifestation. The insurgent politics of crowds and informal public assemblies – the dynamic politics of the people out of doors – has accompanied the history of popular sovereignty at every step of its modern emergence. They are an essential part

[87] Habermas, "Popular Sovereignty as Procedure," 486.

of the contested economies of democratic representation, the tangible forms through which insurgent collective actors make themselves manifest. As such, they should be taken more seriously than they have been by most democratic theorists exploring the concept of popular constituent power.

4

Sovereignty, Action, Autonomy

RAF GEENENS

One of Marx's central and most enduring insights, as concisely expressed in the 1859 preface to his *Contribution to the Critique of Political Economy*, concerns the transformative effects of economic change. As the material forces of production develop, they sooner or later enter into conflict with the existent relations of production and with the political and juridical patterns, the so-called superstructure, in which these relations are expressed. The inevitable consequence, according to Marx, is a period of transformation in which society's superstructure, including its moral, aesthetic, and philosophical forms, is revolutionalized so as to adapt it to the new material circumstances.

This Marxist model of revolution might not be applicable everywhere and at all times, but it does offer an attractive template to explain the current stage of globalization. More so than ever before, capitalism today depends on global mobility – the mobility of goods, capital, services, and people – and this brings capitalism increasingly into conflict with the legacy structures of the nation-state. While the nation-state could in Marx's time be analyzed as a tool at the service of bourgeois power, "a public force organized for social enslavement,"[1] it now seems just an annoying impediment to the dynamics of global capital. Nation-states today hinder capitalism's development in various ways: existent social regulation is incompatible with new business models, national languages and cultures slow down the spread of global services, their attachment to local communities makes individuals less mobile and less flexible than capitalism would like them to be, and so on. In this light, it is not surprising that the political, moral, and cultural patterns associated with the nation-state are steadily being dismantled and replaced

This chapter draws on my "Sovereignty as Autonomy" (*Law and Philosophy* 36(5) (2017): pp. 495–524).

[1] Karl Marx, "The Civil War in France," in K. Marx (ed.), *Later Political Writings* (Cambridge University Press, 1996), p. 182.

by patterns that are more suitable to the workings of global capitalism.[2] For instance, some scholars read the development of EU-law in recent decades as a clear case of ideological adaptation.[3]

This chapter is concerned with just one arena in which glimpses of the ongoing ideological struggle can be witnessed, namely the debate concerning sovereignty as it is currently conducted among philosophers of law. Many legal philosophers today claim that we would be better off without the concept of sovereignty and develop various strategies to eliminate it. My aim here is to go against this trend and defend the concept of sovereignty, albeit in a downsized version. Due to its slow birth out of the vestiges of medieval legal thought, and its long and winding trajectory through centuries of modern politics, the concept has taken on a bulky appearance. What I will try to do is downsize the concept to its bare essentials and uncover its core purpose, which should make it easier to defend the concept against contemporary attempts to dismantle it. It should be noted at the outset that this is not an exercise in historical reconstruction. Rather than trying to "dig up" sovereignty's purported original meaning, I intend to lay bare the aspect of it that I believe to be most valuable, in the sense that it cannot be adequately covered by other concepts, and in the sense that it points to something that we would do well to preserve in our current time.

Surveying the range of anti-sovereignty strategies in legal theory, two types of attacks stand out.[4] The first of these is *empirical* in nature. Its central claim reads that we should abandon the concept of sovereignty because it is impossible to square with our new, multilevel political and juridical reality. Talking in terms of sovereignty made sense within a certain constellation, namely the world of independent nation-states. The notion of sovereignty points to an empirical phenomenon that genuinely existed within this constellation. However, with this constellation gone, the concept is no longer helpful and should better be abandoned. An example of this type of attack is Neil MacCormick's famous statement that "sovereignty and sovereign states, and the inexorable linkage of law with sovereignty and the state, have been but the passing

[2] This is in line with the revolutionary logic described by Marx, but of course only partly in line with Marx's own predictions.

[3] See for instance Alexander Somek, *Individualism: An Essay on the Authority of the European Union* (Oxford University Press, 2008).

[4] Bert Van Roermund identifies the same two anti-sovereignty strategies. He calls them "the Argument from Redundancy" and the "Argument from Incoherence." See Bert Van Roermund, "Sovereignty: Unpopular and Popular," in N. Walker (ed.), *Sovereignty in Transition* (Oxford: Hart, 2003), pp. 33–54.

phenomena of a few centuries."[5] A second anti-sovereignty strategy that can be found in the literature is *conceptual* in nature. The core of this strategy consists in claiming that sovereignty is in principle incompatible with the rule of law. A case in point is Francis G. Jacobs, a former Advocate General of the Court of Justice of the European Union (CJEU). In his book on sovereignty, Jacobs starts by noting that sovereignty "is no longer a viable concept" in today's political and juridical circumstances (this is the empirical strategy), but he goes on to claim that sovereignty was always already incompatible with something that is much more valuable than sovereignty, namely the "rule of law."[6] A recent and intricate formulation of the conceptual challenge is provided by Pavlos Eleftheriadis, who emphatically claims that "[p]hilosophically speaking, sovereignty is and has always been incompatible with the rule of law and with constitutional law itself."[7] According to Eleftheriadis, the very idea of sovereignty is an historical error that stands in urgent need of correction.

Although I believe these challenges to the notion of sovereignty can be read as symptoms of the conflict between the globalizing forces of capitalism and the remaining nation-state forms, their authors of course have diverse purposes and motivations. My main charge against them is that they overlook to what extent the notion of sovereignty, which I will define in terms of collective autonomy, remains uniquely valuable in current circumstances.[8] As I hope to demonstrate, the notion of sovereignty, when properly understood, is not susceptible to their criticisms: sovereignty as autonomy remains practicable in today's multilevel constellation and is normatively compatible with the rule of law.

Below, I start by presenting my account of sovereignty as autonomy, an account that situates the importance of sovereignty at the level of our collective "self-image" or our collective "self-understanding." In three subsequent sections I will describe three main features that I believe to be constitutive for the self-understanding of a political or legal community

[5] MacCormick adds that "their passing is by no means regrettable." See Neil MacCormick, "Beyond the Sovereign State," *The Modern Law Review* 56(1) (1993): pp. 1–18, at p. 1.

[6] Francis Jacobs, *The Sovereignty of Law: The European Way* (Cambridge: Cambridge University Press, 2007), p. 5.

[7] Pavlos Eleftheriadis, "Law and Sovereignty," *Law and Philosophy* 29(5) (2010): pp. 535–569, at p. 539.

[8] In this regard, I agree with Dieter Grimm's affirmation (see for instance Chapter One in this volume) of the contemporary importance of sovereignty. Yet while Grimm seems to see political developments in the supranational realm as the main threat to sovereignty, I believe that economic developments might be an even more important factor.

as sovereign.[9] Admittedly, interpreting our collective "self-image" or "self-understanding" is not an exact science; and those who believe that legal and political theory should stick to rigorous methods might find this modus operandi unnecessarily vague. Yet I believe that such an interpretive exercise is crucial for setting up a conception that captures the normatively valuable aspects of sovereignty, all while being rooted in the historical usage of the term. In this chapter's penultimate section, I explain why I believe my account of sovereignty to be immune against the two dominant lines of criticism. I conclude, in the chapter's final section, by suggesting that the debate on sovereignty is not just one ongoing ideological battle among many others, but might actually be a pivotal one, as should become clear by briefly looking into the ideas of Friedrich Hayek.

1 Sovereignty as Autonomy

The interpretation of sovereignty as autonomy finds its origins in Jean-Jacques Rousseau's *Social Contract*, but it can best be understood by setting up an analogy with Immanuel Kant's account of individual autonomy. In his *Groundwork of the Metaphysics of Morals*, Kant proposes – as is well known – to lay the foundations for a critical examination of pure practical reason. It is in the domain of practical reason that individuals ascribe to themselves autonomy; that is, the capacity to reflect upon norms and to consciously direct their actions based on the outcome of these reflections. This attribution of autonomy is not based on an empirical estimate of the extent to which we actually possess these capacities nor on a perception of this autonomous entity within ourselves. It is rather the assumption on which we operate as soon as we use reason to determine our actions. In Kant's own words, it is a "necessary presupposition of reason in a being that believes itself to be conscious of a will, that is of a faculty ... of determining itself to action as an intelligence and hence in accordance with laws of reason independently of instincts."[10] Thus, in order to speak of autonomous agency, an actor has to adopt a specific perspective: she has to understand herself as an

[9] Bas Leijssenaar develops a somewhat similar inquiry (in his "The Demos as a Plural Subject" in *Netherlands Journal of Legal Philosophy* (46) 1 (2017): pp. 37–64). Using the analytic vocabulary of Margaret Gilbert, he interprets the working of social and political institutions as "organs that provide the capacity for ... agency."

[10] Immanuel Kant, *Practical Philosophy* (Cambridge: Cambridge University Press, 1996), p. 105.

effective cause, capable of steering her own actions on the basis of reasons and thereby transcending the mechanisms of empirical nature.

I believe the Kantian conception of individual autonomy can be translated to the level of collective action and provides a suitable template to understand the notion of sovereignty.[11] Sovereignty then becomes the name for collective autonomy, and a collectivity can be called sovereign when it ascribes to itself the capacity that Kant believes individual actors necessarily ascribe to themselves when taking up the practical perspective: it sees itself as capable of steering its own course of action on the basis of rational considerations and hence as capable of transcending mere societal or economic mechanisms.[12] Rather than pointing to a factual entity endowed with absolute powers, the term "sovereignty" now indicates a specific *perspective* adopted by the members of a political community. Traditionally, whether an entity (an individual, a group of persons, or an institution) can be called sovereign or not depends on empirically observable conditions: does this entity possess a particular set of (factual or normative) powers? Here, whether a community can be called sovereign or not comes to depend on how that community sees itself: does it understand itself as governed by blind laws (be they economic, natural, or sociological), or does it adopt the perspective of autonomy, that is, does it see itself as capable of collective action?

Taking up such a perspective is not a neutral thing to do. Citizens who adopt this perspective see society as a collective subject, a subject that can act on the basis of well-considered reasons and with which they identify themselves. As discussed below, this "collective subject" should not

[11] I will not delve here into the way Kant himself made the transition from individual autonomy to a political philosophy of the state, especially because Kant himself believed the question of sovereignty not to be very important (cf. Howard Williams, *Kant's Political Philosophy* (Oxford: Blackwell, 1983), p. 173 ff.).

[12] This understanding of sovereignty is not disconnected from historical conceptions of sovereignty, such as Bodin's or Hobbes's. For what is crucial for both these authors, is that a group becomes consciously steered, rather than being a loose collection of individuals or animals whose interactions are controlled by the empirical laws of nature. Bodin represents a breakthrough in the genesis of sovereignty for this very reason. Before Bodin, sovereign powers were merely particular powers held by certain individuals. With Bodin, sovereignty became the name for the abstract power to steer society as a whole; an abstract power that – as Bodin discovered – indicates "a unity that was more than the sum of its parts" (Dieter Grimm, *Sovereignty: The Origin and Future of a Political and Legal Concept* (New York: Columbia University Press, 2015), p. 21). In other words, the introduction of sovereignty in the modern sense marks the conscious recognition of society's capacity to act as a united agent, a unity that surpassed its component entities and forces. And this recognition, as Hobbes teaches us, requires the creation of an *image* of sovereignty (cf. Iris Därmann, *Figuren des Politischen* (Frankfurt am Main: Suhrkamp, 2009), pp. 80–97).

necessarily be understood in communitarian or nationalist terms. Believing in the possibility of collective action does not equal believing in a shared identity, let alone that it would require individuals to enthusiastically agree with all of a society's decisions. Yet taking up the perspective of sovereignty does create a new type of relation between the individual and society, a *political* relation that has a separate meaning from other relations the individual is engaged in. According to Martin Loughlin, this is what was at stake, from the very beginning, in carving out the conceptual space for the notion of sovereignty. French jurists such as Bodin sought to establish a type of power and a type of relationship that was independent of (and could be superimposed on) other types of societal relations, in particular: the property relationships of the feudal order.[13] It could be claimed that this remains sovereignty's modus operandi up to this day. By indicating that society is capable of steering itself, a specific type of relationship is established that would otherwise not exist: individuals relate themselves in one way or another toward this steering capacity. This relation can be manifold; it might be an affirmative and cooperative relation, or a more recalcitrant one. But this relation is in any case different from the various relationships – such as family relationships or economic relationships – in which individuals naturally find themselves.

When talking about sovereignty as a "perspective" adopted by citizens, we are clearly looking at the level of the political imaginary. And I think this is indeed where the merits of sovereignty are to be found. Taking up the perspective of sovereignty changes the *image* individuals have of themselves and of society. Rather than simply as a set of individuals, they come to see themselves as political actors involved in a collective undertaking, with a shared responsibility for its working and its effects. But this perspective is not a natural fact, and this points to an important difference between individual autonomy and collective autonomy. As individuals, the standpoint of unified agency is, so to speak, forced upon us. Beings with one material body and endowed with reason have not much choice but to think and act as a unified agent and hence to evaluate, no matter how imperfectly, the acceptability of different possible courses of action. The same is not true for communities, which can perhaps exist without the presence of a genuine sense of collective autonomy. It is conceivable that citizens stop reasoning in

[13] Martin Loughlin, "Ten Tenets of Sovereignty," in N. Walker (ed.), *Sovereignty in Transition* (Oxford: Hart, 2003), pp. 55–86 at pp. 59–63.

favor of or against certain courses of action for society as a whole, and instead withdraw into merely private calculations.[14] At best, we would then be left with forms of order that emerge spontaneously but with no possibility of consciously evaluating their acceptability or correcting their course. In other words, the perspective of sovereignty cannot be assumed as a given. The presence of this perspective is conditional: it depends on whether the necessary infrastructure is in place to sustain this perspective. (Note that I am using the term "infrastructure" here in a decidedly non-Marxian sense).

Below I expand on this definition of sovereignty as autonomy by describing these properties of a community's symbolic or mental "infrastructure" that I believe to be essential for sustaining the perspective of sovereignty. This implies that I am trying to answer the following questions: what are the essential features of a community's decision-making processes, and how does this community need to see and think of itself, if we are to consider this community as sovereign? In answering these questions, I will make use of various contemporary authors who, even if they do not present a fully fledged conception of "sovereignty as autonomy," do understand sovereignty broadly in this same vein. Hans Lindahl[15] and Bert Van Roermund[16] are certainly cases in point, and Martin Loughlin[17] and Neil

[14] Paul Kahn goes one step further and takes the analogy between individual subjectivity and collective subjectivity into the domain of existentialism. He claims that a sovereign political community, like an individual being, has to face its own mortality, in line with Heidegger's understanding of *Sein-zum-Tode*: "The sovereign is the political being characterized by this consciousness of the possibility of its own death. [. . .] It must continue to will itself to be in the face of the acknowledgment of its own mortality. To flee from confronting the possibility of the death of the state is a kind of inauthenticity. To take up that knowledge is to achieve a kind of political authenticity." Paul Kahn, *Political Theology: Four New Chapters on the Concept of Sovereignty* (New York: Columbia University Press, 2011), p. 60.

[15] See Hans Lindahl, "Sovereignty and Symbolization," *Rechtstheorie* 28(3) (1997): pp. 347–371; Hans Lindahl, "Democracy and the Symbolic Constitution of Society," *Ratio Juris* 11(1) (1998): pp. 12–37; Hans Lindahl, "Sovereignty and Representation in the European Union," in N. Walker (ed.), *Sovereignty in Transition* (Oxford: Hart, 2003), pp. 87–114.

[16] See Van Roermund, "Sovereignty: Unpopular and Popular," pp. 44–45; Bert Van Roermund, "First-Person Plural Legislature: Political Reflexivity and Representation," *Philosophical Explorations: An International Journal for the Philosophy of Mind and Action* 6(3) (2003): pp. 235–250.

[17] See Loughlin, "Ten Tenets of Sovereignty"; Loughlin, "Why Sovereignty?," in R. Rawlings, P. Leyland, & A. Young (eds.), *Sovereignty and the Law. Domestic, European and International Perspectives* (Oxford University Press, 2013), pp. 34–49; Loughlin, "The Concept of Constituent Power," *European Journal of Political Theory* 13 (2) (2014): pp. 218–237.

Walker[18] often seem to have something similar in mind when talking about sovereignty.[19] Yet the most elaborate account of sovereignty as autonomy is undoubtedly that of Jürgen Habermas who, in his theory of deliberative democracy, explicitly understands sovereignty through a Kantian lens. In the next section, I will start by taking a closer look at Habermas because he describes two important conditions for collective autonomy: there have to be deliberative procedures for rational collective will-formation, and citizens need to be respected and protected as individuals. I will then, in the two following sections, look at two further properties of sovereign communities: an awareness of one's collective self as a unity, and an awareness of one's collective self as an agent that can choose between various courses of action.

2 First Condition: Rational Will-Formation

The explicit aim of Habermas's deliberative model[20] is to provide a discourse-theoretical reconstruction of the Rousseauist intuition of popular sovereignty. The heart of that intuition is self-authorship of the law: citizens are sovereign if they are subjected to laws that are the outcome of the general will. Again, this is analogous to Kant's idea of moral autonomy. For Kant, we are free when subjected to the moral law because we see ourselves as the author of this law. In the case of individual autonomy, the categorical imperative provides a simple procedure to attain this ideal of authorship. The challenge for Habermas lies in describing the institutional conditions under which the citizens as a whole can, in a similar way, be understood as the author of all rules and public powers to which they are subjected. Habermas will identify two such conditions: citizens need deliberative procedures for collective decision-making and they need to be protected by an adequate system of

[18] See Neil Walker, "Late Sovereignty in the European Union," in N. Walker (ed.), *Sovereignty in Transition* (Oxford: Hart, 2003), pp. 3–32, see in particular pp. 17, 20.

[19] Note incidentally, that all authors in this list are committed to some form of anti-positivism, that is, they believe that understanding social reality is an exercise in reconstruction and interpretation. The object of such a hermeneutic exercise is not so much our empirical political and juridical institutions, but rather the beliefs and attitudes of the human actors who keep these institutions going (see for instance Walker, *Sovereignty in Transition*, p. 16).

[20] As formulated in *Between Facts and Norms* and a number of ancillary publications. See: Jürgen Habermas, "Human Rights and Popular Sovereignty: The Liberal and Republican Versions," *Ratio Juris* 7(1) (1994): pp. 1–13; Jürgen Habermas, *Between Facts and Norms: Contributions to a Discourse Theory of Law and Democracy* (Cambridge: Polity, 1996); Jürgen Habermas, "Constitutional Democracy. A Paradoxical Union of Contradictory Principles?," *Political Theory* 29(6) (2001): pp. 766–781.

rights.[21] Although Habermas admits that there can be variation from society to society, he insists that the broad contours of these two conditions can be derived a priori.

Deriving the first condition is very straightforward. If society is to act on the basis of well-considered reasons, it needs to have the capacity to process reasons in a collective manner.[22] This requires an inclusive public sphere where all opinions and concerns can be expressed, as well as more formal procedures where this input is rationally filtered and where the most relevant arguments ultimately come to determine the content of the law. Habermas emphasizes that this deliberative process needs to be stabilized in solid institutions that are constitutionally entrenched. A second condition is the protection of individual citizens by a robust system of fundamental rights. According to Habermas, the constitutional protection of individual rights is a key precondition of collective autonomy: individuals need to be respected if they are to fully participate in collective deliberations. If, say, you risk being tortured for expressing certain opinions, then the process of decision-making is not particularly rational.[23] The precise content of these rights is not given in advance but should be worked out by citizens themselves in light of their concrete historical circumstances. At best, the philosopher can reconstruct what broad categories of rights will have to be established.[24] The same goes for the condition of deliberative democracy. Habermas sketches a blueprint for a deliberative society in which the ideal of rational will-formation is

[21] A third condition that Habermas mentions is the medium of positive law. Norms need to be crystallized in an empirical medium that has the ability to impose rules backed by the threat of sanctions. Thus, it is only in the form of positive law that society's self-authored norms can take practical effect and genuinely bind all aspects of social life. The choice for the medium of positive law is presented by Habermas as a pragmatic choice for which no alternative exists. Cf. Habermas, *Between Facts and Norms*, pp. 30 ff.

[22] In deriving these conditions, Habermas builds extensively on his earlier, discourse-theoretical work, cf. Habermas, *Between Facts and Norms*, p. 107 ff.

[23] Habermas also hints at a more fundamental connection between collective autonomy and individual rights: If we take all participants seriously as conversation partners in our collective deliberations, we already reject the legitimacy of pre-given, suprahuman truths as possible sources of public authority, and hence accept that citizens are in principle free to select the goals and values of their individual lives. On this more fundamental connection between collective autonomy and individual rights, see Stefan Rummens, "The Co-originality of Private and Public Autonomy in Deliberative Democracy," *The Journal of Political Philosophy* 14(4) (2006): pp. 469–481.

[24] Habermas not only thinks of individual liberties and rights of political membership and participation but also of various social and economic rights that are needed to guarantee the equal enjoyment of more formal rights. See Habermas, *Between Facts and Norms*, p. 121 ff.

realized, but the precise institutional details have to be elaborated by the citizens themselves and will continue to evolve as part of a collective learning process.

It is clear then that for Habermas sovereignty, understood as collective autonomy, can only emerge in specific circumstances. There has to be a stable constitutional setup that maintains a space for an ongoing rational decision-making process and provides all participants with an adequate set of rights. In the absence of these things, the sovereign cannot properly process reasons and arguments, hence has no coherent will, and hence does not exist.

3 Second Condition: Unity

Habermas points out two important conditions for sovereignty. But are these formal conditions sufficient to speak of collective autonomy? Even if there are procedures in place that guarantee that law *is* the outcome of a deliberative process in which all citizens are respected and protected as individuals, it is not self-evident that citizens also *recognize* it as such. Several authors do indeed claim that something more is needed, in particular a conscious image of society as a unity. If citizens are to see laws as the product of a collective effort in which they are involved, then this collectivity needs to have a certain stability throughout time and citizens need to identify themselves with it. What is required, in other words, is some form of collective "selfhood." Habermas for his part strongly resists this step. He repeatedly refuses to link the idea of sovereignty with even the slightest suggestion of a collective "we" or a collective "subject." For Habermas, the rational exchange of arguments as depicted in his deliberative model does not require the idea of a "self"; the subject of sovereignty is simply dissolved into an "anonymous" flow of arguments.[25] Out of fear for nationalist or communitarian echoes, Habermas would rather do without any idea of collective subjectivity. But is Habermas not downsizing the concept of sovereignty *too* much? Is it not possible to rescue the idea of a unit capable of purposive action, a collective subject in which citizens can consciously recognize themselves, without substantializing this collective self and without inflating it into an organic form of societal harmony?

[25] *Ibid.*, pp. 301, 486. Sovereignty, for Habermas, should be "fully dispersed" and "not even embodied in the heads of the associated members" (*Ibid.*, p. 486). See also formulations such as "[T]he 'self' of the self-organizing legal community disappears in the subjectless forms of communication" (*Ibid.*, p. 301).

This would be in line with the idea of moral autonomy as formulated by Kant, for whom agency and subjecthood are closely intertwined. In the *Groundwork*, Kant writes that to be free in the practical domain is to act "*under the idea of freedom*."[26] Christine Korsgaard explains this as follows: "To be an agent, according to Kant, is to be a self-conscious causality."[27] When I act morally, I operate on the assumption that my actions are caused by one specific unit of agency, a unit that I take to be my self. This assumption is not just an accidental by-product of my acting; it is rather the firm ground that carries this whole process. But it does not follow that this self, which is the presumed cause of all my actions, can be experienced by our senses or can be described by theoretical reason. It is rather the standpoint I assume whenever I see myself as acting, that is, whenever I see myself as the cause of events that would not happen without me having the thought of causing them. Kant explicitly warns us against overstepping the bounds of practical reason and believing that this free agent could ever be an object of experience in the sensible world.[28] Thus, for Kant, using reason to reflect upon action is inevitably connected to a consciousness of oneself as an "I," or at least as a "unit" that can be the cause of intentional actions. This consciousness does not depend on a possible definition or empirical perception of this self; it is simply an unavoidable presumption of practical reason: there would be no point in reflecting about the morality of my actions if I do not presume myself to be a *subject* under the moral law.

Could this not provide a helpful cue as to a possible understanding of the subject of sovereignty?[29] Such an understanding would steer clear of the idea of a subject writ large, a people with a substantial, shared identity that can be explicitly defined (which is Habermas's fear). Instead, we would recognize that adopting the perspective of sovereignty implies a consciousness of one's political community as a unity, with a capacity for collective action and hence also with a duty to act responsibly. This also seems to have been the key merit of the modern notion of sovereignty as introduced by Bodin and Hobbes: thanks to the standpoint of

[26] Kant, *Practical Philosophy*, p. 95.

[27] Christine Korsgaard, *Self-Constitution: Agency, Identity, and Integrity* (Oxford: Oxford University Press, 2009), p. 84.

[28] Kant, *Practical Philosophy*, pp. 104–105.

[29] At one point, Christine Korsgaard makes the inverse move and draws an analogy with the idea of state sovereignty (understood as collective autonomy) to clarify her Kantian understanding of the subject of individual autonomy. See Korsgaard, "Personal Identity and the Unity of Agency: A Kantian Response to Parfit," *Philosophy & Public Affairs* 18(2) (1989): pp. 101–132, at p. 114.

the sovereign, we see our political community as capable of acting as a unit. And is this perspective not always presupposed when citizens deliberate, i.e. when they participate in public debates about political decisions, claiming that, for this or that reason, society should act in some or other way? Indeed, how could it not be? There would be no point in advancing arguments in favor of one course of action or against another course of action, if one did not assume that one's political community was capable of acting as a unified agent on the basis of reasons.

Viewed in this light, participating in a public decision-making process implies understanding society as a collective agent, capable of intentional action and with an obligation to act in the right way. Several authors writing on sovereignty are sensitive to this and emphasize that the perspective of sovereignty is indeed interwoven with a sense of collective selfhood; that is, with consciously seeing oneself as part of a larger unity. Moreover, they offer various suggestions as to how such a collective self-representation can be produced. Hans Lindahl for instance, in an essay on the European Union's slow self-constitution, emphasizes the importance of performative language use. His prime example is the Treaty of Rome, and in particular the Treaty's Preamble, which, although officially making claims *about* European unity (in a constative manner), tacitly helps bringing this unity into being.[30] New collective self-representations can also be produced by performative language use in judicial contexts. Lindahl cites the important *Costa* v. *ENEL* and *Van Gend & Loos* rulings by the European Court of Justice ("ECJ"). In these rulings, the ECJ "seized the initiative" and, by *describing* EU-law as an autonomous legal order, at the same time *created* this order.[31] Bert Van Roermund similarly emphasizes the importance of unity, and also sees this unity primarily as an effect of self-referential language use, for instance by judges.[32]

Lindahl and Van Roermund are largely correct. Sovereignty should be understood in connection to a community's conscious awareness of itself as a unity, and performative language use in public settings is indeed crucial in constructing such a sense of unity. This is also in keeping with

[30] Lindahl, "Sovereignty and Representation in the European Union," p. 101 ff.

[31] *Ibid.*, pp. 105 ff.

[32] For Van Roermund, individual autonomy and collective autonomy are analogous precisely because both individuals and collectivities can *refer to* themselves as a self. See Van Roermund (2003), pp. 45ff. There is a strong similarity with the writings of Michael Saward, who describes the work of political representation as a work of "claim-making," see Michael Saward, *The Representative Claim* (Oxford: Oxford University Press, 2010).

the vast literature on the role of representation and symbolic forms in social life (e.g., Ernst Cassirer).[33] However, it is doubtful that unity is enough. Is the sheer observation that a political or legal community consciously understands itself as a unity sufficient to apply the label of sovereignty? In the next section I will argue that something more is needed: for a community to see itself as genuinely autonomous it also needs to have an awareness that it can act, and that it can act freely, i.e. that it can choose among various courses of action. By and large, the need for such a sense of agency seems to elude Lindahl and Van Roermund.

4 Third Condition: Agency

In order to explain why unity is not enough, allow me to use a somewhat odd nautical metaphor.[34] Imagine a number of people, not on a genuine ship but on a floating platform in the open sea. They drift sometimes in one direction, sometimes in another direction, depending on the wind and the ocean's currents. The people on this platform might have a strong vision of themselves as a unity, with a shared past and a shared (rather bleak) destiny. But this is clearly not the same as seeing oneself as an autonomously acting unit. In this situation, the addition of a motor and a steering wheel would make a world of difference. With these elements added, the group acquires the capacity to sail in various directions. If the raft now sets course in one specific direction, this is no longer a mere effect of natural mechanisms, but it can be understood by the rafting crew as an act of collective autonomy. This points to a key element in the self-image (or in the "symbolic constitution") of a sovereign collectivity: its members need to have a vivid awareness that their "raft" can travel in various directions, and that the direction in which it eventually goes is not a matter of immovable natural laws but will be the effect of a conscious choice. Does this require that they have the absolute liberty to travel in whatever direction that pleases them? I do not think so. The presence of limitations does not have to be fatal to the awareness of autonomy. On boats it most certainly is not. The fact that there are empirical limits (steering upwards to the sky, for instance, is

[33] This literature is constantly lurking in the background of Lindahl's and Van Roermund's work. See for instance Lindahl (1997); Lindahl, "Authority and Representation," *Law and Philosophy* 19(2) (2000): pp. 223–246.

[34] There is of course a long and venerable history of comparing polities to boats, started by Plato, continued by Aquinas, and most recently taken up by Habermas and James Tully, among many others.

impossible) as well as normative limits (maritime law forbids, inter alia, crashing into another vessel) does not normally taint one's awareness of being on a ship that is able to purposely steer in a specific direction.[35]

Turning from boats to actual societies, I submit that the *staging of political conflict*, as practiced in representative democracies, produces exactly this effect on our collective self-image.[36] A visible conflict about society's future allows citizens to consciously see themselves as sovereign because it vividly reminds them of the fact that societal norms and policies are not predetermined but require a collective decision. This is also what makes representative democracy special. All human communities are shot through with potential tensions and divisions, but many societies are conflict-shy and deploy a variety of strategies to maintain an appearance of social unanimity. Democratic societies are different in that they do not muffle or deny the existence of societal oppositions. Instead, they openly acknowledge the presence of conflicts and opposing forces and even make them publicly visible at the heart of their most important institutions. The presence of multiple parties on the political stage is especially important in this regard. Every party embodies a specific ideological position and translates this position into concrete policy proposals that have the potential to push society in a specific direction. Thus, the conflict between different parties constantly shows us that our society can move in different directions: our future as a collectivity is open and it is up to us to decide in what direction our society will evolve. By confronting us with the undecidedness of our future, the multiplicity of representatives clearly keeps at bay the idea that we are on a predetermined path. This latter idea is very widespread, and there exist many versions of it (such as the belief that we are governed by material laws of history or by economic necessity). The best protection against such views is precisely a staged conflict between representatives, which constantly stimulates our sense of collective agency. Of course, the public brawling of politicians is often a far cry from the rational republic that many Kantians have in mind. Yet I believe a visible, staged conflict is

[35] The same goes, by the way, for the autonomy of individual persons. There as well, the presence of various physical and normative limitations does not necessarily imply the absence of moral autonomy.

[36] In what follows, I am heavily leaning on ideas of the late French philosopher, Claude Lefort. See Lefort, *Democracy and Political Theory* (Cambridge: Polity Press, 1988) and see my "Political Representation: The View from France," in L. Disch, M. van de Sande and N. Urbinati (eds.), *The Constructivist Turn in Political Representation* (Edinburgh University Press, 2019), pp. 89–103.

essential if we want to reproduce, at the collective level, the consciousness of being a free agent that Kant described so well for the level of individual action. As mentioned before, Lindahl and Van Roermund are not attentive to this intrinsic connection between collective agency and political conflict, nor is Habermas.

5 Challenges

This, then, gives the complete account of sovereignty as autonomy, an account that is primarily concerned with what happens at the level of our collective imaginary. Taking my lead from Kant's description of individual autonomy, I have distinguished three elements that I believe to be essential for collective autonomy. (1) If a collectivity is to see itself as capable of acting on the basis of reasons, it needs to have the capacity to process reasons in a collective manner. This requires deliberative procedures and the adequate protection of participants. (2) This capacity cannot be uncoupled from a conscious awareness, on the side of citizens, that they are part of a larger unity. (3) Citizens also need to be aware that this unit is an agent of intentional action. This awareness can be activated by political conflict, which confronts us with the openness of our future and thus with the possibility of (and the need for) collective decisions.

Can this account of sovereignty rise to the empirical challenge ("sovereignty has no place in a multilevel world") and to the conceptual challenge ("sovereignty is incompatible with the rule of law") mentioned at the beginning of this chapter? I believe it can. Let me start with the conceptual challenge, which was formulated most cogently by Pavlos Eleftheriadis.[37] According to Eleftheriadis, the term "sovereignty" is only meaningful when it refers to an empirical entity (a thing, a person, or a group of persons) that is the supreme source of all norms. Building on this assumption, he demonstrates that all potential uses of the term run into severe conceptual problems. Take for instance John Austin's description of the sovereign, as a ruler who is obeyed by all and obeys no one. Such an Austinian sovereign inevitably depends on rules (as listed by H.L.A. Hart: rules of succession, rules that distinguish random orders from legitimate edicts, and so on) which she did not make herself and which therefore rob her of her claim to sovereignty. According to Eleftheriadis, other uses of the term "sovereignty" run into similar difficulties and are, therefore, equally incoherent. The word

[37] Eleftheriadis, "Law and Sovereignty."

"sovereignty" can for instance indicate the highest lawmaking office within a constitutional framework (think of the sovereignty of Parliament in the United Kingdom) or to indicate the role of the people in a democracy (i.e., popular sovereignty). In all these cases the operations of sovereignty depend on procedures and norms that are prior to the sovereign, both in a chronological sense (these rules have to be in place before the sovereign can exist or act) and in a normative sense (these rules impose limits on the exercise of sovereignty). Thus, a constitutional regime has no place for the idea of a sovereign who is truly the first source of all rules and who stands normatively above all rules. Eleftheriadis concludes that the notion of sovereignty might have a place in an absolutist, lawless regime, but is utterly incompatible with a constitutional setup, where constitutional norms are always the higher authority to which all institutions and persons remain subjected.

In spite of its plausibility, this argument need not force us to give up the idea of sovereignty. As Habermas has amply demonstrated, generating the collective will depends on the presence of deliberative procedures and on protecting their participants. This means that the sovereign will can only appear when there are solid constitutional rules in place. Are these rules an external limitation on sovereignty, a limitation that deprives the self-governing community from its claim to autonomy? Certainly not, and claiming so would be highly counter-intuitive. The analogy with individual autonomy is again enlightening. The exercise of moral autonomy by an individual person clearly depends on the presence of certain biological elements (most importantly: a brain) as well as certain symbolic elements (a certain self-image). Similarly, the exercise of collective autonomy depends on the presence of specific material and symbolic elements. And just as these supporting elements might be wanting in some individuals and more strongly present in others, some collectivities might have a reduced capacity to act autonomously whereas others might have a more established constitutional framework that enables a higher degree of collective autonomy. Yet if collective autonomy increases to the extent that constitutional rules are stronger, then it is incoherent to claim that such rules limit the sovereign will or diminish its sovereign quality. Enabling conditions can simply not be equated with limitations.

Moreover, constitutional rules are not limitations imposed from the outside. It is the citizens themselves who establish and continue to refine their own constitutional framework in order to further their autonomy. Habermas emphatically describes constitutional democracy as a learning process: citizens realize in concrete and changing circumstances the abstract normative requirements of collective autonomy. As they improve their interpretation of these requirements, they gradually approach the ideal of complete autonomy. Think again of individual autonomy. Children start without autonomy, yet they do gradually become autonomous as they critically work through the norms carried over during the formative years. From an empirical perspective, full autonomy will never be reached. But this does not threaten the fact that, when dealing with other adults, we act "under the idea" that they are now autonomous.

Let me now turn to the empirical challenge. Assuming that sovereignty involves supreme legal or political powers, the empirical critics argue that sovereignty can by definition no longer exist today, as legal and political powers are now spread out over multiple levels. However, if one is willing to abandon the connection between sovereignty and political or legal supremacy and instead accept that, in a democratic world, sovereignty is short for the perspective adopted by a self-governing polity, then things start to shift. I previously compared collective autonomy to having the feeling of sitting on a ship that is able to steer its own course. In our multilevel world, one should probably imagine sitting on several ships at once, all of them self-steering (for instance, a European nation-state, an autonomous region within that state, the European Union, and the rudimentary global order). Critics might argue that this image is flawed because these different layers are not independent ships, all happily steering their own course in a sea of their own. In fact, some of these levels of government are hierarchically superior to others, restrict the maneuvering space of the lower levels of government in important ways, and thereby taint the autonomy of these smaller units.

I believe this criticism to be misguided. For starters (and as already mentioned above), the presence of limitations does not necessarily alter our sense of being aboard a ship that deliberately steers its own course. Actual boats also need to take into account a whole host of physical and normative limitations. Moreover, it is not just the lower levels of government that have to accept limitations and restrictions. In a well-ordered global order, all boats have to accept that they can hinder each other's paths and therefore have to conclude binding agreements that might have deep constitutional effects and limit everyone's purported supremacy, even that of the higher levels of government.[38] Most importantly,

[38] In other words, the different levels of government stacked in a federal or confederal order need not be hierarchically ranked. Ideally, they have clearly delineated sets of

the vertical stacking of multiple legal or political orders does not imply that limitations emerging higher up (e.g., EU-norms that restrict a member state's policy range) are constraints that are imposed from the outside by an unaccountable foreign power. In principle, these decisions result from an exercise of our collective autonomy as well. We have to imagine ourselves as sitting on *all* these different ships, given that these different constitutional layers are all meant to be vehicles of our autonomy. Naturally, this requires that each of these layers is institutionally arranged in such a way that we can indeed recognize them as an expression of our collective autonomy, a condition that is hardly realized in today's world. I also silently assume that citizens can have an active sense of political identification with more than one decision-making level at the same time. Authors who are skeptical of our postnational constellation tend to deny that this is possible. But I think that both our own experiences (with political commitments often running from local town politics to global affairs) and the literatures on federalism and on multiculturalism confirm that stacked and dispersed identifications are feasible.[39]

In sum, it is important to turn attention away from these aspects of sovereignty that have relatively little to offer to democratic societies (absolutely supreme political and legal powers) and instead focus on what I take to be the normative core and the most valuable element in the cluster of ideas and concepts that has coalesced around the term sovereignty, namely: sovereignty as the name for the perspective a community adopts when it sees itself as collectively autonomous. The concept of sovereignty, defined in this way, is perfectly able to withstand the dominant criticisms to which it is exposed.

6 Why Does It Matter?

In this concluding section I would like to explain why it so important to rescue the notion of sovereignty. As mentioned at the beginning of this

competences so as to prevent them from colliding. And when constitutional matters are to be decided (for instance regarding the transfer of competences from one level of government to another level), they ought to treat each other as equals. See Geenens and De Schutter, "A Tripartite Model of Federalism" (unpublished manuscript).

[39] See for instance Luis Moreno, *The Federalization of Spain* (Frank Cass, 2001); Mathew Mendelsohn, "Measuring National Identity and Patterns of Attachment: Quebec and Nationalist Mobilization," *Nationalism and Ethnic Politics* 8(3): pp. 72–94 (2002); Helder De Schutter, "Federalism as Fairness," *The Journal of Political Philosophy* 19(2) (2011): pp. 167–189.

chapter, the political, moral, and cultural patterns of the nation-state stand under increasing pressure, as these patterns hinder the smooth functioning of global capitalism. That "hindrance" might occur in a variety of ways, but my hypothesis would be that the nation-state is particularly impeding to capitalism because it offers a context where collective autonomy can emerge. Thus, if the nation-state's institutional and cultural infrastructure is slowly being chipped away, this might ultimately not just be because nation-states harbor irritating labor regulations or because they hinder the frictionless mobility of individuals, but rather, more fundamentally, because this infrastructure continues to enable a sense of collective authority over the future.

Why would collective autonomy be such a significant enemy to the functioning of global capitalism? The answer is to be found in a conceptual distinction that was sacred to Hayek, neoliberalism's most important prophet, namely the distinction between "cosmos" and "taxis" as he presents it in *Law, Legislation and Liberty*. For Hayek's purposes, these two terms refer to two radically different types of order: "cosmos" stands for orders that develop and grow spontaneously, whereas "taxis" stands for orders that are the product of deliberate design. According to Hayek, social order (including a society's legal and moral norms) is, to a much larger extent than usually assumed, a form of cosmos. Constructive rationalists (his term for thinkers like Hobbes) would want us to believe that society is *made*, but in fact most of it simply *grows* through processes that, even though human beings are actively involved, can best be described in the terms of adaptation and selection which Hayek borrows from biological theories of evolution. In fact, he does not *borrow* these terms; he genuinely claims that social order *is* an extension of biological order, without any real discontinuity between the two. Moral rules, for instance, far from imposing a categorical *ought*, are just a continuation of action patterns that *are* successful.[40] Even the complex institutions of modern society, according to Hayek, can only be explained as the fruit of spontaneous evolution.[41]

Hayek deploys the opposition between "cosmos" and "taxis" against everyone who believes that society, as a whole, can form judgments about what is "just" or "unjust," can "act" and have a "purpose," or could be "responsible" for anything.[42] Such an "intentionalist" way of looking at

[40] Friedrich Hayek, *Law, Legislation and Liberty* (London and New York: Routledge, 2013) pp. 18–19, 76–77.
[41] *Ibid.*, pp. 42ff., 48, 72.
[42] *Ibid.*, p. 27.

collectivities is misguided, according to Hayek, because it suggests that social norms can be attributed to a "sovereign" entity that has consciously deliberated about them, as if society could act in the same way as an individual person.[43] One good look at nature is enough to dispel such fictions. In biological systems, Hayek tells us, one finds combinations of functions and operations that are not less complex than those of human society, and yet they lack any awareness of purpose and have been created without "deliberate co-ordination" and without "conscious reason" being involved.[44] Unfortunately, these intentionalist fictions are omnipresent and constantly incite men to try and "pursue common ends," which – in Hayek's eyes – leads to disastrous consequences.[45] In the field of law, Hayek's position translates into a strong preference for common law. Whereas legislation connects law to conscious decisions by a political community, the slow process of common law resembles nature in that it gradually selects and enforces the most efficient practices. Echoing early natural law, Hayek writes that it is no coincidence that the term law can refer both to an observed regularity in physical nature and to a norm for human behavior.[46] Hayek sometimes aims his wrath directly at the notion of popular sovereignty. Not only does he dislike the concept of sovereignty, which he equates with the idea that laws derive from the will of an entity with unlimited power, but he especially derides the "fairy tale" idea that the people could ever be "acting together" and that this would somehow be "morally preferable to the separate actions by individuals."[47]

This latter remark makes very clear what is at stake. Ultimately, Hayek's claims about the nature of social order have an unambiguous practical message: society should be organized in such a way that the spontaneous actions of individuals can work their magic and can, through mechanisms that elude full understanding, result into forms of order that are superior to what could ever be achieved through conscious deliberation. This means that society should mostly refrain from interfering in the life of its members; at most, it can impose rules that are conducive to the emergence of spontaneous order. While the preference for individual action over collective action could be just a value choice that Hayek urges upon us, he eagerly emphasizes that

[43] *Ibid.*, pp. 27, 32.
[44] *Ibid.*, pp. 28–29, 40.
[45] *Ibid.*, p. 31.
[46] *Ibid.*, p. 70.
[47] *Ibid.*, p. 377.

hard scientific proof shows spontaneity to be more efficient and more productive than collective rationality, which is in any case impossible to achieve.

This message is strangely contradictory. Hayek literally writes that it is important that *we* become *aware* of the scientific evidence in favor of spontaneous individual action, so that *we* can organize the world accordingly.[48] He thereby assumes that there is a "we" to which he can address himself, a "we" that can process reasons and that can ultimately order society in a specific way. In other words, he presupposes the possibility of collective autonomy, while at the same time urging collective autonomy to deny itself and to abdicate in favor of quasi-biological modes of collective order. The performative contradiction that appears here in philosophical form is none other than the well-known lie of contemporary neoliberal capitalism, which presents itself as a policy choice that is sufficiently supported by economic evidence so as to make normal democratic legitimation superfluous. In fact, it is not even a choice. Ever increasing competition, modeled on nature itself, is simply the most efficient mode of production ("there is no alternative") and hence there is no need to subject neoliberal policies to a democratic political process. In such a process, neoliberal policies would be assessed in light of public standards of justice and would of course be unmasked as just one possible course of action among others. Global capitalism seems bent on undermining the possibility of such moments of collective consciousness. Ideally, there would just be individuals competing against each other, without anyone thinking or judging in the name of society as a whole. Such a competition still needs some rules, but these could possibly be maintained without being connected, as legislated laws are, to the collective will of a political community.

I believe this to be the real background to contemporary philosophical debates about sovereignty. The concept of sovereignty, stripped to its core meaning and detached from specific historical contexts such as that which produced Marx's critique of bourgeois nationalism, refers to the very possibility of consciously steering society. Accordingly, citizens can be called sovereign when they do adopt such a perspective upon themselves, that is, when they see themselves as a collective agent that is capable of autonomously choosing its own course. Discarding the notion of sovereignty in favor of a globalized rule of law implies a realignment of law according to the wishes of

[48] See for instance *ibid.*, p. 37.

contemporary capitalism as laid out by, for instance, Hayek. Thus, rather than just innocently helping us to dispose of an outmoded legal concept, the philosophical critics of sovereignty are, knowingly or unknowingly, helping to counteract the emergence of collective autonomy.

PART II

History of Theory

5

Liberal Governmentality and the Political Theology of Constitutionalism

MIGUEL VATTER

1 Introduction: 'The King Reigns But Does Not Govern' as Formula for Constitutionalism

'The king reigns but does not govern'. This formula, which according to Carl Schmitt was coined by Adolphe Thiers, a French liberal historian and politician, enemy of Bonapartism yet suppressor of the Paris Commune, has become today the most important formula in the study of liberalism.[1] Michel Foucault and Giorgio Agamben both understand this formula as capturing something essential about liberalism as a form of governmentality that guides the conduct of individuals either in the absence, or beyond the reach, of the sovereign power and its legislation through normative and normalizing orders that escape democratic control.[2] Although not discussed as such, this formula also underlies recent attempts by jurists and historians of political ideas such as Martin

[1] See the discussion of the formula in: C. Schmitt, *Politische Theologie II: Die Legende von der Erledigung jeder Politischen Theologie* (Berlin: Duncker & Humblot, 1996), 41–45. For an unsurpassed reconstruction of nineteenth-century French liberalism that provides the immediate context for the formula, see: L. Jaume, *L'individu effacé ou le paradoxe du libéralisme francais* (Paris: Fayard, 1997), 158–169, 186–192.

[2] See G. Agamben, *The Kingdom and the Glory: For a Theological Genealogy of Economy and Government* (Stanford: Stanford University Press, 2011), 70–108; M. Foucault, *Security, Territory, Population: Lectures at the Collège de France 1977–1978* (New York: Picador, 2009), 76. For commentary on the formula in this context, see J. Whyte, 'The king reigns but he doesn't govern'. Thinking Sovereignty and Government with Agamben, Foucault and Rousseau' in T. Forst (ed.), *Giorgio Agamben: Legal, Political and Philosophical Perspectives* (London: Routledge, 2013), 143–161 and M. Dean, *The Signature of Power: Sovereignty, Governmentality and Biopolitics* (London: Sage, 2013) 123–124, 193–195. The concepts of governmentality and governance both attempt to capture a development in the idea of government once sovereignty and the nation-state is decentred, but they do so from vastly different analytics of power. On the concept of governance, see M. Bevir, *Key Concepts in Governance* (London: Sage 2008).

Loughlin and Richard Tuck to bolster the sovereignty of the state against new forms of governing without the state that emerge in neoliberalism.[3] This chapter proposes a new reading of this formula by situating it on the terrain of constitutionalism, rather than on that of sovereignty. In so doing, it seeks to bring together in a meaningful exchange these two different critical approaches to neoliberalism, and the emerging debates they harbour. One debate is between those who advocate a Foucauldian and biopolitical and those who adopt an Agambenian and politico-theological analysis of neoliberal governmentality.[4] The other is the one between advocates of a republican, constitutional approach to democracy and those who argue for the revival of popular sovereignty on the basis of new 'democratic' interpretations of Bodin and Hobbes.[5]

The formula 'The king reigns but does not govern' was already employed by Charles McIlwain in his 1940 classic *Constitutionalism, Ancient and Modern*, not in order to capture the essence of modern liberal government, but as the scheme for modern constitutionalism.[6] McIlwain's hypothesis is that modern constitutionalism finds its roots in medieval royal law as interpreted by the thirteenth-century English jurist Henri Bracton. On this view, Bracton theorized that the monarch abstains from governing so that he can bind himself to a constitution, thus giving rise to his sovereignty or 'reign' in the form of a constitutional or limited government. Hardly a decade after McIlwain's liberal reading

[3] See M. Loughlin, *Foundations of Public Law* (New York: Oxford University Press, 2010) and R. Tuck, *The Sleeping Sovereign: The Invention of Modern Democracy* (New York: Cambridge University Press, 2016). For an earlier formulation of the distinction between state and government in light of neoliberal developments, see Q. Skinner, 'A Genealogy of the Modern State', *Proceedings of the British Academy* 162 (2009), 325–370. Conversely, see G. Duso, 'La democrazia e il problema del governo', *Filosofia Politica* 20 (3) (2006), 367–390, for the opposite strategy in the critique of neoliberalism which turns on the recovery of a 'medieval' conception of government against the sovereignty of the modern state.

[4] For examples of the former, see W. Brown, *Undoing the Demos: Neoliberalism's Stealth Revolution* (New York: Zone Books, 2017) and M. Cooper, *Family Values: Between Neoliberalism and the New Social Conservatism* (New York: Zone Books, 2017). For examples of the latter, see J. Vogl, *The Ascendancy of Finance* (New York: Polity, 2017) and E. Santner, *The Weight of All Flesh: On the Subject-Matter of Political Economy* (New York: Oxford University Press, 2015).

[5] For the former, see P. Pettit, *On the People's Terms: A Republican Theory and Model of Democracy* (New York: Cambridge University Press, 2013); for the latter, apart from Loughlin and Tuck, see now D. Lee, *Popular Sovereignty in Early Modern Constitutionalism* (New York: Oxford University Press, 2016).

[6] C. H. McIlwain, *Constitutionalism: Ancient and Modern* (Ithaca: Cornell University Press, 1947), 77.

of the formula, Ernst Kantorowicz developed a new interpretation of Bracton in *The King's Two Bodies* that assigned constitutionalism quite a different, enabling role with respect to the powers of government. By returning to the discussion between McIlwain and Kantorowicz, this chapter traces how constitutionalism transitions from a discourse on the limits to government to a discourse that serves to undo all such limitations. It is in this latter function that constitutionalism makes possible the passage to neoliberal governmentality. McIlwain's account of liberal government rests on a republican approach to constitutionalism, whereas the more recent attempts by Loughlin and Tuck to delimit the range of government depend on a non-republican conception of popular sovereignty. The discussion of McIlwain thus permits us to address the second debate mentioned above, the debate between neo-republican and neo-populist approaches to democratic constitutionalism. The analysis of Kantorowicz's use of political theology to displace constitutionalism from a discourse on the limits of sovereignty to a discourse on unlimited governmentality can be productively compared with Loughlin's attempts to employ political theology for the sake of bolstering the claims of popular sovereignty. The discussion of Kantorowicz also permits us to address the first debate mentioned above, which turns on the relation between political theology and neoliberalism.

The development of an alternative genealogy of limited or constitutional government is a particularly urgent task in the context of legal developments after 9/11 and the on-going War on Terror. For these events and the processes they have set off seem to have led to the implosion of constitutional government, in the sense that they have given rise to a paradoxical coincidence of unlimited government by emergency decrees under the increasing supremacy of constitutional courts.[7] Foucault had foreseen, at least in part, this development when he noted, in volume1 of the *History of Sexuality*, that the spread of

[7] For the rise in emergency government at the heart of post-Second World War constitutional governments, see the argument in G. Agamben, *State of Exception* (Chicago: University of Chicago Press, 2005).

For its connection to global constitutionalism, see accounts like the ones offered by A. Negri and M. Hardt, *Empire* (Cambridge: Cambridge University Press, 2001) and now H. Lindahl, *Authority and the Globalisation of Inclusion and Exclusion*, (Cambridge: Cambridge University Press, 2018). For treatments of constitutionalism in the age of the 'state of exception', see S. Holmes, *The Matador's Cape: America's Reckless Response to Terror* (New York: Cambridge University Press, 2007); D. Dyzenhaus, *The Constitution of Law: Legality in a Time of Emergency* (Cambridge: Cambridge University Press, 2006);

biopolitics (and, thus, of liberal governmentality) was shadowed by 'a whole, continual and clamorous legislative activity: these were the [constitutional – MV] forms that made an essentially normalizing power acceptable'.[8] However, neither the Foucauldian nor the Agambenian genealogies of neoliberal governmentality have focussed on the role played by the medieval tradition of constitutionalism in this process.[9]

This chapter seeks to shed light on the paradox pointed out by Foucault, that governmentality goes hand in hand with a constitutionalization of social spheres, by returning to the interpretation given by Kantorowicz of the formula 'the king reigns but does not govern'. Kantorowicz's masterpiece, *The King's Two Bodies*, has been the object of sustained interest on the part of political, literary and cultural theorists, in particular with respect to his discussion of the 'mystical body' of the Crown and its application to modern popular sovereignty and democratic government.[10] Unfortunately, these readings leave more or less untouched the way in which Kantorowicz brings the method of political theology to bear on the origins of western constitutionalism.[11]

'All significant concepts of the modern theory of the state are secularized theological concepts not only because of their historical

B. Ackerman, *The Decline and Fall of the American Republic* (Cambridge, MA: Harvard University Press, 2013).

8 M. Foucault, *The History of Sexuality: Volume I: An Introduction* (New York: Vintage Books, 1990), 144.

9 The only partial exception is found in Agamben's discussion of the 'canonistic notion of *plenitudo potestatis*' in G. Agamben, *The Kingdom and the Glory: For a Theological Genealogy of Economy and Government* (Stanford: Stanford University Press, 2011), 100–103, but even here the approach is not constitutional.

10 See V. Kahn, 'Political Theology and Fiction in The King's Two Bodies'. *Representations* 106 (1) (2009), 77–101; E. Santner, *The Royal Remains: The People's Two Bodies and the Endgames of Sovereignty* (Chicago: The University of Chicago Press, 2011). Previously, Kantorowicz's interpretation of the 'two bodies' had found its most fertile reception in France, starting with the debates between C. Lefort, *Writing: The Political Test* (Durham, NC: Duke University Press, 2000), M. Gauchet, *The Disenchantment of the World* (Princeton: Princeton University Press, 1999), and P. Rosanvallon, *Le peuple introuvable* (Paris: Gallimard, 1998) on the absence/presence of the body of the People in popular sovereignty. On these themes, see now S. Nässtrom, 'Democratic Representation Beyond Election', *Constellations* 22 (1) (2015), 1–12.

11 As coined by Carl Schmitt, 'political theology' designates the historical phenomenon of the migration of theological concepts to jurisprudence and vice versa. For the meanings of political theology, see M. Vatter, 'The Political Theology of Carl Schmitt' in J. Meierhenrich and O. Simons (eds.), *The Oxford Handbook of Carl Schmitt* (New York: Oxford University Press, 2017), 245–268, and Montserrat Herrero, *The Political Discourse of Carl Schmitt: A Mystic of Order* (Lanham, MD: Rowman & Littlefield, 2015).

development – in which they were transferred from theology to the theory of the state ... – but also because of their systematic structure'.[12] Schmitt's famous methodological definition of political theology found its first application in his own interpretation of modern sovereignty as a function of the legal establishment of a state of exception to law. But it is not often remarked that the Anglo-American historiography of medieval political and legal thought in the twentieth century also employed the methodological understanding of political theology, without always recognizing or acknowledging it.[13] Unlike in Schmitt and in Agamben, this historiography thematized politico-theological motifs more in relation to constitutionalism than to sovereignty or government. For instance, in one of his last books on the theological foundations of modern constitutionalism, Brian Tierney explains that 'the typical process that occurred was the assimilation of a text of Roman private law into church law, its adaptation and transmutation there to a principle of *constitutional* law, and then its reabsorption into the sphere of secular government *in this new form*'.[14] The claim is structurally identical to Schmitt's methodological understanding of political theology, except that Tierney emphasizes the linkage of political theology to constitutionalism, rather than to sovereignty.

This 'constitutionalist' path taken by political theology in the Anglo-American debate since the 1940s climaxes in Kantorowicz's critique of McIlwain's theses on Bracton. The second section explains why this mid-century debate on Bracton is so significant for the genealogy of modern constitutionalism, working backwards from the current debate on sovereignty and government in Tuck and Loughlin. The third and fourth sections take up, respectively, the standpoints of McIlwain and Kantorowicz. The conclusion explains the significance of this alternative genealogy for the understanding of neoliberal ideas of governmentality.

[12] C. Schmitt, *Political Theology: Four Chapters on the Concept of Sovereignty* (Cambridge: MIT Press, 1988), 36.

[13] As far as I know, the first use of the phrase 'political theology' in this literature (other than Kantorowicz) occurs in F. Oakley, 'Jacobean Political Theology: The Absolute and Ordinary Powers of the King', *Journal of the History of Ideas* 29 (3) (1968), 323–346.

[14] B. Tierney, *Religion, Law and the Growth of Constitutional Thought 1150–1650* (Cambridge University Press, 1982), 25 emphasis mine.

2 Eyes Wide Shut: On Sleeping Sovereigns and All-Seeing Executives

In their efforts to defend the sovereignty of the state against the onslaught of neoliberal governmentality, a group of contemporary historians of political ideas ranging from Tuck and Loughlin to Eric Nelson and Kinch Hoekstra have recently argued that an absolutist conception of sovereignty lies at the origin of modern republican constitutionalism. In what is perhaps the most audacious claim of all, Nelson opens *The Royalist Revolution* by adopting McIlwain's thesis that the American patriots began their rebellion against the English Parliament in 'a sincere desire to rebalance the English constitution in favour of the Crown' only to argue, against McIlwain, that 'the turn to the royal prerogative was *the* formative moment in the history of what would emerge as American constitutionalism'.[15]

This new historiography on sovereignty, ultimately, revisits the dilemma first formulated by Otto Gierke's foundational presentation of the development of modern political thought out of the medieval context. For Gierke, the natural right tradition that gave rise to early modern 'public law' in Bodin, Grotius and Hobbes could never escape the fact that 'the contractual relation must always involve a duality of persons; a personality of the Ruler must always emerge by the side of the personality of the People, equally essential to the existence of the State'.[16] Gierke identified the originality of Hobbes's theory in his attempt to use the idea of social contract in order to eliminate one of these two fictional Persons.

> He substituted for the two original contracts a single contract by which each pledges himself to each to submit to a common Ruler, who, on his side, takes no part in the making of the contract. This assumption destroyed, in the very germ, any personality of the People . . . The personality of the People died at its birth . . . With a logical inevitability all public right is absorbed, in every possible form of the State, by a Sovereignty of the Ruler which is absolutely unlimited and illimitable.[17]

In an ironical footnote, Gierke added:

[15] E. Nelson, *The Royalist Revolution: Monarchy and the American Founding* (Cambridge, MA: The Belknap Press, 2017), 6–7. Nelson's book is framed by the formula 'the king reigns but does not govern' – see footnote 14 at page 344. For his part, Tuck claims that 'a sovereign people can act *like a monarchical sovereign* through the process of majority voting' on a legal constitution. Tuck, *The Sleeping Sovereign*, 257. (Emphasis mine).

[16] O. Gierke, *Natural Law and the Theory of Society 1500 to 1800* (Cambridge: Cambridge University Press, 1934), 53.

[17] *Ibid.*, 60.

> Hobbes's account of the similarity and difference between the monarchical and the republican sovereign illustrates particularly how much he identifies the 'personality' of the Ruler with the physical substance of a man or a body of men. The republican sovereign only really exists for him as long as it is actually in session; in the interval it sleeps, and this sleep becomes death if the right of meeting at its own discretion be lost.[18]

In his recent book, *The Sleeping Sovereign*, Tuck has tried to resuscitate the image of the 'sleeping sovereign' – which for Gierke placed the people in a permanent state of suspended animation – as the true essence of modern popular sovereignty. Tuck assigns to Bodin's articulation of absolute sovereignty the honour of making possible modern constitutionalism by installing a principled separation between state (viz. sovereignty) and government.[19] Bodin reversed the (allegedly) Aristotelian idea of constitution (*politeia*), whereby it is not the 'body' of the self-governing citizens (the *politeuma*) but only the 'head' of the sovereign, entirely absolved from the tasks of government, that can give a 'form' or 'constitution' to the practice of government. Tuck's account minimizes the Aristotelian, Conciliarist and Machiavellian contributions to the development of popular sovereignty on the grounds that they confuse sovereignty with government since they adopt to varying degrees the (allegedly) Aristotelian idea of constitution as referring to the *politeia* understood as a 'form' of government, where only one part of the city is *kurios* or 'dominant'.[20]

Tuck's account faces the daunting task of explaining how a Bodinian sovereign who has 'all the power to appoint and dismiss the officers and to give laws to every one' can also be the fountainhead of rule of law or constitutional government.[21] Viewed from the neo-Roman republican tradition, such a task is internally contradictory because, at least since Polybius, the point of a constitution is precisely to create a republic characterized by a 'mixture' of monarchical, aristocratic and democratic elements thanks to which there is no single, absolute and ultimate site of legislative power. Unsurprisingly, Tuck concentrates the main burden of

[18] *Ibid.*, 267 fn 153.

[19] 'Before Bodin, democracy implied *government* by citizens, in a legislature of some kind, and though it was widely supposed that in some sense "the people" lay behind all political structures, they did not do so as legislators. After him, the citizens could be thought of (if one wished) as Bodinian sovereigns, formally authorising a set of fundamental laws'. Tuck, *The Sleeping Sovereign*, 249.

[20] On Aristotelian *politeia* see Tuck, *The Sleeping Sovereign*, 12–16. On the critique of Conciliarism and Marsilius see *ibid.*, 49–56.

[21] Bodin, *Republique* bk. II, ch. 7 (1576 ed., p.281) cited in Tuck, *The Sleeping Sovereign*, 19.

proof on Bodin's unorthodox interpretation of the Roman Republic and its constitutional order. Bodin breaks with the traditional republican understanding of the Roman Republic because for him the mixed political body does not define the Roman 'state' (which is in turn identified with the idea of *status rei publicae*) but merely expresses the way in which the activity of 'government' was exercised in the Roman state.[22] The Roman republican 'state', on this Bodinian view, is never divided or mixed because it consists of the undivided, sovereign power of the *populus* according to the formula *potestas in populo.*[23]

Hoekstra, for his part, argues that the Hobbesian conception of sovereignty leads to a modern form of constitutionalism because the emphasis on a unique rather than mixed idea of sovereignty defended by early modern absolutism does not contradict, and indeed may call for, a mixed, i.e. 'limited', idea of government.[24] Hoekstra shows how Hobbes defended this reading of the Roman constitution by claiming that

[22] 'The state can be a monarchy, and nevertheless be governed as a democracy' citing Bodin, *Republique* 1576, pp. 233–234, cited in Tuck, *The Sleeping Sovereign*, 21. Tuck seems to accept without question Bodin's misleading equivalence between sovereign, state and the Roman expression, *status rei publicae.* On this point, see M. Vatter, 'Republics are a Species of State: Machiavelli and the Genealogy of the Modern State', *Social Research* 81 (1) 2014, 217–241.

[23] The Bodinian and Hobbesian readings of Roman constitutionalism were most likely heavily influenced by their reception of medieval civilian interpretations of Roman law. However, what this influence amounts to is disputed in the literature. Ralph Giesey, for instance, argues that Bodin's reliance on the *mos italicus* (i.e., the early tradition of legal scholarship in mediaeval Europe) explains why his sovereign is actually limited by law, in this case, by 'natural law'. But since for Italian legists, natural law flows into the law of nations and Roman civil law, the *mos italicus* 'had been concerned to establish a workable constitution for independent communes by establishing juridical limitations upon the *segnoria* (the word, incidentally, given as the Italian equivalent of *souveraineté* in the opening sentence of *Répub.* I,8)'. See R. E. Giesey, 'Medieval Jurisprudence in Bodin's Concept of Sovereignty', in J. Franklin (ed.), *Jean Bodin* (London: Routledge, 2006) 105–122, at 117. On this view, whatever constitutionalism is still found in Bodin is of medieval origin. Conversely, Daniel Lee has argued that Monarchomachs defended an *absolutist* conception of popular sovereignty (the inverse mirror of the absolutist conception of princely sovereignty in Bodin and Hobbes) by adopting the civilian conception according to which *dominium* belongs to the people as a corporation (*universitas*) and trumps the *imperium* of the prince. See D. Lee, 'Private Law Models for Public Law Concepts: The Roman Law Theory of Dominium in the Monarchomach Doctrine of Popular Sovereignty', *The Review of Politics* 70 (2008), 370–399. Here the legists become precursors of absolutism, not constitutionalism. For a similar strategy applied to Hobbes, see also D. Lee, 'Hobbes and Civil Law', in D. Dyzenhaus and T. Poole (eds.), *Hobbes and the Law* (Cambridge: Cambridge University Press, 2012), 210–135.

[24] K. Hoekstra, 'Early Modern Absolutism and Constitutionalism', *Cardozo Law Review* 34 (2013), 1079–1098 at 1082–1083.

potestas in populo refers to something like sovereignty held by 'simple democracy', whereas *auctoritas in senatu* refers to the derivative authority of 'a council aristocratical', viz., merely one branch of government.[25]

These readings of the Roman republican constitution made by early modern proponents of undivided sovereignty tend to abstract from the point that the Roman *populus* has *potestas* always already under law because the *populus* is composed of *sui iuris* citizens, i.e. individuals capable of bearing a common law, with its rights and duties. This is the point of Cicero's famous definition of the Roman *res publica*: 'For the people, according to his [Cicero's] definition, is an assembly of the multitude associated by a consensus of laws and by a community of interests [*populum enim esse definivit coetum multitudinis iuris consensu et utilitatis communione sociatum*]'.[26] Augustine's report of the Ciceronian conception of the Roman constitution would assure its widespread transmission as the medieval idea of *lex* as *constitutio populi*, meaning a 'natural' because uncoerced ordainment of a people according to the contribution of their social function to the satisfaction of social needs and according to long-held customs (*consuetudinis*).[27] Unlike the Hobbesian shift from multitude to people, which can only occur through the *unification* of many wills into one sovereign will (both in *De cive* and in *Leviathan*), in Cicero the unification into a people passes through a *community* of law and interests, without the need to artificially create a sovereign will (that is, in turn, creative of the political body or *civitas*).[28] From this republican perspective, one can say that the Roman Republic is characterized by a constitutional separation of power (*imperium*) from

[25] Hobbes, *Elements of Law* bk. 2.1.17 cited in Hoekstra, 'Early Modern Absolutism', 2013. For another discussion of the same thesis, see P. Springborg, 'Hobbes, civil law, liberty and the Elements of Law', *Critical Review of International Social and Political Philosophy* 19 (1) (2016), 47–67. I owe this reference to Gonzalo Bustamante.

[26] Augustine, *The City of God* (New York: Penguin, 1984), 19.21 On the reception of this passage in medieval and renaissance political thought, see M. S. Kempshall, '*De Re publica* 1.39 in Medieval and Renaissance Political Thought', in J. A. North and J. G. F. Powell (eds.), *Cicero's Republic* (London: Institute of Classical Studies, University of London, 2001), 99–135.

[27] On the medieval conception of law, see in general P. Grossi, *L'ordine giuridico medievale* (Bari: Laterza, 2004). On the Ciceronian roots of medieval constitutionalism, see C. J. Nederman, 'Nature, Sin, and the Origins of Society: The Ciceronian Tradition in Medieval Political Thought', *The Journal of the History of Ideas* 49 (1988), 3–26 and 'Rhetoric, Reason and Republic – Republicanisms: Ancient, Medieval, and Modern', in J. Hankins (ed.), *Renaissance Civic Humanism: Reappraisals and Reflections* (Cambridge University Press, 2004), 247–269.

[28] See the discussion in V. Arena, 'Popular Sovereignty in the Late Roman Republic', in R. Bourke and Q. Skinner (eds.) *Popular Sovereignty in Historical Perspective* (New York:

equal law (*aequus ius*), which is institutionalized by the granting of *auctoritas* to the senate and veto powers to the tribunate of the plebs.

The key to Roman and neo-Roman constitutionalism is the separation of *potestas* from *auctoritas*, whereas modern Bodinian and Hobbesian sovereignty unites both in one (representative) person who, as Hoekstra admits, must be 'one umpire who *ultimately decides* disputed cases, and *this judge* is the one who has sovereign *authority*'.[29] Only by relying on Bodin's and Hobbes's partisan or interested readings of the Roman Republic can Tuck cast doubt on what one could call the standard and long-lasting republican tradition that sees in constitutionalism an anti-sovereign ideal.[30] Indeed, for the republican understanding, a constitution is primarily the mechanism that *disallows* the construction of one site in which power (*potestas*) and authority (*auctoritas*) are unified as the ultimate instance of law-giving. By way of contrast, the new historiography of sovereignty employs the distinction between state ('the king reigns') and government ('but does not govern') in order to eviscerate republican constitutionalism.

In so doing, these contemporary historians give an interpretation of the formula 'the king reigns but does not govern' that is very distant from its medieval interpretation. The medieval conception of sovereignty, or of the 'king who reigns', is premised on the existence of 'fundamental' laws that cannot be at the disposal of the king because they are not made by the king. The sphere of these laws is, therefore, referred to by the term *iurisdictio* and opposed to the idea of *legislatio*, the latter being an activity that a king or prince may engage in, as well as other representative bodies. The opposite is the case with Bodin and Hobbes, where sovereignty

Cambridge University Press, 2017), 73–95, which is, however, vitiated by an anachronistic employment of the language of sovereignty. Arena interprets Cicero's claim in *De re publica* 1.39 that '*res publica,* then, is the property of a people (*res populi*)' to mean that 'the people were de facto owners of their own property, which they could administer as they wished – in other words, were the sovereign power in the commonwealth' (quoted in Arena, 77). Here it is as if the civilian conception of the people qua *universitas* and having absolute *dominium* is conjoined with a Hobbesian reading of the *lex regia* (*Quod principi placuit, legis habet vigorem*) and projected back onto Cicero.

29 Hoekstra, 'Early Modern Absolutism', 1083, emphasis mine. Notice the sublation of authority into sovereign power through the identification of the legislating king with the king as a judge. As Giesey correctly states, 'The king as judge is medieval; the king as legislator, modern'. Giesey, 'Medieval Jurisprudence', 119.

30 See the defence of a 'mixed constitution' in both P. Pettit, *On the People's Terms: A Republican Theory and Model of Democracy* (New York: Cambridge University Press, 2012) and H. Arendt, *On Revolution* (New York: Penguin, 1990), despite the great differences in what they understand by the term.

becomes the supreme and sole legislative power. For Bodin and Hobbes, sovereignty is an absolute power that makes for law, whereas for medieval conceptions of sovereignty, it is law that makes for the supreme power of the king.[31] The medieval constitutional roots that reappear in modern republican constitutionalism, viz., the reference to a 'fundamental' or 'basic' law that spells out how the power of the state is to be established, under what limits and for what aim is left aside in Bodin and Hobbes.

As mentioned in the first section, one of the reasons that impel scholars interested in the development of modern constitutionalism to delve into the *arcana* of medieval political and legal thought concerns the continuities with or, perhaps better, the roots drawn from medieval constitutionalism. Particularly in relation to the history of constitutionalism, as opposed to the idea of the state or of political economy, it is difficult to support claims that allege a *radical* discontinuity between modern and medieval thought. This consideration, of course, does not decide at all the methodological question of whether these continuities (and, *a fortiori*, the discontinuities) with medieval constitutionalism are best addressed through a 'history of ideas' approach (Oakley and Tierney) or a 'Cambridge School' approach (Pocock, Condren, early Skinner) or a 'genealogical' approach (Foucault, Agamben, late Skinner), or a *Begriffgeschichte* (i.e. conceptual history) approach (Koselleck, Duso).[32] This chapter does not take sides with any particular approach. All of them have made valuable contributions to our understanding of how modern constitutionalism emerged from medieval constitutionalism.

However, questioning the medieval/modern dichotomy does encounter an obvious objection. This objection has been perhaps best phrased by

[31] The point was already made by Gierke: 'the original negative conception [of medieval sovereignty – MV] – the conception of a power which is not externally subject to any Superior – is made to assume a positive form by being as it were turned "outside in", and used to denote the relation of the State to everything which is within itself. From the quality of being the "supreme" earthly authority [i.e., the quality of being simply the *highest* authority], there is deduced the whole of that absolute omnipotence [i.e., the quality of being the *only* authority, and therefore unlimited and all-powerful] which only the modern State demands for itself'. Gierke, *Natural Law*, 41.

[32] On these traditions, see M. Richter, *The History of Political and Social Concepts: A Critical Introduction* (Oxford: Oxford University Press, 1995) and now E.J. Palti, 'The "Theoretical Revolution" in Intellectual History: From the History of Political Ideas to the History of Political Languages', *History and Theory* 53 (3) (2014), 387–405. For genealogy and archaeology in the history of political ideas, see the overview in R. Whatmore and B. Young (eds.), *A Companion to Intellectual History* (Chichester, West Sussex: Wiley Blackwell, 2016) and the theoretical statement in G. Agamben, *The Signature of All Things: On Method* (New York: Zone Books, 2009).

Cary Nederman in his critique of Francis Oakley's claim that modern constitutionalism owes its origin to canon law by way of Conciliarism.

> Although sixteenth- and seventeenth-century authors may have cited the authority of conciliar theorists . . . their references were necessarily partial and distorted: the issues animating the former – the distribution of power among earthly authorities and peoples for the sake of temporal public welfare – were fundamentally distinct from the conceptual underpinnings of the latter – the reform of the Church for the sake of reconciling believers, individually and as a community, with God.[33]

Nederman's claim, then, is that modern constitutionalism is essentially a secular enterprise, whereas medieval constitutionalism remains embedded in a theologico-political matrix from which it cannot disentangle itself.

The problem with Nederman's objection to Oakley's claim has become clearer thanks to two decades of complex debates on the nature of 'secularization' and, indeed, on whether there ever was such a thing.[34] The significance of approaching the history of modern political thought through the perspective of political theology is that the emergence of 'secular' political concepts in early modernity is seen as a function of the transference of concepts from the field of theology to that of jurisprudence. Political theology is one way to maintain the salient difference that Nederman posits between medieval and modern constitutionalism without undermining the possibility that crucial continuities or 'roots' or 'signatures' are nevertheless carried over from medieval to modern constitutionalism. An entirely different question is whether Schmitt articulated correctly the logic and the possibilities of political theology. As we shall see, Kantorowicz, in his own study on political theology, did not think so.

Martin Loughlin's *The Foundations of Public Law* adopts Schmitt's politico-theological understanding of constitutionalism in order to reconstruct a complex history of the continuities and discontinuities between medieval and modern constitutionalism. Unlike Tuck's position, Loughlin's defence of the claims of (modern) sovereignty against

[33] C.J. Nederman, 'Constitutionalism – Medieval and Modern: Against Neo-Figgisite Orthodoxy (Again)', *History of Political Thought* 17 (2) (1996), 179–194.

[34] On secularization and its critique, see, among others, J. Casanova, *Public Religions in the Modern World* (University of Chicago Press, 1994); T. Asad, *Formations of the Secular: Christianity, Islam, Modernity* (Stanford University Press, 2003); C. Taylor, *A Secular Age* (Cambridge: Harvard University Press, 2007); H. de Vries and L. Sullivan (eds.), *Political Theologies: Public Religions in a Post-Secular World* (New York: Fordham University Press, 2006).

(medieval) government is undertaken in conversation with the literature on the 'theological' origins of modern sovereignty. Indeed, the book begins with a reconstruction of the long-lasting struggle between the 'Papal monarchy' of the Church and the 'theocratic kingship' of the Empire.[35]

As is well known, Neville Figgis's account of *Political Thought from Gerson to Grotius* identified the crucial impetus for the establishment of a 'secular' political sphere in the first effective separation of the Church from the State during the Investiture struggle. For Figgis, this development was propelled by the Papacy, not the Empire, and eventually led to the Conciliar movement and to modern Parliamentarism.[36] The reason why the Church became 'secular' before the Empire has been explained by Francis Oakley in terms of the durability of the Hellenistic conception of 'sacral kingship' in the Imperial political imagination. Until the English Revolution, monarchs understood themselves as representatives of God on earth and as having sacramental powers unified in their person.[37] Legal historian Harold Berman claimed that in his struggle against the Emperor, Pope Gregory VII actually triggered a Papal 'legal revolution' that led to what sociologists call the 'functional differentiation' of law from politics, a key signature of modern civil society.[38]

Loughlin rejects this narrative and instead adopts the claim made famous by Walter Ullmann that the Papacy was always the dominant force in the medieval Church, and the Papacy, from Saint Peter onwards, was essentially a legalistic theocracy.[39] However, Loughlin does hold on to the thread of 'sacral kingship' in medieval thought proposed by

[35] Loughlin, *Foundations*, 19–28. Loughlin's book is the object of a recent collection of critical essays found in M.A. Wilkinson and M.W. Dowdly (eds.), *Questioning the Foundations of Public Law: A Critical Review* (Oxford: Hart Publishing, 2018). However, none of the essays takes up centrally the question of the politico-theological sources of modern constitutionalism in Loughlin's account.

[36] N.J. Figgis, *Studies of Political Thought from Gerson to Grotius 1414–1625* (Cambridge: Cambridge University Press, 1916).

[37] On sacral kingship, see F. Oakley, *Kingship: The Politics of Enchantment* (Oxford: Blackwell, 2006); *Empty Bottles of Gentilism: Kingship and the Divine in Late Antiquity and the Early Middle Ages (to 1050)* (New Haven: Yale University Press, 2010); *The Watershed of Modern Politics* (New Haven: Yale University Press, 2015).

[38] See H. Berman, *Law and Revolution: The Formation of the Western Legal Tradition* (Cambridge: Harvard University Press, 1983) and for the wide-ranging implications of the Papal legal revolution, see H. Brunkhorst, *Critical Theory of Legal Revolutions: Evolutionary Perspectives* (London: Bloomsbury, 2014).

[39] Loughlin, *Foundations*, 20. I cannot here enter into the long debate between the Ullmann school and the Figgis school on the structure of Papal government, which finds one of its latest expressions in the polemics between Oakley and Nederman.

Oakley. This allows Loughlin to understand the conflict between Pope and Emperor as a competition between two distinct claims to unify power and authority on the basis of two claims to privileged access to God's providential order.[40] Loughlin's thesis is that modern constitutionalism effects a break from medieval constitutionalism thanks to the modern conception of sovereignty which restructures the political community free of any reliance on God's will by putting in its place, so to speak, the will of a people. Given that for *droit politique* 'the authority of the state . . . is absolute',[41] Loughlin argues that the modern conception of sovereignty manages to unify, at least at a national level, *potestas* with *auctoritas*, thus fulfilling the medieval theologico-political aspiration in a radically changed, 'secular' context.

If the first narrative argues that modern sovereignty, so to speak, pacifies and reunites, at the national level, the absolutism contested by Papacy and Empire, then the second narrative at work in Loughlin brings together an account of how the transition from medieval to modern constitutionalism is a process of 'secularization' (in the Schmittian sense of the term) that is best expressed or culminates in the emergence of the new idea of 'public law'. By modern 'public law' or *droit politique* Loughlin understands a doctrine according to which 'no concept of fundamental law that binds the state can exist' because the absolute state is 'itself the source of law'.[42] However, even in modern public law the medieval roots are still visible. For Loughlin, the medieval idea of a 'fundamental law' at the basis of political power does not simply vanish under conditions of modern sovereignty but itself splits into two contrary understandings of 'constitution': the constitution of the state or sovereignty, which Loughlin calls *droit publique* proper and the 'constitution of the office of government', by which he refers to the received understanding of modern constitutionalism as based on the creation of written constitutions understood as legal documents intended to check the powers and policies of government by means of judicial review mechanisms.[43]

As Loughlin readily admits, this curious distinction of two meanings of the modern constitution comes from Carl Schmitt's *Constitutional Theory*. Indeed, Loughlin's main thesis is that the doctrine of 'political

[40] Hence medieval political thought is characterized by 'the theological-political question'. Loughlin, *Foundations*, 18.

[41] *Ibid.*, 209.

[42] *Ibid.*, 209.

[43] *Ibid.*, 210.

jurisprudence' or 'public law' ought to follow Schmitt in establishing the priority of the first or 'material' constitution of the sovereign over the second or 'formal' constitution of government through the rule of law.[44] As in Tuck, Loughlin is also faced with a double bind: how to employ law in order to 'constitute' a power of the state that is 'absolute' with respect to law? How is it possible to 'legally' constitute a supra-legal absolute power?[45] Loughlin's answer is to say that the first meaning of law is equivalent to *droit politique*, whereas the second meaning of law is equivalent to ordinary or parliamentary legislation. But in order for the answer not to rely on a simple trick of homonymy, and for the meaning of *droit* in *droit politique* to have some family resemblance to what we call 'positive' law, Loughlin actually has to return to the early modern debates on kingship that fed into the formula 'the king reigns but does not govern'. That is why his attempt is an important background for the alternative genealogy proposed in this chapter.

Loughlin is keen on recovering medieval constitutionalism as what justifies the modern sovereignty-based separation between state and government precisely because he believes that 'the medieval notion of fundamental law – which in the modern world finds its analogy in public law as political right – has become submerged' by a legalistic understanding of constitutionalism.[46] Loughlin's polemic is directed against the 'legalistic' or 'normativist' idea of the modern constitution as a higher law standing above the state that he sees exemplified in the famous US case of *Marbury*. 'Through Marshall's work (in Marbury – MV), not only was the ancient sense of the constitution as fundamental law buried; so too was the idea that the modern constitution was a form of *droit politique*. Instead the Constitution was transformed into a new type of positive law'.[47] *Marbury* and the institution of judicial review stand for 'the judicial usurpation of politics . . . [because] the judiciary has taken upon itself the task of interpreting not only ordinary law but also public law'.[48]

44 See now also M. Loughlin, *Political Jurisprudence* (New York: Oxford University Press, 2018).

45 I put 'legally' in quotation marks because it becomes clear that for Loughlin 'legally' stands for a concept of 'right ordering'. See Loughlin, *Foundations*, 91. This seems to be his own rendition of Schmitt's idea of *nomos*, discussed below.

46 Loughlin, *Foundations*, 297.

47 *Ibid.*, 293.

48 *Ibid.*, 299.

The key to Loughlin's critique of the judicial interpretation of the Constitution as a control on both legislative and executive powers is his radical reevaluation of the idea of the prerogatives of government. Loughlin claims that these prerogatives originate in the medieval distinction between the king's absolute and legally conditioned powers, where absolute power is linked to government's pursuit of *salus populi* beyond the rule of law.[49] The distinction between statutory law and executive prerogative is drawn back to the medieval distinction between *iurisdictio* and *gubernaculum*.[50] This is the point where Loughlin's argument touches on McIlwain, who was among the first to point out the cruciality of this distinction in his famous interpretation of Bracton.

But from Loughlin's perspective, McIlwain's presentation of Bracton and medieval constitutionalism is too caught up with the 'Whig' interpretation of constitutional monarchy, which relies on the 'medieval idea of the king as feudal lord', to be kept bridled by the other feudal nobles and the *lex terrae*, viz. common law. Loughlin's interpretation of Bracton has an entirely different agenda. The modern conception of sovereignty which makes a 'constitutional' use of the power of prerogative to establish the state, even when law recedes, owes its lineage to Bracton's interpretation of the 'body of royal law (*lex regia*)' but only on condition that one understand Bracton as having posed the decisive question for the very idea of public law: 'how can the king be both *legibus solutus* and *sub lege*?'[51]

The outlines and stakes of this agenda are clearly set out in Loughlin's discussion of Locke, which adopts Harvey Mansfield's curious hypothesis according to which Locke subscribes to the rule of law *merely* to check 'the ordinary prerogative powers of government' but 'still leaves intact the absolute (or regal) prerogative powers of the government'.[52] In this way, Loughlin can place Locke's theory of prerogative in continuity with his reading of Schmitt's theory of the state of exception. Schmitt famously claimed that, in the state of exception to constitutional norms and rights, 'the state remains, whereas law recedes'. Loughlin accepts this claim as

49 *Ibid.*, 378ff.

50 *Ibid.*, 379. Loughlin does not credit McIlwain with this step.

51 *Ibid.*, 40. The literature on Bracton is very large; see C. J. Nederman, 'Bracton on Kingship Revisited', *History of Political Thought* 5 (1) (1984), 61–77 for a recapitulation of the debate and one of its last salvos. Within the confines of this chapter, I shall be able to discuss only some of the main contributors to this debate. For the debate on Bracton in the seventeenth century, see now C. J. Nederman, *Lineages of European Political Thought: Explorations Along the Medieval/Modern Divide from John of Salisbury to Hegel* (Washington: Catholic University of America Press, 2009), ch. 19 *passim*.

52 Loughlin, *Foundations*, 385.

valid and explains it as follows: 'he [Schmitt] is claiming that there are moments when the workings of public law (*droit politique*) require that the rules of positive law be set aside, suspended, or modified. Positive law recedes, but *droit politique* remains'.[53] For Loughlin, *droit politique* understood as the 'constitution of the state', and not merely as constitutional laws that nominally 'limit' government, is a 'dynamic' that works 'within a public sphere of both absolute and conditioned power'.[54] In other words, *droit politique* is a conception of constitutionalism that is deployed in the space of 'prerogatives' of government with respect to positive legislation, rather than offering the limits to these prerogatives.

Evidently, for Loughlin, *pace* Tuck, the sovereign is not 'asleep' at all but very much awake and attentive to those 'emergencies' and 'crises' and 'threats' that no ordinary legislative power can hope to cope with and that calls forth the imperious necessity for some representative of the person of the state to act before and besides the rule of law. In Loughlin, the formula 'the king reigns but does not govern' means that sovereignty, under the doctrine of *droit politique*, does not have to submit itself to the rule of law, which rule, instead, remains binding only for the acts of a parliamentary government or of the government of a King-in-Parliament.

What makes it possible to overturn the tradition of constitutionalism so dramatically, such that the resources of this tradition come to be pitted *against* the project of limiting government, whether through bolstering a decisionistic return to state sovereignty (as occurs in Tuck and Loughlin) or through clearing the path for the hegemony of neoliberal economic governmentality (as occurs in Foucault)? In order to answer this question, it is time to turn to the discussion between McIlwain and Kantorowicz. For it is here that one can clearly see at work the shift from an idea of constitutionalism that rejects the Schmittian claim that where law recedes the 'concrete order' of the *nomos* remains to an idea of constitutionalism that is instead worked out on just that Schmittian basis, an idea that has become increasingly dominant in our days.

3 McIlwain and the Antinomy of Liberal Constitutionalism

In order to understand the implications of *The King's Two Bodies* for liberal constitutionalism, it is useful to start from one of the main

[53] *Ibid.*, 401.
[54] *Ibid.*, 402.

polemical objects of Kantorowicz's masterpiece, none other than McIlwain's *Constitutionalism, Ancient and Modern*, published in 1940 at the height of the Battle of Britain.[55] McIlwain develops a genealogy of liberal constitutionalism in which the constitutional 'rule of law' of *iurisdictio* (captured by the phrase 'the king reigns') has supremacy over the liberal 'rule by law' of *gubernaculum* (captured by the phrase 'but he does not govern'). McIlwain formulated the principles of liberal constitutionalism on the basis of a celebrated interpretation of Bracton. Bracton argued for the sovereign 'prerogatives' that assured the king could not be judged in any law court, while at the same time he seems to have believed that the king remained 'bridled' by legal commitments to the law and to the nobles, as reflected in documents like the Magna Carta. It is McIlwain who first sees in Bracton's formulation the expression of a paradox of sovereignty: How could one and the same king be 'above the law' and yet 'law-bound'? The paradox can also be phrased as follows: the 'rule of law' presupposes that law is 'sovereign', yet sovereignty is an attribute of a public person, of the state. The sovereignty of law is paradoxical because it requires that the person (of the state) stand above law itself while law stands above all (natural) persons that compose the state and are subject to it.

McIlwain's ingenious solution of this paradox appealed to Thiers's formula. He claimed that in the English 'ancient constitution',[56] the king was 'above the law' only in the sense of his power of *gubernaculum*, or administration, which often required the king to take exception to standing legislation when confronted by situations of emergency. However, for McIlwain the employment of royal prerogatives was strictly limited to the sphere of *gubernaculum*. The sovereign exercise of unlimited *gubernaculum* was carefully separated from the authority of *iurisdictio*, namely, from the fundamental rights or basic constitutional limits of all governments, which remain *ultra vires*, that is, beyond the power of any king or minister to alter. As McIlwain states, in Bracton, sovereignty is only 'the highest *legal* power

[55] Kantorowicz does not mention McIlwain's reading of Bracton directly in his book. However, as discussed below, his argument can be understood as a systematic inversion of McIlwain's proposals. On the polemical structure of political theory, see the reconstruction of Hobbes's system in Q. Skinner, *Liberty before Liberalism* (Cambridge: Cambridge University Press, 1997) and Q. Skinner, *Visions of Politics: Volume 3: Hobbes and Civil Science* (Cambridge: Cambridge University Press, 2002).

[56] For the concept, see the classical study J. G. A. Pocock, *The Ancient Constitution and the Feudal Law: A Study of English Historical Thought in the 17th Century* (Cambridge: Cambridge University Press, 1987) and now M. Loughlin, *The British Constitution: A Very Short Introduction* (New York: Oxford University Press, 2013).

in a state, itself subject to no law'.[57] Bodin re-interprets the medieval idea of sovereignty as the *legally determined* highest power into the modern idea of sovereignty as the *absolute power to make* the highest law. In Bodin, unlike in Bracton, the power of the sovereign takes the place of the authority of *iurisdictio* or fundamental law. This leads to the dilemma confronted by Tuck and Loughlin: whether to represent the people in the sovereign or give a self-identifying ('homogeneous') people the sovereign power of plebiscitary constitution-making. Both options fall squarely within the Schmittian framing of modern constitutionalism, defanging it of any capacity to limit the claims of sovereignty. McIlwain's return to Bracton, in 1940, had tried, probably for one last time, to conjure up the doctrines of medieval constitutionalism in order to resist the modern Leviathan's descent into Behemoth.[58]

McIlwain's innovative interpretation of Bracton was based on his solution to the tension existing between two pieces of Roman Imperial public law that held together the entire edifice of medieval public law jurisprudence, the *lex regia* and *lex digna*. These two laws constituted an antinomy because one made the king stand under law while the other allowed the king to stand over law. The *lex regia* stated, in the formulation by Ulpian: 'Quod principi placuit, legis habet vigorem; utpote cum lege regia, quae de imperio eius lata est, populus ei et in eum omne suum imperium et potestatem conferat' (*Digest* 1, 4, 1).[59] For Bracton, the *lex regia* was a 'king-making' law: it stated that only in and through law did the king receive the power to make whatever laws he saw fit to make ('quod principi placet legis habet vigorem').[60] On McIlwain's reading of Bracton, the *lex regia* meant that the king had no authority to go against, or take exception to, the constitutional provisions that turned him into an 'absolute' sovereign.[61] This reading of the *lex regia* made sense of

[57] McIlwain, *Constitutionalism* 28–29.

[58] F. Neumann, Behemoth. *The Structure and Practice of National Socialism*, 1933–1944 (Oxford University Press, 1942).

[59] 'A decision given by the emperor has the force of a statute. This is because the populace commits to him and into him its own entire authority and power, doing this by the *lex regia* which is passed anent his authority'. A. Watson (trans. and ed.), *The Digest of Justinian*, vol. I (Philadelphia: University of Pennsylvania Press, 1985), 14. See also discussion in McIlwain, *Constitutionalism*, 156, n.5. For the most recent discussion of the reception of the *lex regia* in medieval political and legal discourse, see Lee, *Popular Sovereignty*, ch.1 passim.

[60] 'What has pleased the prince has the force of *lex*'. See McIlwain, *Constitutionalism*, 70ff.

[61] A similar strategy is offered in B. Tierney, 'Bracton on Government', *Speculum* 38 (2) 1963, 295–317 and '"The Prince is not Bound by the Laws". Accursius and the Origins of the Modern State', *Comparative Studies in Society and History* 5 (4) 1963, 378–400.

Bracton's puzzling text, the famous, *addicio de cartis* (II, 110) which stated that 'The king has a superior, namely God. *Also the law by which he was made king.* Also his court, namely the earls and barons because earls are so called as being companions of the king, and who has a companion has a master [*magister*]. And therefore if the king should be without a bridle, that is without a law, they ought to put a bridle on him'.[62] At the same time, McIlwain interpreted the *lex digna* as regulating the acts of a 'law-making' or sovereign king: according to this law, it befitted the dignity or elevated rank of the king to follow the laws that he has made, except when emergencies called for taking exception to them for the sake of the *salus populi*.[63]

The antinomy of the *lex regia* and *lex digna* was thus a double one. For McIlwain, the *lex regia* appears to make the king absolute with respect to the law because whatever pleases him has the force of law, but in reality the *lex regia* actually states the king's subjection to the *iurisdictio* of law. Conversely, the *lex digna* appears to say that the king must always rule by laws, but in reality this law frees his government from having to rule by laws, allowing the king to govern through exceptional means, through royal prerogatives, whenever exceptional circumstances require it. Having formulated Bracton's doctrine in the terms of a Kantian transcendental antinomy, McIlwain proceeded to resolve the contradiction in Kantian fashion, namely, by assigning validity to both laws, but in separate spheres of application. In the sphere of *iurisdictio* or constitution, the *lex regia* is valid; in the sphere of *gubernaculum* or government, the *lex digna* is valid, but not conversely.

For purposes of comparison it is instructive to see the fate of *iurisdictio* (corresponding to *lex regia*) and *gubernaculum* (corresponding to *lex digna*) in Tuck and Loughlin. For them, modern democracy turns on a division between two legislative powers, not two laws: one power (sovereign) to make constitutional laws (corresponding to *lex regia*), the other power (government) to make ordinary legislation (corresponding to *lex digna*). Contrary to republican constitutionalism, this separation of extraordinary from ordinary powers of legislation has no internal

[62] I do not have space in this essay to enter into the details of a very complicated debate on Bracton's *addicio de cartis* that extended from the 1930s until the 1980s.

[63] In Tierney's translation of the *Digna vox* (*Digest* 1, 3, 31; Codex 1, 14, 4): 'It is a statement worthy of the majesty of a ruler for the Prince to profess himself bound to the laws. So much does our authority depend on the authority of the law. And indeed it is greater for the *imperium* to submit the principate to the laws. And by the declaration of the present law we indicate what we do not permit ourselves'.

relation to the authority of law: in both cases, law is whatever the power who makes them says it is. If the power belongs to the sovereign, the laws are constitutional; if the power belongs to government, the laws are merely legislation or decrees. The authority of the law corresponds to the unity of power. This is exactly opposite to the medieval idea of limited government, as well as being opposed to the republican understanding of constitutionalism, where law has authority only when power is divided against itself, which is only possible under a constitution.

4 Kantorowicz and the Constitutionalization of Government

Kantorowicz's discussion of Bracton in *The King's Two Bodies* subverts entirely McIlwain's solution to the antinomy of medieval constitutionalism. There is no space here to discuss the background of Kantorowicz's argument.[64] Suffice to say that throughout his career, starting with his famous biography of Frederick II, Kantorowicz sides with the Imperial position in the Investiture struggle against the Papacy.[65] Kantorowicz sees the origins of the modern *Rechtsstaat* in the cause of the Germanic-Norman Hohenstaufen Emperors against the theocratic Popes. He occupies a standpoint that is diametrically opposed to the Figgisite narrative as well as to Berman's interpretation of the Papal legal revolution. Kantorowicz is probably the most sophisticated representative of the school of thought according to which constitutionalism in the West flourished not thanks to the attempted separation of the Church from the Empire but despite it. Only thanks to the rejection of the Papal party in the new absolutist monarchies could a modern 'rule of law' emerge.

Kantorowicz's solution to the antinomy of medieval constitutionalism is the reverse of McIlwain's. Whereas the latter sees the *lex regia* as source of limitation of the king's powers of jurisdiction, Kantorowicz argues that the king, in accordance with the *lex regia*, is '*not legally* bound to law, yet bound himself to the Law and lived voluntarily in accordance with the law', in accordance to the *lex digna*.[66] Where in McIlwain the *lex digna*

64 See now R. Lerner, *Ernst Kantorowicz: A Life* (Princeton: Princeton University Press, 2017).

65 It is a piquant detail, not noted by Tuck, that the image of the 'sleeping sovereign' does not originate with Hobbes at all, but originally refers to the medieval legend of Frederick's early death according to which he had not really died but lay asleep in some mountains, waiting for the right time to reconquer his Empire. See W. Köhler, 'Emperor Frederick II., The Hohenstaufe', *The American Journal of Theology* 7 (2) 1903, 225–248.

66 E. H. Kantorowicz, *The King's Two Bodies: A Study in Medieval Political Theology* (Princeton: Princeton University Press, 1997 [1957]), 105. Emphasis mine.

designates the sphere of government (*gubernaculum*) and the *lex regia* that of the constitution (*iurisdictio*), in Kantorowicz it is the opposite: *iurisdictio*, the king's dependence on given, fundamental law, is left up to the *lex digna* and is a matter of the king voluntarily placing himself under law in order to give place to the administration of justice. *Gubernaculum*, the condition of being free from law, now belongs to the sphere of the *lex regia* or to constitutional law. In other words, the constitution, which for McIlwain is supposed to bind the king to law, has become for Kantorowicz the instrument that 'legally' unbinds the king from law.

Unlike Loughlin's claim that constitutionalism, understood as the discourse on fundamental law, permits the separation of sovereignty from government, and assigns supremacy to the former over the latter, Kantorowicz shows exactly the opposite: constitutionalism allows government to usurp the place of the sovereign under the cover of sovereignty. With this hypothesis, Kantorowicz seems to anticipate the thesis made famous by Niklas Luhmann according to which the legal interpretation of the Constitution and the mechanism of judicial review is not only the apex of a self-referential and self-producing legal sub-system but also represents the attempt by the political sub-system to take back and exert control over the 'functional differentiation' of the legal subsystem.[67] From Kantorowicz's perspective, constitutionalism should not be seen as the limit to governmental action. But it is also something much more than an enabler of government.[68] Kantorowicz's account helps us to see how constitutionalism becomes liberal government's most subtle and dangerous weapon against a republican political life.

But how can a constitution 'legally' make it possible for the king to be 'not legally bound to law'? This is where Kantorowicz's discourse picks up from Schmitt's constitutional theory. Schmitt argues that a constitution is primarily the expression of a people's (political) decision, not a basic norm or rule for the generation of norms or rules. The constitution is a decision, among other things, concerning the substantive 'identity' of a people: who shall have which basic rights and

[67] See the argument in N. Luhmann, 'Verfassung als evolutionäre Errungenschaft', *Rechthistorisches Journal* 9 (1990), 176–220. Luhmann's thesis is that the constitution functions as a 'structural coupling' between the political and legal subsystems, making possible a 'juridical' solution to the self-referential problem of the political system and a 'political' solution to the self-referential problem of the juridical system (sect.4). But precisely the 'balancing' effect of the constitution betrays its hyper-political function.

[68] This corresponds to Holmes's 'positive' understanding of constitutionalism in S. Holmes, 'Constitutions and Constitutionalism', in M. Rosenfeld and A. Sajó (eds.), *Comparative Constitutional Law* (New York: Oxford University Press, 2012), 189–216.

privileges, and who shall not have them.[69] Expressed differently, every constitution has as its primary stake that of designating the person (of the state), what Kantorowicz calls the 'king's second body'. This person of the state must stand above the laws because it is that person who *decides and embodies* the fundamental principles and values embedded in the constitution, which in turn alone provide for the government to administer justice, to distribute goods in accordance with those constitutional principles and values. The sovereign is 'the very Idea of Justice which itself is bound to law and yet above law because it is the end of all law'.[70]

Kantorowicz's insight is that the Bractonian theory of the constitution, whose intention is entirely anti-ecclesiastical, is actually structured entirely in theological terms. Kantorowicz argues that Bracton could place the person of the state, in and through its constitution, above the law only because he conceived of the king's 'second body' in analogy to the Trinity. Here Kantorowicz reverses Schmitt's understanding of political theology and the process of secularization. In one sense, Kantorowicz's political theology is Schmittian in so far as it aims to destroy the liberal constitutionalism advocated by McIlwain, whose central tenet is that the rule of law stands above the rule of the sovereign. But in a deeper sense, Kantorowicz's political theology is anti-Schmittian for two main reasons. In *Political Theology, Roman Catholicism as Political Form* and *Political Theology II* Schmitt argued that the modern state constitutes itself as another Church: the role of the sovereign in the modern secular state is a politico-theological one.[71] In Schmitt's technical vocabulary, the function of the modern sovereign is to keep secular modern society 'open' to a transcendent, theological instance, while the sovereign's confessional 'neutrality' keeps the peace between different ecclesiastical claims to have a privileged access to this transcendence or 'mystery'.[72] For Kantorowicz, on the contrary, the modern state makes

[69] See the discussion in A. Kalyvas, *Democracy and the Politics of the Extraordinary: Max Weber, Carl Schmitt, and Hannah Arendt* (New York: Cambridge University Press, 2009), 131–136.

[70] Kantorowicz, *The King's Two Bodies*, 96.

[71] In the *Nomos of the Earth* this role is identified with the theological concept of *katechon* or 'restrainer' of the Antichrist: C. Schmitt, *The Nomos of the Earth in the International Law of Jus Publicum Europaeum* (New York: Telos Press, 2003). On this concept, see now M. Cacciari, *The Withholding Power: An Essay on Political Theology* (London: Bloomsbury Academic, 2017).

[72] See the discussion of Hobbes's diamond in C. Schmitt, *The Leviathan in the State Theory of Thomas Hobbes: Meaning and Failure of a Political Symbol* (Chicago: University of Chicago Press, 2008) and, in general, H. Meier, *The Lesson of Carl Schmitt* (Chicago: The

a political use of the 'mysteries' of Christian theology in order to replace the very institution that gave rise to theology, namely, the Universal Church. The theological 'mystery' is replaced by the political 'secrets' of state sovereignty.[73] The second reason why Kantorowicz is anti-Schmittian is that he offers an entirely different solution to a problem that Schmitt's *Constitutional Theory* had originally pointed out, but that Schmitt was incapable of resolving throughout his career. The problem consists in explaining how one and the same constitution can articulate its monarchic and democratic principles, or, what is the same, how a constitution can join the function of political representation to the function of political identification.[74]

As discussed above, Schmitt popularized the story that it was the Papacy which started to employ Roman Imperial public law in order to separate itself from the temporal power of the Emperor and of the kings. By splitting itself from the State, the Church established not only its autonomy but also the autonomy of the legal system over and above the political system, thus, in due course, giving rise to the idea of a counter-majoritarian, liberal constitutionalism. Kantorowicz's treatise tells the opposite story: he shows how the monarchical state employs Trinitarian theology in order to undermine the autonomy of the Church with respect to the State, thereby turning the medieval 'Christian people' that compose the *corpus mysticum* of the Church into the modern 'people' of the nation-state. In attacking the

University of Chicago Press, 1998). This hypothesis of an 'immanent frame' of modern society that must be 'opened' by a theological instance has been taken up by J. Milbank, *Theology and Social Theory* (London: Blackwell, 2006) and Taylor, *A Secular Age*.

73 For a version of this thesis, see E. H. Kantorowicz, 'Mysteries of State. An Absolutist Concept and its Late Medieval Origins', *The Harvard Theological Review* 48 (1955), 65–91. A contemporary example of the functioning of such 'mysteries' of state is expressed in the Australian *Mabo* case that recognized 'native title' to Aboriginal and Torres Straits Islander peoples and overthrew the doctrine of *terra nullius* at the level of common law while at the same time upheld it in some form as a 'secret' or 'mystery' tied to 'acts of state' of the Crown, which are non-justiciable in Australian legal courts. See D. Ritter, 'The "Rejection of *Terra Nullius*" in *Mabo*: A Critical Analysis', *Sydney Law Review* 18 (5) 1996, 1–33; I. Hunter, 'Native Title: Acts of State and the Rule of Law', *The Australian Quarterly* 65 (4) 1993, 97–109; and L. Popic, 'Sovereignty in Law: The Justiciability of Indigenous Sovereignty in Australia, the United States and Canada', *Indigenous Law Journal* 4 (2005), 117–157.

74 For the problem, see C. Schmitt, *Constitutional Theory* (Durham, NC: Duke University Press, 2008). This is the same problem tackled by E. Laclau in *On Populist Reason* (London: Verso, 2005). The recent literature on sovereignty, from Loughlin to Tuck and Nelson, can also be understood in terms of the effort to explain the coincidence of monarchy and democracy within a constitutional framework, but all of them adopt quasi-Schmittian motifs that do not resolve the problem.

supremacy of the Church, the modern state sought to undermine the 'autonomy' of the legal sphere with regard to democracy. In so doing, it establishes the ground for monarchical and then democratic sovereignty as the sole source of legitimate law-making or jurisdiction. This is the very process that Tuck and Loughlin celebrate, but do so in the mistaken belief that sovereignty was separated from government thanks to constitutionalism, whereas in reality constitutionalism (viz. 'public law') turns sovereignty into the instrument of government.

In *The Kingdom and the Glory*, Agamben puts forward the hypothesis that liberal governmentality secularizes Trinitarian political theology in that the sovereignty of the Father is always already an aspect of the government of the Son, which takes the secular form of the providential dispensation of the free market economy.[75] Kantorowicz, instead, shows the Trinitarian foundations of modern constitutionalism. For Kantorowicz, the analogy between the king and God the Father is meant to found the king's power of *iurisdictio*, not the king's power of *gubernaculum*. As Father of Justice, the king is 'above' the law through the *lex regia*: the king (or person of the state) is *legibus solutus* in a constitutional sense, and not in a merely administrative sense, as McIlwain naively thought. Interpreted according to Trinitarianism, the formula 'the king reigns but does not govern' means that God the Father/King, who is above the law, surrenders the administration or government of Justice to the Son, Jesus (as) Christ, the 'mortal' God. It is in the form of this Second Person that state power comes to stand 'under' law and becomes a legislative and administrative state. The Father ('who reigns but does not govern') maintains His sovereignty only by sacrificing Himself (as the Son) on the Cross of government. Analogously, the king sacrifices his jurisdictional power by giving up his jurists and lawyers to the autonomous subsystem of law and rights of civil society, which has its finality in 'administering' justice according to positive, statutory law. The sacrifice of government on the part of the sovereign is juridically represented by the employment of the *lex digna*: 'the element of Son-ship to law of prince or emperor is found in the *lex digna*'.[76] Ultimately, the sacrifice of the Father or sovereign on behalf of the Son or

[75] See Agamben, *The Kingdom and the Glory*, 1–16 for the formulation of his hypothesis. For commentary, see D. Leshem, *The Origins of Neoliberalism: Modelling the Economy from Jesus to Foucault* (New York: Columbia University Press, 2016) and N. Heron, *Liturgical Power: Between Economic and Political Theology* (New York: Fordham University Press, 2018).

[76] Kantorowicz, *The King's Two Bodies*, 104.

government has the purpose of transferring the idea of justice away from the constitutional sphere and towards the sphere of administrative action.[77] This is the remote origin of the curious phenomenon that citizens demand social justice from the arbitrary and always changing nature of government public policy rather than from the courts of justice. It lies at the basis of the recurrent 'crises of legitimacy' occasioned by the insurmountable conflict between the principles of the welfare state and those of so-called liberal constitutionalism that so exercised social theorists in the 1970s.[78] In other words, the 'administration' of justice (what McIlwain calls *gubernaculum* and places under *lex digna*) is in Kantorowicz identical to the dispensation of a 'mystery' of state; that is, of prerogatives of government that establish a permanent state of exception in the form of rule by administrative decrees.

5 Conclusion: From Sovereign Constitutionalism to Economic Constitutionalization

Kantorowicz's interpretation of Bracton purports to show that it is the profane government of the State, rather than the sacred government of the Church, which is the true inheritor of Trinitarianism in law. In so doing, he subverts the Schmittian secularization thesis. Public law is not the sphere where the sacred finds its new abode amidst the profanity of modern liberal politics and economics, as Schmitt mistakenly assumed. Instead, seen from Kantorowicz's viewpoint, public law appears as a device that makes it possible for the modern state to govern its citizens from within an entirely 'immanent frame', where previous forms of 'governing' human beings in the western tradition, as Foucault's studies on governmentality have shown, turned on a pastoral model that

[77] Compare Loughlin's interpretation, who adopts Gaines Post's claim that the 'Christological theme in Bracton, neglected in many accounts, provides a central motif in his analysis of the status of the king. Just as Christ and the Virgin were free from the law, so too was the king. And just as Christ and Virgin by their own *voluntas* submitted to the laws, so should the king, by his own will, adhere to the laws of the realm'. See Loughlin, *Foundations*, 41 following G. Post, 'Bracton as Jurist and Theologian on Kingship', in S. Kuttner (ed.), *Proceedings of the Third International Conference of Medieval Canon Law, Strasbourg 3–6 September 1968* (Rome: Biblioteca Apostolica Vaticana, 1971), 113–130.

[78] See the formulations in J. Habermas, *Legitimation Crisis* (Boston: Beacon Press, 1975) and C. Offe, 'Some Contradictions of the Modern Welfare State'. *Critical Social Policy* 2 (5) 1982, 7–16. For a recent recovery of these hypotheses, see W. Streeck, *How Will Capitalism End? Essays on a Failing System* (London: Verso, 2016).

promised to lead each individual to their individual salvation. Through public law, theologians lose their utility as interpreters of the 'mystery' of salvation because this mystery is now a 'mystery of state' and requires the 'ministering' of justice through public policy. The bourgeois revolutions replaced priests with lawyers and jurists in this ministerial function, but this, as we begin to realize today, may just have been an intermediary step: the constitutional logic of government requires that lawyers be replaced by economic managers, as occurs with the imposition of a neoliberal economic *nomos*.[79]

What difference does it make if one adopts Schmitt's use of political theology, as Loughlin does, or the one proposed by Kantorowicz, to help make sense of neoliberal transformations of the public sphere? Loughlin argues that the economicism of liberalism corrodes western democratic constitutionalism because it undermines the 'public law' conception of sovereignty. Sovereign power has a 'constitutional' dimension because it can be understood as a 'constituent power', defined as the extra-ordinary power to make the highest law that establishes the absolute sovereignty of the state in its radical separation from government.[80] This key motif in Loughlin's jurisprudence deploys Schmitt's later attempts to render his early conception of sovereignty in terms of the ancient Greek idea of *nomos basileus*, which contains in one formula both the meaning of a power that is absolute with respect to law and the meaning of being a ground of the rule of law:

> It would appear that state (the political unity), constitution (the status of unity and order) and *nomos* (the order of a concrete spatial unity) are, to all intents and purposes, synonyms ... If state highlights unity and constitution the form of that unity, then *nomos* accentuates the motive forces that shape the form of that unity: it is 'the full immediacy of a legal

[79] See the trend toward a 'managerial mindset' in constitutional and international law discussed by M. Koskenniemi, 'Constitutionalism as Mindset: Reflections on Kantian Themes About International Law and Globalization', *Theoretical Inquiries in Law* 8 (1) 2007, 9–36.

[80] Loughlin, *Foundations*, ch.8 *passim*. This is a similar claim to the one made by Tuck. However, Tuck argues that Sieyes, who first coined the term 'pouvoir constituant', was not a defender of sovereignty in the manner of Hobbes and Bodin, since he thought that constituent power could be represented by a national assembly rather than remaining dormant with the people as 'sleeping sovereign'. Tuck, *The Sleeping Sovereign*, 162–180. For the problematic consequences of Tuck's advocacy of a plebiscitarian idea of constituent power, see B. Garsten, 'From Popular Sovereignty to Civil Society in Post-Revolutionary France', in R. Bourke and Q. Skinner (eds.), *Popular Sovereignty in Historical Perspective* (New York: Cambridge University Press, 2016), 236–269, at 257–259.

> power not mediated by laws'; it is a constitutive historical event – an act of *legitimacy*, whereby the legality of a mere law first is made meaningful.[81]

The antinomian idea of a 'legal power not mediated by laws' is called *nomos* by Schmitt and *droit politique* by Loughlin.

Yet Loughlin's public law framework cannot account for the overlap between the Schmittian conception of *nomos* and the employment of the concept of *nomos* by a neoliberal thinker like Hayek in order to designate the 'right ordering' produced by free markets and other such 'spontaneous orders'.[82] The emergence of 'nomothetic' thinking in the neoliberal rationalization of state sovereignty, thematized by Wendy Brown in terms of the shift from *homo politicus* to *homo economicus*, seems to indicate that the rational choice allocation of goods has become synonymous with *iurisdictio*. The interpretation of Kantorowicz offered above suggests that the realization of the idea of justice through markets can best be explained if one reverses the causal story proposed by Loughlin. It is not state sovereignty that employs constitutionalism in order to limit government, but, conversely, government employs constitutionalism, viz., *droit politique*, in order to limit the political life of citizens, and embed their *res publica* in self-steering, autopoietic normative orders that free peoples can no longer hope to control.[83]

Loughlin seems to believe that only an appeal to the Schmittian doctrine of state of exception can keep in check the neoliberal *nomos* of the free markets.[84] Kantorowicz's interpretation of Bracton disallows such a sovereign solution to neoliberal governance; that is, a Schmittian

[81] M. Loughlin, 'Nomos' in D. Dyzenhaus and T. Poole (eds.), *Law, Liberty and State: Oakeshott, Hayek, and Schmitt on the Rule of Law* (Cambridge: Cambridge University Press, 2015), 65–95.

[82] On the 'neoliberal' aspects of Schmitt's juridical thought see R. Cristi, *Carl Schmitt and Authoritarian Liberalism: Strong State, Free Economy* (Cardiff: University of Wales Press, 1998); on *nomos* in Schmitt and Hayek, see M. Vatter. 'Neoliberalism and Republicanism: Economic Rule of Law and Law as Concrete Order (*nomos*)' in M. Cooper, D. Cahill, M. Konings, and D. Primrose (eds.), *The SAGE Handbook of Neoliberalism* (London: Sage, 2018), 370–383.

[83] For a theologico-political reconstruction of the phenomenon of market-embedded states see H. Brunkhorst, 'All Nightmares Back: Dependency and Independency Theories, Religion, Capitalism and Global Society' in M. Vatter (ed.), *Crediting God: Sovereignty and Religion in the Age of Global Capitalism* (New York: Fordham University Press, 2010).

[84] According to his doctrine of public law, 'constitutional laws are valid only because they presuppose an underlying "material" constitution [i.e., the constitution of the sovereign] . . . This point leads . . . to a recognition of the legitimacy of provisions that authorize the suspension of constitutional laws during a "state of exception" since such provisions preserve the material constitution'. Loughlin, *Foundations*, 215.

conception of a legal ('material') constitution that establishes a supra-legal absolute power (viz., sovereignty). Kantorowicz's reading of the formula 'the king reigns but does not govern' points in a different direction. Rather than eliminating constitutionalism, the onslaught on sovereignty by neoliberal governmentality has managed to make sovereign constitution-making an intrinsic part of liberal governmentality. The significance of Kantorowicz's genealogy of constitutionalism lies in having shown how government comes to fuse itself with constituent power, thus preparing the way for liberal forms of government to be carried out by something that can be called 'constitutionalism without republicanism'. System-theoretic legal scholars refer to this phenomenon in terms of a shift from 'constitution' to processes of 'constitutionalization' (which can be plural and also enter into 'regime collisions' with one another).[85] If the hypotheses outlined in this chapter are valid, then the recovery of public law mythologemes like 'sleeping sovereigns', 'royal revolutions' and quasi-constitutional executive 'prerogatives' might not be the best strategy to counteract the symbiosis of neoliberalism and global constitutionalism.

[85] G. Teubner, *Constitutional Fragments: Societal Constitutionalism and Globalization* (New York: Oxford University Press, 2012).

6

Popular Sovereignty

The People's Two Bodies

PASQUALE PASQUINO

The following chapter has two main sections that partially overlap. Perhaps they just convey the same idea in two different ways. In the first section I present a conceptual analysis of the terms people, sovereignty, and popular sovereignty to reach the conclusion that *in a constitutional democracy* sovereignty, and so political authority, is divided and shared among different state organs, contrary to Rousseau's conception, and that the "people" – the voters – are only *one* of the *constituted* powers.[1] In the second section, I argue that the concept of popular sovereignty as *constituent* power of the people, rather than transposing onto the subject "people" the idea of absolute power of a monocratic institution (the Kingship), is instead the foundational principle of the framework of limited power typical of the contemporary constitutional state.[2] The "people," I therefore conclude, have to be understood as occupying a vital double role within our constitutional imaginary – supplying both the constituent power and a constituted power.

1 Conceptual Analysis

I shall begin with a brief conceptual analysis of the two words composing the expression *popular sovereignty*.

[1] In the following remarks, I use the distinction between constituent and constituted power as it was systematized by Emmanuel Sieyes (on this point I should refer to the second chapter of my book *Sieyes et l'invention de la constitution en France*, Paris, 1998, pp. 31–52). The conceptual core of this dichotomy is the idea that the *constituted* powers exercise a limited authority, defined by the constitution, which is a superior norm, because it was supposedly decided by a more authoritative political actor: the *pouvoir constituant*.

[2] More precisely *état de droit constitutionnel, verfasungsmaessiger Rechtstaat* – expressions not easy to translate in English; *rule of law* is too vague, because it can be predicated of a country like the UK which has no rigid constitution and no "hierarchy of norms."

(a) People

People is a term used in our western culture[3] to designate a variety of collective agents/actors. First, it is used as the equivalent of the archaic Greek term[4] and, more precisely, of the Aristotelian *demos*.[5] Here, "people" refers to the lower social classes, to those, notably, who controlled the majority in the Athenian *ekklesía*[6] – the meetings of citizens where collective decisions concerning the life of the polis were taken. In ancient Rome, the acronym SPQR – *Senatus populusque romanus* – signaled that the *populus* was only a segment of the Roman republican *civitas*, not the totality of the citizens. Senators (*patricii*) were the other segment, comprising both the

[3] My colleague Yile Zhang has sent me a set of observations concerning the Chinese term/concept of people that I will summarize, as they are of interest in relativizing the western conceptions.

The English word "people" has in Chinese mostly the two following meanings: first, "人们" (Ren Men), which is the plural word for "人" (Ren). It means "persons" and is a neutral word without any specification. Second, "人民" (Ren Min), which is a collective noun in Chinese, and it has political meaning: it is the opposite of "敌人" (Di Ren, enemies).

In its original sense (during the Zhou Dynasty), Min meant those who have the lowest social status in the country – slaves, the mob, etc. Later, according to the Origin of Chinese Characters (《说文解字， Shuo Wen Jie Zi), "人" (Ren) and "民" (Min) acquired totally different meanings: while Ren is the most valuable creature in the world, which has the best characteristics above all, Min is the most common creature. Min usually referred to the mob in ancient China.

In contemporary China, Ren Min assumed its political meaning for the first time. According to Mao Zedong, Ren Min are "all socialist working people, builders of the socialism," "the patriots who support the Chinese Communist Party and the Socialism with Chinese characteristics," and "the patriots who stand for the reunification of the motherland." Since 1949, Chinese "Ren Min" "have taken control of state power and become masters of the country." Article 2 of the Chinese Constitution even states that "all power in the People's Republic of China belongs to the people (Ren Min)." And Ren Min exercise state power via the National People's Congress and the local people's congresses at various levels.

A lot of names of Chinese collective bodies – in the economic domain, the academic domain, and in the press – use this political word "Ren Min." For example, the Party's press "People's Daily" (《人民日报》, Ren Min Ri Bao), the People's Bank of China (中国人民银行, Zhong Guo Ren Min Yin Hang), People's University (人民大学, Ren Min Da Xue, or Ren Da), People's Congress (人民代表大会, Ren Min Dai Biao Da Hui, or Ren Da), and so on.

[4] See P. Chantraine, *Dictionnaire étymologique de la langue grecque*, Paris, 1999, pp. 273–274.

[5] H. Bonitz, *Index Aristotelicus*, Berlin, 1870, p. 176.

[6] See M. H. Hansen, *The Athenian Democracy in the Age of Demosthenes*, University of Oklahoma Press, 1999, pp. 125–160.

social structure and the institutional architecture of political authority in the ancient Roman Republic.[7]

Secondly, the term is used, in the language imposed by contemporary representative government, as a synonym of *voters*, meaning the list of those who according to the constitution and the laws of a given country have political rights – the equivalent of the Athenians *politai.*[8] Hereby political rights is meant the active right to vote. In that (legal) sense the people is an organ of the state, a *constituted power* – applying Sieyes' distinction between constituted and constituent power – at least in any democratic society. By this I mean that, in a representative democracy, the "people" thus conceived do not exist prior to the constitutional positive law.[9] The catalogue, with number and names, of those who have the right to vote is decided by some political authority preexisting the act of voting. In this perspective, there are no people without a government – even if it may be just a provisional political power or an old, fading, and vanishing one.

Thirdly, by the word "people," we may instead refer to the population at large, to the inhabitants of a territorial state, without other legal or social specifications. This version of the people has a role to play in the working and stability of any non-despotic political system, through its cooperation, acceptance, or even passive acquiescence.[10] This

7 On this point, see the still very important study of Claude Nicolet, *Le métier de citoyen dans la Rome républicaine*, Paris, Gallimard, 1976, notably, p. 289 ff.

8 How many inhabitants are citizens, i.e. full members, of this "people," varies from a very small number (as in Athens: not more than one tenth of the inhabitants of the polis; or at the beginning of the nineteenth century at the time of the *suffrage censitaire*, when only citizens with *Besitz und Bildung* (i.e., property and education) had the right to vote) to all the adult people (excluding only immigrants, children, and sometime prison inmates (UK)) in contemporary democracies. On this point, see J. A. Schumpeter, *Capitalism, Socialism and Democracy*, New York, 1975, pp. 243–245.

9 See, for example, Giuseppe Ugo Rescigno, in his contribution to Vezio Crisafulli and Livio Paladin (eds.), *Sovranità del popolo e fonti del diritto nel pensiero di Carlo Esposito*, Padova (2003), p.8, speaking of this question with reference to the Italian constitution says "The main thesis [of C. Esposito] is that sovereignty is not something that preexists and is limited by the law (*diritto*), but a reality which is constructed by the law: 'the provision of the art. 1 of the Italian Constitution does not mean that the Constitution puts extrinsic limits over the exercise of a preexisting popular sovereignty [. . .] but on the contrary that the popular sovereignty exists only inside the limits and forms in which the Constitution organizes, recognizes and makes it possible and as far as it is exercised in the forms and limits of the constitutional law: Independently from the Constitution and the law there is no sovereignty but only the arbitrary power of the people, there is no sovereign people, but the crowd with its passions and weaknesses'" http://archivio.rivistaaic.it/materiali/convegni/20030619_padova/rescigno.html (my translation).

10 Relevant to this third conception of the "people," we also speak sometimes of *public opinion* – which is nowadays a by-product of polls and surveys.

"people"[11] may, moreover, play a significant role by *supporting* the elite during a regime change or a revolution. That support may take the form of a violent rebellion helping to get rid of an existing declining régime – we can think of the French, Russian, and Chinese revolutions – or it may consist of the more or less vigorous approval of or passive compliance with a regime change. As an example of popular active approval and support, we may think of the collapse of the Soviet system in Central and Eastern Europe in 1989, which was mostly nonviolent but involved the actions of a significant number of citizens.[12]

Note that the first and the third meanings just considered refer to concepts of a societal nature. The first designates a social class/group and the third the membership in general of a nation or political community. The second meaning instead is primarily a legal concept connected with the function of *authorization*. This is a point to which I will later return. Moreover, in the second section of my remarks, I claim that there is a crucial *fourth* sense of the word "people" which, in combination with the idea of constituent power, establishes the principle of "limited government."

(b) Sovereignty

The word *sovereignty* needs, in turn, to be defined to avoid misunderstandings.

Independently from the externally oriented meaning of *self-governing political territorial entity* (*stato libero*, in Machiavelli's parlance),[13] in the language of modern public law, the term "sovereignty" refers to the agent (Monarch) or agency (Parliament, for instance) supposed to exercise "supreme authority," an entity which has the last word, at least from a legal point of view, in exercising authority inside the political community. This is the rough equivalent of the Aristotelian *ho kyrios*. It is, then, a conception of sovereignty – or lordly power – which as originally

[11] Or at least an active section of it.

[12] This is evidently not an exhaustive list of the used meaning of the term people (see for a conceptual history of the word the entry *Volk* in Reinhart Koselleck, Fritz Gschnitzer, Karl Ferdinand Werner, Bernd Schönemann, "Volk, Nation, Nationalismus, Masse," in: Reinhart Koselleck, Werner Conze, Otto Brunner (eds.), *Geschichtliche Grundbegriffe: Historisches Lexikon zur politisch-sozialen Sprache in Deutschland*. Bd. 7, Klett-Cotta, Stuttgart 1992, pp. 141–431.

[13] This sense of *national sovereignty* is nowadays again the object of a political debate between the nationalist/*souvrainistes* political forces inside the members-states of the EU and the pro-Europeans (federalist) ones.

conceived could refer to one, few, or many members of the polis and from which derives the old standard taxonomy of forms of government: monarchy, oligarchy, democracy.

In contemporary democracies, political authority – an expression I prefer to sovereignty, a term never used by Sieyes except in the derogatory sense of "the absolute power" – is exercised in different forms and with different competences, by a variety of actors and constituted powers – as they are specified in the written constitution. Their decisions are *collectively*[14] legally compelling. This is what is best understood as sovereign;[15] legally binding on all, at least temporarily, because these decisions can always be modified.[16] The voters, whose choices must be obeyed,[17] may after a while – at the time of next elections – modify their choice concerning who will be their representatives, and these elected representatives have the power to enact new legally binding decisions. Moreover, agencies such as Constitutional Courts, independent[18] both from citizens and elected officials, have the constitutional competence to modify in part or *in toto*, through interpretation or veto, the legal decisions made by elected officials. In addition, they possess the power to modify their own opinions over time.[19] Hence, they share with the Parliament the legislative or general law-making power – which may also be exercised directly by voters from time to time through referendums.

[14] This specification is important. All the decisions of state organs are binding, but the verdict of an ordinary judge binds only the parties to a litigation and the discretionary decisions of the administration only those immediately affected. Here I am referring to primary legislation, or other legal decisions binding *erga omnes*.

[15] For the reason to be discussed in the main text, claiming that the sovereign is the agency which has "the last word" does not fit with the political reality. In the absolute state the sovereign could say *sic volo sic jubeo, stat pro ratione voluntas* (this I wish, thus I order, my will stands in place of reason). Nowadays in a constitutional democracy the only agent that can decide without any justification is the voter, the microscopic fragment of the baroque sovereign: he or she does not have to justify or give arguments for his or her choice.

[16] The decisions, but not necessarily the concrete consequences of them; the invasion of Iraq or the death of someone sentenced to capital punishment but discovered to be innocent after execution, as is possible in some states of the US, are decisions which cannot be recalled and reversed.

[17] At least when the electoral law produces a majority, which is not necessarily the case; where there is a proportional electoral law, it happens that there are different possible coalitions to create a majority and the choice of one of them is in the hands of the elected representatives, not the voters.

[18] "Independent" in the legal sense: members of the Constitutional Court are not elected by the citizens and are not legally accountable either to them or to elected officials.

[19] Precedents are binding on the inferior courts, but they typically bind the apex courts only if relatively recent.

It follows that the people as voters (in Sieyes' language, a *pouvoir commettant*) are only one of the agencies exercising high political authority in a structure of constitutional representative democracy. For typically, this takes the form of a mixed government; more precisely one that can be defined (to avoid conflating it with the classical theory of *memigmene politeia*)[20] as *shared/divided power* or, if we want to use the classical term, divided sovereignty.[21]

(c) *Popular Sovereignty*

Putting together our two terms, we may observe that the expression *popular sovereignty* is sometimes used also in conjunction with the so-called *pouvoir constituant* of the people. Now, in order to make sense of this conjunction, it seems that it is necessary to begin by distinguishing between two functions or activities associated with a modern constituent power, which, since the Philadelphia Convention, has been identified with the idea of writing and establishing a new documentary constitution in a democratic *constitutional decision-making process*. I have suggested elsewhere[22] to call these two functions *authorship* and *authorization*.

The "people," whatever meaning we give to this word, have never written a constitution.[23] At best the citizens-voters *authorize* the constitutional text through a variety of possible (*ex ante* or *ex post*) legal mechanisms. Modern constitutions, starting from the end of the eighteenth century, have been written instead by a small group of individuals consisting of both political actors[24] and legal experts.[25] We offer just

[20] Which presupposes the existence of *unequal* members of the political community; see Pasquale Pasquino, "Machiavelli and Aristotle: The Anatomies of the City," (2009) 35 *History of European Ideas*, pp. 397–407.

[21] The thesis that sovereignty, or political authority, cannot be divided/shared is a mysterious dogma of Rousseau's political philosophy; unified political authority may only be necessary in special and exceptional situations like civil wars – the historical context when Jean Bodin and Thomas Hobbes were considering political order. It is possible that Rousseau's hostility to divided sovereignty had something to do with his rejection of the mixed government of the constitution of England.

[22] See the article in fn 23 below.

[23] Concerning the unsuccessful attempt of a constitution written with *some* contributions by the citizens, see my article "Constituent Power and Authorization: Anatomy and Failure of a Constitution-making Process," in Valur Ingimundarson, Philippe Urfalino, Irma Erlingsdóttir (eds.), *Iceland's Financial Crisis: The Politics of Blame, Protest, and Reconstruction*, Routledge, 2016, pp. 230–238.

[24] In the twentieth century, the political actors were in general organized and chosen by political parties.

[25] In the twentieth century, essentially public/constitutional law professors.

a few examples, citing some major personalities: Antoine Barnave and Guillaume Thouret, both *avocats au barreau*, legal experts, and also crucial political actors inside the *Assemblée Nationale Constituante* that produced the French constitution of 1791; the social democratic leader Friedrich Ebert, plus academics like Max Weber and Hugo Preuss for the Weimar *Reichsverfassung* of 1919; King Carlo Alberto and the members of the king's council, notably Giacinto Borelli[26] for the *Statuto Albertino* (1848), which was the constitution of the Kingdom of Sardinia and then of Italy (from 1861) until the collapse of the fascist regime; De Gasperi and Togliatti, the leaders of the two major political parties present in the Constitutional Assembly, plus the constitutionalist Costantino Mortati for the Italian republican constitution written between 1946 and 1947; De Gaulle plus Michel Debré and other legal advisors for the French constitution of the Fifth Republic in 1958.

While it is evident that modern constitutions have been written by few individuals, starting from the tiny group of members of the Philadelphia Convention, nonetheless those constitutions that were not simply *octroyées* – and so granted by the existing sovereign power (like the *Statuto Albertino* or the French Charters of 1815 and 1830)[27] – have been *authorized* by a citizens' vote. This is achieved either *ex ante* through the election of an assembly with the explicit mandate to write the new constitution (as was the case in Weimar Germany, 1919, and in Rome, 1946) or *ex post* through a popular ratification (direct as in the case of most French constitutions or indirect, as in the US and Germany, 1949).[28]

Note, however, that the "people" ratifying a written constitution (likewise the list of individuals qualified as voters for the establishment of

[26] See the entry G. Borelli, in *Dizionario biografico degli italiani*, vol. 12 (1971), sub voce.

[27] On this distinction see: C: Schmitt, *Verfassungslehre* (1928), Engl. trans. *Constitutional Theory*, Duke University Press, 2008, pp. 126–130.

[28] In some rare cases – like the French constitution of 1791 – there was no popular formal legal authorization at all. It is not wrong to claim that there was at its origin a legal *coup d'etat*: the *Serment du Jeu de Paume* of June 20, 1789. Another special case is supplied by the Russian and Chinese non-liberal democratic constitutions; the fundamental charters of these countries were written some years after the defeat of the old regime and the civil war (1936 in Soviet Union, 1954 in the communist China). Why these authoritarian regimes wrote a constitution *ex facie* similar to the constitutions of liberal democracy (characterized by citizens' rights and the separation of powers) is a fascinating question that I cannot discuss here. It is worth noting that the fascist regimes mostly did not bother to write their own constitutions; they just ignored the existing ones (in the case of the Fascists, the *Statuto Albertino*, in Italy; in the case of the Nazis, the Weimar Constitution, in Germany).

a constituent assembly) have always been a legal artefact; it is a list including a specific set of the inhabitants of a territorial state that the written constitution, through its *authors*, designates as "citizens"/voters. In case of election of the constituent assembly before the writing and ratification of the constitution, the composition of the authorizing body is the result of a decision made either by some previous existing authority (the King in France in 1789 – even though the Estates General convoked in Versailles were not supposed to write a constitution) or a provisional authority (the *Luogotenente del regno* and the provisional government, in Italy, after the collapse of the fascist regime). It is these prior authorities, rather than the "people" themselves, who decide, through specifying a list of names, who is going to be member of the "people" *qua* authorizing body. In this perspective, therefore, it is not the "people," as a legal entity, which produces a constitution, but the constitution, or some previous legal decision that invents the "people."

I should add that legal authorization and stable popular endorsement/popular support are different concepts and different realities. Without the latter, a constitutional order established and authorized by the constitutional document will not survive.[29] To take but one notable example, the republican constitution of the French Revolution in its basic tenets was definitively accepted by the French society only one century later with the establishment of the Third Republic.[30] A revolution and a significant regime change[31] are, indeed, transformative processes that take often a long time to produce a relatively stable political order, one that the constitution tries to codify. The enactment of a written constitution is a legal event, and the content of it can either last for a very long time (US, 1787; Belgium, 1831) or die immediately (Naples, 1799).

[29] Note that "people" here means the set of members of the political community (i.e., our third sense), the endorsement of which is necessary to guarantee societal acceptance and support of the legal prescriptive document that we call in the contemporary world *Constitution*. "People" in this sense includes the decisive social forces – including the army where it is a politically active and not a neutral actor.

On this point, see the still very relevant text of Ferdinand Lassalle, *Über Verfassungswesen* (1862), Europäische Verlagsanstalt, Hamburg, 1993.

[30] As persuasively argued by Francois Furet, *Revolutionary France 1770–1880* (Oxford, Oxford University Press, 1995).

[31] Notably when the principle of legitimacy is radically modified (e.g., from a traditional monarchy or a despotic regime to a liberal democracy).

(d) A Note on Popular Will

In ordinary – non-constituent – political circumstances the notion of popular sovereignty is connected and overlapping with the meaning of the expression *popular will*, since popular sovereignty seems, at least *prima facie*, the sovereign will of the people. Hence, we should pause on this concept, which in turn needs some clarification.

It is relatively easy to figure out what is the will (or preference) of an individual – at least if he or she has one; it is much more complex to identify the will of a collective body. I consider here the will of that specific collective body made up by voters in a democracy. We could assume that the will of the voters is the same as the will of their elected representatives, thanks to a quite mysterious mechanism of transposition of individual wills – though in general we view the relationship between the voters and their representatives under the more prosaic label of "accountability."[32] If the representative body consists of one or more than one collective institutions – as in bicameral systems – the question of the locus of collective identity is just shifted from the will of the voters to the will of an assembly.[33] But in any event, we need to consider the algorithm that allows the transformation of a large number of individual wills into a "collective" one.

In the case of a binary choice, if the issue can be reduced to only two options, the rule of aggregation is simple: democracies (but not only democracies[34]) use majority rule. Citizens can answer a question by *yes* or *no*, and in case of two candidates, choose one of them.[35]

[32] Rousseau may have been right in claiming that the will cannot be transferred and represented. The fact is that by voting, in general, the people simply authorize some individuals to exercise the will in their place. In representative democracies, using a synecdoche, we use the words "people" or "voters" to refer to a majority or often even a plurality (i.e., the largest minority) of them. Who makes up this majority or plurality depends on the electoral law. The synecdoche is doubled by assuming that the will of the majority of the representatives is the will of the Parliament.

[33] I'm not going to discuss here this question (actually the questions involved are two: the first one is the so-called agency problem: meaning the questionable identity between the will of representatives and the will of the represented; the other concerns the specific different rules for decision-making of the representative assemblies – the standing orders of parliamentary procedure).

[34] On majority rule in aristocratic regimes see Pasquale Pasquino, "Samuel Pufendorf: Majority Rule (logic, justification and limits) and Forms of Government" (2010) 49 *Social Science Information* (Collective Decision-Making Rules), pp. 99–109.

[35] Note that in the case of the choice of a single position, we need a rule transforming the votes for multiple candidates into a single choice: e.g., plurality, in Chile at the time of

For the election of representative assemblies, the algorithm that aggregates a huge number of individual choices/wills/preferences of the voters into the small number of seats to be assigned to the members of a representative assembly, namely the *electoral law*, plays a critical role. If we change the algorithm, for instance from a majoritarian to a proportional electoral system, the "will of the people" will be immediately different![36] With a strongly majoritarian electoral law, as in the UK, usually a single party gets the majority of seats in the Commons; with proportional representation, instead, coalition governments are de facto inevitable – especially in a parliament fragmented among a multiplicity of political parties, as Belgians, Italians, Israelis, and Spaniards, for instance, know well. Moreover, different coalitions will express different collective wills.

With this in mind, we should appreciate that the so-called popular will, even in the ordinary democratic context, does not exist as such, independently of the electoral law and its particular mechanism for aggregation of single wills, and of the decision by political actors choosing the partner(s) of a governmental coalition. Hence, there is, in general, no popular will without representation, the configuration of which depends massively on the electoral law. It is the will of the representative majority, with the relevant sense of a "majority" dependent in turn on the rules structuring the decision-making procedures of legislative assemblies.

As to the mythology of direct/immediate democracy in our contemporary societies, I can here only add that it supposes some special group of individuals (a sort of equivalent of the Athenian *boulé*) asking questions that the citizens will have the possibility to answer (via internet) with a *yes* or a *no, without deliberation among them*. Accordingly, it would need rules to choose the people initiating the process and the quorum of citizens answering, not to speak of the complex structure necessary to enforce the decisions.[37]

Allende's election; run off/ballotage, in France, since 1962; electoral college, in the US. In single member districts, the rule is often *first-pass-the-post* or some version of run off.

36 This explains why debates about electoral law are in general ferocious, since they change the supposed popular will; in reality the power relations among political parties and their representatives.

37 In Italy a political party (*Movimento 5 Stelle* – the 5 Stars Movement), which suggests moving from representative to direct democracy, asked its members to approve, on its internet platform, the governmental alliance it sought to make with another party after the 2018 general election. 42,274 persons answered, who were apparently considered "representative" of the 11 million of citizens that voted for the 5 Stars. So, this is an

2 The People's Two Bodies

So far, I have been trying to tease out some different meanings that "people," "popular will," and "popular sovereignty" have in our political language. In this shorter second section of my remarks I will revisit and develop my main claim. I will ask in what sense, from the vantage point of the doctrine of the state and the constitution, when we refer to popular sovereignty in the specific context of the *constitution-making process*, we can speak of *people's two bodies*, mimicking the title of the famous book by Ernst Kantorowicz.[38]

I said that the people as the body made up of a nominative list of voters is a *constituted power*, a power created by the constitution; it exercises in a representative democracy essentially the function of selecting the representatives through the mechanism of electoral law. Emmanuel Sieyes designated this function as *pouvoir commentant* – that is to say, the power of appointment/authorization *pro tempore* of the elected representatives.

Sieyes, as already noted, was also the author of the broader distinction between *pouvoir constituant* and *pouvoirs constitués*.[39] So far, I have been claiming that the "people," at least from the legal point of view, is always a *pouvoir constitué*, not only when they select the legislative representatives, but even when they ratify a constitution; since in any event the "people" does not write the constitution and can only reject it if there is a process of *ex post* ratification – as, for instance, in the case of the first constitutional charter of the French Fourth Republic in 1946. In one sense, therefore, we should agree with Hobbes, in that the un-constituted people are, if not necessarily a *dissentiens multitudo*, at least a subject that cannot have much more than an undefined, unarticulated *Wille zur Verfassung* – a will to have a constitution.[40] Moreover, and now against

example of a representative procedure (by a party critical of the very idea of representation!) where the representatives, the ratifying people, are not even chosen by the represented ones. On direct democracy and referendums, see the important book by Yannis Papadopoulos, *Démocratie directe*, Paris, Economica (coll. "Politique comparée"), 1998; and the classical texts by Carl Schmitt, *Volksentscheid und Volksbegehren: Ein Beitrag zur Auslegung der Weimarer Verfassung und zur Lehre von der unmittelbaren Demokratie*, de Gruyter, Berlin-Leipzig, 1927 and Erich Kaufmann, *Zur Problematik des Volkswillens*, de Gruyter, Berlin-Leipzig, 1931.

38 *The King's Two Bodies: A Study in Medieval Political Theology*, Princeton University Press, 1957.

39 See Pasquale Pasquino, *Emmanuel Sieyes et l'invention de la constitution en France*, Paris, Editions Odile Jacob, 1998.

40 On this point Carl Schmitt, note 27 above, p. 131.

Hobbes, we could say that the "people" cannot become either the author or an actor[41] in a constitution-making process but only the authorizing public approving or rejecting the constitution.

So, we are left with the question: what, if anything, *is* the constituent power of the people and its *sovereign* nature? My answer to such a question is set out schematically in Figure 6.1. It holds that what I have called authorization[42] has indeed a twofold dimension. On one side, the popular authorization through ratification of a constitutional text is performed, as suggested, by a constituted power, the members of the ratifying body, which makes authorized and legally valid the decision of a constitution-making actor[43] that is *not* identical with the "people." On the other side, there is a dimension of this distinction between constituent and constituted power that is the foundation of the liberal principle of *limited government*. This latter dimension can be designated, for want of a better adjective, as the *negative* meaning of the classical legal concept of "popular sovereignty."

But how can we make sense of the concepts of popular sovereignty and the constituent power of the people, which is utilized in the rhetoric of most of contemporary liberal-democratic constitutions,[44] if it is not to become just another way to describe acquiescence?[45] Discussing the doctrine of constituent power of the people in an important article, E.-W.

[41] See *Leviathan*, chapter 16.

[42] I cannot present here the origin of this idea of authorization in the contractarian political theory of Thomas Hobbes and its concretization at the end of the eighteenth century, when the legitimacy of political authority began (in America and in France) to be grounded in the legal mechanism of popular elections. It is enough to say that this idea presupposes the assumption of *political equality* among citizens and the artificial nature of political power – where by "artificial" is meant that no one has by nature a power *sui juris* to enact and impose binding orders upon the members of the community, if he or she is not authorized by those who must obey them. The political authority is not a *Patriarch* any more but an artificial institution, an artifact established by authorization to protect and guarantee subjects' equal natural rights. See Pasquale Pasquino, "Modern Representative Democracy: Intellectual Genealogy and Drawbacks" in B. Kapossy (ed.), *Markets, Morals, Politics*, Harvard University Press, 2018, pp. 111–135.

[43] An example among many others is of the French citizens ratifying the text of the Constitution of the Fifth Republic, written by De Gaulle and his legal advisors.

[44] We can think, for example, of the Preamble to the American constitution: "*We the People of the United States*, in Order to form a more perfect Union, establish Justice, insure domestic Tranquility, provide for the common defense, promote the general Welfare, and secure the Blessings of Liberty to ourselves and our Posterity, *do ordain and establish this Constitution* for the United States of America."

[45] It seems that the Schmittian dichotomy between the constituent power of the people and the constituent power of the King (*Constitutional Theory*, pp. 130–131) capture a relevant aspect of the concept. In the latter case, the citizens are like children, who obey a more or

the (so-called *sovereign*) *people* act

I. legally as
constituted power (a) electing ordinary representatives
(b) ratifying the constitution (1)

II. sociologically as
(a) the social-political forces supportive of the constitutional *status quo*
(b) the social-political forces supportive of a constitutional change/revolution (2)

The doctrine of *constituent power of the people* has a double dimension:

On one side, it refers to II(b), on the other, to the idea that *no constituted power* can exercise an unlimited power (3), which owes its meaning to the idea of the people as a normally absent and inactive actor, emerging only in exceptional circumstances and acting legally through its representatives and in the form of I(b) but here only as a constituted power.

The concept of *popular sovereignty, in nuce*, covers three different realities.

(1) as a constituted power acting in the process of the ratification of a constitution or in the authorization of a constituent assembly
(2) as the active social-political force supportive of a constitutional change
(3) as the founding principle of the liberal constitutionalism: the limitation of all constituted powers (including the power of the people as voters)

Figure 6.1 Popular sovereignty and constituent power

Böckenförde suggested a possible answer, one similar to what I found working on the constitutional-political theory of Sieyes[46] when he laid out the systematic foundations of the concept of constituent power. Behind and beyond the constituted powers, representatives, and voters exercising political authority, there is something other: *an external subject, which absorbs and monopolizes the absolute power, so that no authority exercising power under the constitution can pretend undivided sovereignty for itself.*

Alongside the "people" exercising the constituted *pouvoir commettant* (the voting power), which has legal limits like any constituted power,[47] there is a transcendent "people" that by its very presupposition makes impossible the concrete exercise of an absolute sovereignty. In a representative democracy this other body of the people takes the

less benevolent Father, whereas in the former case they are somehow partners in a collective enterprise.

46 See E.-W. Böckenförde, *Die verfassungsgebende Gewalt des Volkes*, Frankfurt a. M., 1986, now translated as "The Constituent Power of the People: A Liminal Concept of Constitutional Law," in Mirjam Künkler and Tine Stein (eds.), *Constitutional and Political Theory*. Selected Writings by Ernst-Wolfgang Böckenförde, Oxford University Press, 2017, chapter VII, and Pasquale Pasquino, "Constitution et pouvoir constituant: le double corps du people," in *Figures de Sieyes*, Paris, Presses Universitaires de la Sorbonne, 2008, pp. 13–23.

47 Depending, as I said, on the terms of the constitution and on the character of the electoral law, which is not decided by the people themselves!

place that God had in medieval theories of limited monarchy. Hans Baron in his dissertation on Jean Calvin[48] showed that according to the Genevan reformer no king in the Christian Europa could assign to himself an unlimited power, since such a power is the prerogative only of God; so that the absolute power of God makes limited the power of a Christian King.

That this other transcendent "people" is rhetorically described as the constituent power does not tell us much about its real power, which, from the legal point of view, overlaps with the ratification function of a normative document produced by a political-legal elite; it means nonetheless that the constituted powers, the ordinary State organs, including the *pouvoir commettant* exercised by the voters, can only be conceived of as limited segments of a divided power. The formula of "popular sovereignty," (re) invented[49] and used by political actors at the end of the eighteenth century and systematized during the following one by constitutional theorists, supplied a necessary rhetoric. Based on the legal mechanism of authorization (ratification), it was used both to justify the political power of a new elite and as a way to limit its power. On one side, the authorization of repeated elections of representative state organs destroyed any form of power *sui juris* (whether preemption, genealogy, or divine right); on the other side, the attribution of the sovereignty to an abstract entity – the people or the nation – implied the denial of undivided concrete sovereignty, and so absolute power, to any single state organ.

Article 3 of the French Declaration of 1789 writes: "*Nul corps, nul individu ne peut exercer d'autorité qui n'en émane expressément*" – that is to say, no body or individual may exercise authority if this does not emanate from the national sovereignty. Beyond this metaphysical language, we discover the modern constitutional principle of a "limited government." The transposition of sovereignty from King to "people," therefore, effectively brought about the destruction of the early modern idea of absolute sovereignty.

One could add, in conclusion, that the principle of limited government is but one form and one result of the awakening of the sleeping sovereign.[50] It is the result that prevailed in the post-Hobbesian western

[48] *Calvin Staatsanschauung und das konfessionelle Zeitalter*, Berlin, München, R. Oldenburg, 1924.

[49] I am thinking here of precedents such as G. Lawson, *Politica Sacra et Civilis* (1660) and Marsilius of Padua, *Defensor Pacis* (1324).

[50] On this see the suggestive book by Richard Tuck, *The Sleeping Sovereign. The Invention of Modern Democracy*, Cambridge University Press, 2016.

culture. Starting from the English and French civil wars (the Great Rebellion and the French Revolution), the constitutionalization of sovereign power declared (with uneven success) the end of power without limits. Yet elsewhere, most notably in Russia and in China, the awakening of the sovereign instead produced despotic regimes.

Now, in many places – West and East, the sovereign whose energy once produced the revolutionary transformation – liberal or otherwise, has fallen back into a deep sleep.

7

Nations against the People

Whose Sovereign Power?

OLGA BASHKINA

1 Introduction

The end of the twentieth century saw the temporary decline in the importance of the concepts "sovereignty" and "nation-state." As the hopes for a cosmopolitan post-national world unraveled, "sovereignty" and "nation-state" were deemed to be outdated and obsolete for at least two reasons. On the one hand, globalization and internationalization have allegedly transformed the Westphalian world order of independent sovereign states, bringing about a future of post-state cosmopolitan universalism. Sovereignty, a concept co-original with the statist imaginary, was believed to be destined to wither away together with the nation-state. On the other hand, sovereignty was targeted for its incompatibility with the principles of constitutionalism and the rule of law. Perhaps, sovereignty, understood as the highest absolute indivisible power, was fit for the old regime of contesting nation-states. However, it was claimed, it is alien to contemporary constitutionalism with its core principles of separation of powers, constitutional limitations, and international cooperation.

But now that the cosmopolitan utopia has been challenged by conflicting national sovereignty claims, liberal theory has brought back the sovereignty discourse and attempted to reimagine it in light of earlier criticisms. A variety of theorists have come to a renewed agreement that sovereignty remains indispensable in a world of constitutional democratic states. After several decades of being doubted and questioned, the significance of the concepts of sovereignty and nation-state appears to have been rehabilitated.

The turmoil of continuous doubt has been addressed through the technique of neutralizing the conflictual content of "sovereignty" and "nation-state." This way of arguing implies that "sovereignty" and "nation-state" are concepts pertaining to symbolic unity and cooperation, and not to domination and discrimination. Skepticism toward sovereignty, it is said, results from widespread scholarly confusion between governmental power and sovereignty.[1] If sovereignty is conflated with the power of government exclusively to control the state of affairs in a given territory, it would be rejected based on the observation that such an absolute and indivisible control does not exist. Yet, sovereignty in the contemporary sense of the word, it is claimed, does not signify this kind of power anymore. Instead, "sovereignty" now stands for symbolic representation of the unified authority, the assumed legal supremacy of the state.[2] In this understanding, "sovereignty" is also compatible with processes of political and legal integration, e.g., the European Union, as it exemplifies the possibility of the unity of law and self-determination of a political community without presupposing territorial exclusivity and monopolism of decision-making.[3] Interestingly, this newly asserted meaning of sovereignty, even as it claims to reflect a novel contemporary reality, has not moved far from the classics of state theory. This is well illustrated by Hegel's definition of sovereignty in his *Philosophy of Right*:

> Since sovereignty is the ideality of every particular authority, it is easy to fall into the very common misunderstanding of regarding this ideality as mere power and empty arbitrariness, and of equating sovereignty with despotism. But despotism signifies the condition of lawlessness in general, in which the particular will as such, whether of a monarch or of the people (ochlocracy), counts as law (or rather replaces law), whereas sovereignty is to be found specifically under lawful and constitutional conditions as the moment of ideality of the particular spheres and functions within the state.[4]

Both the recently emergent defenses of sovereignty and Hegel's *Philosophy of Right*, then, emphasize sovereignty's symbolic and ideal

[1] M. Loughlin, "Why Sovereignty?," in *Sovereignty and the Law: Domestic, European and International Perspectives*, ed. R. Rawlings, P. Leyland, and A. Young (Oxford University Press, 2013), 34–39.

[2] *Ibid.*

[3] R. Geenens, "Sovereignty as Autonomy," *Law and Philosophy*, 36 (2017), 495–524; Neil Walker, "Sovereignty Frames and Sovereignty Claims," in *Sovereignty and the Law: Domestic, European and International Perspectives*, ed. R. Rawlings, P. Leyland, and A. Young (Oxford University Press, 2013), 18–33.

[4] G. W. F. Hegel, *Elements of the Philosophy of Right* (Cambridge University Press, 2003), 315–16.

character. Hegel additionally observed that sovereignty as "ideality" is only possible if it is grounded in subjectivity, which in Hegel's case means the concrete individual subjectivity of the monarch.[5] This, Hegel argued, is necessary in order to give legitimation and concrete representation to a complex system of separated powers and forces. This observation reveals that "sovereignty," analyzed from a philosophical point of view, is a concept that appeared in modern philosophy in correlation with the idea of subjectivity. In contemporary liberal thinking, the idea of the subject of sovereignty has been reimagined along the same neutral lines as the concept of sovereignty itself. The transformation of the modern understanding of sovereignty is narrated as the shift from personal power of command to an abstract signifier that "symbolizes the unity of ordering,"[6] where, in the name of separation of powers, sovereignty is refused to a ruler, an office of government, or even to the people as a concrete entity. Instead, in this modern liberal understanding the people may be understood as a purely legal denominator, as a very general and "thin" expression of a unitary sovereign subject.

In a somewhat fuller but still abstract version of the liberal narrative, the symbolic subject of this impersonal nonviolent sovereignty can be the people united by constitutional patriotism, as in Jürgen Habermas' famous theory. There, sovereignty is described as an attribute of a democratic "tradition-building," a "self-correcting learning process," which encompasses past and future generations involved in the shared project of self-governing community.[7] Or, to cite a further option, the subject of sovereignty can be the nation carefully defined in inclusive terms by theories of liberal or civic nationalism. In this case, collective subjectivity forms around shared constitutional values, where the "nation" provides the core for more meaningful forms of citizenship.[8] Either way, the sovereign people or nation are portrayed as participating in a cooperative project in the framework of the rule of law in a harmonious conflict-free fashion.

I want to bring to the fore the problematic character of this neutral cooperation engrained in many liberal theories of sovereignty and its subject. The neutrality of the liberal project has been famously

[5] *Ibid.*, 317.

[6] Loughlin, "Why Sovereignty?," 48.

[7] J. Habermas, "Constitutional Democracy. A Paradoxical Union of Contradictory Principles?," *Political Theory*, 29, 6 (2001), 766–81.

[8] R. Brubaker, "In the Name of the Nation: Reflections on Nationalism and Patriotism," *Citizenship Studies*, 1, 2 (2004), 115–27.

denounced by Carl Schmitt.[9] More recently, Habermas's agreement-oriented model has been criticized by Ernesto Laclau and Chantal Mouffe, who employed Schmitt's friend/enemy distinction in order to construct their vision of agonistic democracy.[10] I follow a similar path and problematize the neutral understanding of sovereignty and its collective subject. I do this by analyzing the work of Carl Schmitt's older contemporary from Strasbourg, a French constitutional theorist Raymond Carré de Malberg. His theory greatly influenced the development of the rule of law tradition. Crucial for my purposes is that it makes explicit the conflictual and oppressive character of sovereignty. Contemporary liberal constitutional theory draws significantly from the tradition of French constitutional thought – in particular from Carré de Malberg's programmatic work on the theory of state *Contribution à la Théorie Générale de l'Etat* (1920). Yet, as the reception of constitutional patriotism and civic nationalism as only modestly different strands of contemporary liberal constitutionalism rather indicates, it has too rarely been observed and little appreciated why, within this French tradition, the distinction between "people" and "nation" as subjects of sovereignty matters for understanding the oppressive nature of the sovereignty of a constitutional state.

That key distinction in French legal thought between popular and national sovereignty is seen as epitomizing the process of sovereignty's modernization from concrete power to abstract legal framework. The narrative of the opposition between "people" and "nation" in this process was developed in its most refined form by Carré de Malberg. The transformation from people to nation happens, so his story goes, when an earlier conception of direct popular sovereignty formulated by Jean-Jacques Rousseau is replaced by a new one, born during the French Revolution. A more progressive version of sovereignty, in line with developing liberal and constitutional values, is then theorized over the course of the French Revolution, specifically exemplified by Abbé Sieyès' theory of representation. The new theory places sovereignty in the hands of the nation, a constructed symbolic community, where sovereignty ceases to be exercised directly by the entire citizenry and instead stands for the combination of all powers exercised in the name of this community.

[9] C. Schmitt, *The Concept of the Political* (Chicago: University of Chicago Press, 2007).

[10] E. Laclau and C. Mouffe, *Hegemony and Socialist Strategy: Towards a Radical Democratic Politics* (London; New York: Verso, 2014).

Yet, Carré de Malberg's take on the transformation of the people into the nation is not merely a historical argument. Indeed, he aimed to demonstrate the impersonal nature of sovereignty in the liberal representative state based on the principle of separation of powers, which brings him close to the neutral project of contemporary theory. However, he also used the concept of the nation in order to demonstrate the inevitable dual nature of sovereignty; standing both for mutual cooperation of national citizens and oppressive criminalization of popular resistance. In what follows, I explore two points. First, using the example of Carré de Malberg's theory, I show how the people might be refused the role of the subject of sovereignty due to the incompatibility of such an attribution with the maintenance of the oppressive element of sovereignty. Secondly, I show how national sovereignty is meant not only to provide a neutral framework of cooperation but also to impose an oppressive control, excluding and penalizing deviance.

2 Can the People Be Sovereign?

Carré de Malberg's work belongs to the genre of the general theory of the state developed at the end of the nineteenth century. This short-lived genre saw several prominent figures (Carré de Malberg, Jellinek, Kelsen, etc.) and perished after World War II with the rise of political science.[11] While the general theory of the state appeared in Germany as a contribution to the ongoing state building process, in France it took the form of a response to the tendencies of democratization. Expanding suffrage and an increase of social conflicts led to a questioning of the validity of representative claims and of the correspondence between the legal will of the government and the real will of the people.[12] As one of the four canonical theorists of French constitutional thought (together with Adhémar Esmein, Léon Duguit, and Maurice Hauriou), Carré de Malberg treated issues of sovereignty and its subject as key. The distinction between the people and the nation as subjects of sovereignty, which is the focus of my analysis below, does not originate with Carré de Malberg.[13] Yet he brought it to its full theoretical explication.

[11] O. Jouanjan, E.Maulin «Introduction – La théorie de l'État entre passé et avenir. Journées en l'honneur de Carrés de Malberg », *Jus Politicum*, n° 8, http://juspoliticum.com/article/Introduction-La-theorie-de-l-Etat-entre-passe-et-avenir-Journees-en-l-honneur-de-Carres-de-Malberg-549.html.

[12] *Ibid.*

[13] G. Bacot, *Carré de Malberg et l'origine de la distinction entre souveraineté du peuple et souveraineté nationale* (Paris: CNRS éd., 2001). Bacot argues not only that the distinction

A crucial question in Carré de Malberg's conception of the state is who should be deemed the subject of sovereignty – the concrete and tangible people or the more abstract nation, devoid of the dangerous excesses of power. In defending the nation as the subject of sovereignty that can guarantee its stable unwavering character, Carré de Malberg first repudiates the people as a potential sovereign. His analysis of popular sovereignty and the people revolves around a critique of Rousseau's theory of popular sovereignty, which, according to him, posits the people, considered as a concrete assemblage of individuals, as the source of absolute and indivisible sovereignty. Carré de Malberg sees Rousseau's theory of sovereignty as representative for a wide variety of theories, such as those of the monarchomachs and that of Hobbes. He also sees this theory as standing behind the American Constitution and the French Constitution of 1793.

Carré de Malberg's account of popular sovereignty is formed around a series of critiques that he directs at Rousseau's theory. The first one pertains to Carré de Malberg's claim that popular sovereignty is born as a result of the combination of the individual sovereignty of citizens. He understands Rousseau's idea of the social contract to rely on the premise that there exist atomized individuals who are sovereign in their own will, which allows them to participate equally in contracting and so creating a new sovereign power out of their individual sovereignties. Although Carré de Malberg's exaggeratedly arithmetical reading of popular sovereignty misses Rousseau's central distinction between *volonté de tous* and *volonté générale,* it illustrates how in this discourse the non-constituted people are conceived as monadic individuals incapable of forming any organization of their own. The idea of social contract, or individuals creating collective sovereignty, appears to Carré de Malberg as containing a logical contradiction. If individual sovereignty is posited, he believes, it can hardly be combined with the general will as total collective control, for one cannot submit oneself to the rule of others without losing one's own sovereignty: "sovereignty and subjection to the will of the other are two incompatible things."[14] It illustrates Carré de Malberg's

between popular and national sovereignty was not Carré de Malberg's invention, but also that he had misidentified the source of this distinction. Carré de Malberg associates the doctrine of popular sovereignty with the theory of Rousseau, and national sovereignty with the constitutional thought of the French Revolution, while Bacot claims that the distinction comes in later: most significantly with the counter-revolutionary tendencies during the Bourbon Restoration and the political thought of the Doctrinaires.

[14] R. Carré de Malberg, Contribution à La Théorie Générale de l'Etat (Dalloz, 2003), II, 156: "*Souveraineté et sujétion à la volonté d'autrui sont deux choses inconciliables.*"

fear that if people are actually endowed with sovereignty, they will not submit to the domination of the state. Thus, the logical contradiction of popular sovereignty manifests itself in the troubled relationship between the one and the many. The many, Carré de Malberg argues, are logically incapable of forming the one, where the one is posited to be the state with centralized power.

The second criticism of Rousseau and popular sovereignty, following from the first, is based on an analogy Carré de Malberg's draws between popular sovereignty and the confederation of states. If a confederation of states does not form a new sovereign state, a confederation of citizens does not form a state properly speaking either:

> if it were true that the democratic state, in accordance with Rousseau's ideas, was analysed as a pure association or confederation of sovereign citizens, it must be immediately inferred that the democratic state is not a true state; for a confederation of individuals is no more able than a confederation of states to form a state. ... The doctrine of Rousseau, far from founding the state and sovereignty, implies denial of the one and the other.[15]

Just as he claims that if the state in the Rousseauian vision were to be found on popular sovereignty, it could not be a real state, Carré de Malberg also invokes Rousseau's theory of popular sovereignty to undermine the idea of the democratic state. He argues that "democracy" and "state" are fundamentally incompatible, since democracy is a system with an institutional structure that is completely dependent on the unstable will of the people, while a proper state is defined by its durable organization. Whereas the states forming a confederation are free to leave any time they please, the same does not apply to the people forming a state. But if individual persons are granted sovereignty, then the association they form – the state – is vulnerable to their decision to remain part of it or to destroy it,[16] rendering the dominating power of the state "*impuissant*"[17] (impotent).

[15] *Ibid.*, II, 165: "*Si il était vrai que l'État démocratique s'analyse, conformément aux idées de Rousseau, en une pure association ou confédération de citoyens souverains, il faudrait aussitôt en déduire que l'État démocratique n'est pas un État véritable: car, une confédération d'individus ne peut pas plus qu'une confédération d'États former un État.* < ... > *La doctrine de Rousseau, bien loin de fonder l'État et la souveraineté, implique dénégation de l'un et de l'autre.*"

[16] *Ibid.*, 166.

[17] *Ibid.*, 165.

This results in a third and final criticism following from Carré de Malberg's assumption that Rousseau believes popular sovereignty is capable of founding the democratic state. In fact, democracy and popular sovereignty are not synonymous for Rousseau, since they are separated by Rousseau's major distinction between sovereignty and government. While advocating popular sovereignty, Rousseau theorizes democracy as a type of government which is not co-original with popular sovereignty. Nevertheless, while Rousseau never defended democracy and did not envision democracy as a universally applicable form of government, Carré de Malberg's equivalence of popular sovereignty and the democratic state allows him to further elaborate on his point that the people cannot be the source of sovereignty properly speaking. He calls this a "political" argument and concludes that it is impractical to describe the outcomes of the decisions of those in power as made in the name of the people since, in that case, people would be able to question those decisions and potentially challenge the whole system that leads to their production.[18] This argument amounts to the rejection of what some today call "strong popular sovereignty," that is, of popular sovereignty as constituent power preexisting the constitution as opposed to "the outcomes of the democratic process governed by constitutional law."[19] Except that popular sovereignty for Carré de Malberg is always "strong" and so always potentially destructive for the state.

The observations above show that Carré de Malberg denies the people sovereignty on account of his particular aggregative understanding of the people: if the people were to be endowed with sovereignty, it would be based on the sum of their individual sovereignties. This is, on the one hand, an over-stretched interpretation of Rousseau and, on the other hand, a disregard of other possible takes on "the people." For instance, Neil Walker singles out nine different ways how the term "people" can be understood as constitutionally implicated, including people as drafters (as popular participants in drafting the text of the constitution), people as legislators (as popular involvement in a constitutionally prescribed law-making process), and people as editors (as participants in constitutional revision).[20] Pierre

[18] *Ibid.*, 166.

[19] L. Vinx, "The Incoherence of Strong Popular Sovereignty," *International Journal of Constitutional Law*, 11, 1 (2013), 101–24.

[20] N. Walker, "Post-Constituent Constitutionalism? The Case of the European Union," in M. Loughlin and N. Walker (eds) *The Paradox of Constitutionalism. Constituent Power and Constitutional Form*, (Oxford University Press, 2008). The other six ways to understand the category "people" are people as datum (pre-given sociological existence), people as totemic inference (the existence of a written constitution is believed to be a sufficient ground, a totem, for uniting people), people as authors (the text of the constitution is

Rosanvallon,[21] discussing the constitutional debate at the outset of the French Revolution, concludes that there exist three alternative ways to conceive of the people in representative democracy. "People" can be explained in the sense of a democracy of opinion where representatives are subject to constant popular surveillance. "People" can also serve as an instance of balancing out the functioning of representatives through the power of ratification. Finally, by separating the constituent power and ordinary government, "people" can be seen as present only at the original moment of the political community.

Still the fact that Carré de Malberg chooses to see "people" as atomized individuals is significant when it comes to their relationship to sovereignty and the state. He uses his version of Rousseau to get the point across that the relationship between people, their mutual feelings, associations or agreements, cannot be considered the source of sovereignty in the constitutional state. For him, there are logical, political, and practical inconsistencies in assuming that people are sovereign. The inconsistencies that Carré de Malberg deduces in the concept of popular sovereignty are premised on his conviction as to the primacy of the state as the system of centralized domination. Since he does not see the people as a simple legal category, he concludes that the "people" is fraught with unrest, disagreement, and instability; their identity is fluctuating and does not guarantee a firm ground and longevity to the constitutional state. Yet, of course, this does not make him reject the state, but instead he looks for another theory of the subject of sovereignty more compatible with his envisioned model of sovereignty as domination.

Carré de Malberg's take on the people as a shapeless aggregate of dispersed individuals who are nothing without state organization is indirectly critiqued by Laclau and Mouffe who place popular sovereignty in the pot of democratic struggle.[22] They find precisely in the people's lack of identity the foundation of their subjectivity and popular sovereignty. Chantal Mouffe in her most recent book, *For a Left Populism*,[23] revives the argument from *Hegemony and Socialist Strategy* for a non-essentialist

authorized or endorsed by institutions representing popular will), people as narrators (symbolic identification with the narrative of "We, the People" in the constitutional text), people as subjects (people as "beneficiaries" of the system of government), peoples as reflexive interpreters (ongoing engagement in public sphere and public discourse).

21 P. Rosanvallon, *La Démocratie inachevée: Histoire de la souveraineté du peuple en France* (Paris: Folio, 2003), 41–2.

22 Laclau and Mouffe, *Hegemony and Socialist Strategy*.

23 C. Mouffe, *For a Left Populism* (London; Brooklyn, NY: Verso, 2018).

approach to a democratic subject composed of "the multiplicity of struggles against different forms of domination."[24] The people is a fluctuating category that defines itself, in line with Schmitt's friend/enemy distinction, through and against conflict with its adversary. Popular sovereignty here is placed in the struggle for radicalization of democracy where partaking "in a 'we' of radical democratic citizens does not preclude participation in a variety of other 'we's'."[25] Mouffe, again, calls for the Left to unite under the aegis of radical democracy where the unity of the radical political subject will combine the diversity of anti-domination movements. The defender of the liberal state, Mouffe sees the state as a space where popular sovereignty can be exercised. Unlike Carré de Malberg, she does not treat people's plural identity as incompatible with the viability of the state. This seems to be rooted in the fact that Mouffe's agonistic approach depicts the state as an instrument for the struggle for hegemony which a united Left should properly employ. Carré de Malberg is far from being a radical democrat, hence his refusal to ground sovereignty on popular conflict. Instead, he portrays conflict as anti-democratic, so making the people the enemy of the nation.

3 Nation and the State

As Margaret Canovan points out, nationhood is a tacit premise of almost all political thinking.[26] It clearly is in the case of Carré de Malberg. It informs his thinking all along in theorizing the nation as an alternative subject of sovereignty. In the following sections, I explain how in Carré de Malberg's theory the nation is introduced not as an impersonal neutral alternative to the people. The nation, as I aim to show, is supposed to serve as a controlling restrictive super-ego imposing itself over fractious popular drives. Carré de Malberg finds the roots of the French national sovereignty doctrine in the theory of representation of Abbé Sieyès. When Carré de Malberg approaches Sieyès' thought, he interprets it in connection with the parliamentary debates that took place in the National Assembly in 1789. First and foremost, separating the ideas of king and state, previously so tightly conjoined ("*L'État, c'est moi*"), French revolutionaries set the ground for a new way of conceiving of state and sovereignty, where the sovereignty of the monarch is replaced

[24] *Ibid.*, 16.
[25] *Ibid.*, 127.
[26] M. Canovan, *Nationhood and Political Theory* (Edward Elgar, 1996), 1.

by the sovereignty of the French nation. As the French Constitution of 1791 proclaimed, sovereignty, literally, belongs to the nation: "Sovereignty . . . belongs to the Nation; no section of the people, no individual, can usurp its exercise. The Nation, from which all the powers emanate, can exercise them only by delegation."[27] Although the participants of the debate about the novel organization of public powers are numerous, for Carré de Malberg it was Sieyès who "defined the representative government, at the beginning of the new era of public law, with an accuracy and precision that has not been exceeded since then."[28] Carré de Malberg is particularly interested in the sitting of September 7, 1789, when Sieyès presented his position on the ongoing dispute about the meaning of representation and the role of the imperative mandate. In Carré de Malberg's view, the originality of Sieyès lies in his distinguishing representative government from democracy and proclaiming the indivisible anti-federalist character of the French nation.[29] This comes to fruition where, according to Carré de Malberg, Sieyès proposes the theory of national sovereignty:

> I know that because of various distinctions and confusion we have come to consider the national will as if it could be something else than the will of the representatives of the nation, as if the nation could speak other than through its representatives. Here false principles become extremely dangerous. They are meant only to fragment, to tear France into an infinite number of small democracies which would then unite only by the ties of a general confederation. France is not an assemblage of states, it is a unique whole composed of integral parts.[30]

For Carré de Malberg, this emphatically anti-federalist intention is key to understanding Sieyès and the overall conception of the nation that

[27] www.conseil-constitutionnel.fr/les-constitutions-dans-l-histoire/constitution-de-1791, "*la Souveraineté . . . appartient à la Nation; aucune section du peuple, ni aucun individu, ne peut s'en attribuer l'exercice. La Nation, de qui seule émanent tous les Pouvoirs, ne peut les exercer que par délégation.*"

[28] Carré de Malberg, *Contribution à La Théorie Générale de l'Etat*, II, 257: "*Ce discours définit le gouvernement représentatif, dès le début de l'ère nouvelle du droit public, avec une sûreté et une précision qui n'ont pas été dépassées depuis lors.*"

[29] *Ibid.*, II, 254–59.

[30] *Ibid.*, II, 254: "*Je sais qu'à force de distinctions et de confusion, on en est parvenu à considérer le vœu national comme s'il pouvait être autre chose que le vœu des représentants de la nation, comme si la nation pouvait parler autrement que par ses représentants. Ici, les faux principes deviennent extrêmement dangereux. Ils ne vont à rien moins qu'à morceler, qu'à déchirer la France en une infinité de petites démocraties, qui ne s'uniraient ensuite que par les liens d'une confédération générale. La France n'est point une collection d'États; elles est un tout unique, compose de parties intégrantes.*"

predominated among constituents in 1789. From this definition Carré de Malberg concludes that the nation as the indivisible and united body is where "exclusively resides sovereignty" and that "the general will that forms the expression of sovereignty cannot be understood as the sum of particular wills coming from each of the districts, but this general will is itself part of the unity and indivisibility of the nation."[31] It has been shown that Sieyès himself deliberately avoids ascribing sovereignty to any agent or institution,[32] distancing himself both from Rousseau's account of popular sovereignty and from more radical positions during the French Revolution. On the few occasions where he does use the concept of sovereignty, it has negative connotations and is usually employed to criticize his opponents.

There is, however, one case in which he gives a positive definition of sovereignty. He asks:

> what is sovereignty? Do the associates put together and represent all their forces and means? Of course not. Thus, sovereignty understood as a supreme power that would dominate and embrace everything does not exist. It is not found in the mass of all public officers taken together, and if the constitution separates powers, if each of them bound by their special mission cannot go beyond it without usurpation and crime, where can one place the gigantic idea of sovereignty? It is clear that under the terms of supreme or sovereign authority one can only understand the final decision of many special authorities whose judgement is of the last resort.[33]

This definition resembles Carré de Malberg's own vision of sovereignty, where sovereignty does not belong to any concrete institution or person

[31] *Ibid.*, II, 255: "*La volonté générale, qui forme l'expression de la souveraineté, ne peut s'entendre comme une somme de volontés particulières, émanant de chacun des bailliages; mais cette volonté générale participe elle-même de l'unité et de l'indivisibilité de la nation.*"

[32] P. Pasquino, *Sieyes et l'Invention de La Constitution en France* (Edile Jacob, 1998); L. Rubinelli, "How to Think Beyond Sovereignty: On Sieyès and Constituent Power," (2019) 18 *European Journal of Political Theory*, 47–67. https://doi.org/10.1177/1474885116642170.

[33] E. Sieyes, "Bases de l'Ordre Social," in *Sieyes et l'invention de La Constitution en France*, ed. P. Pasquino (Paris: Odile Jacob, 1998), 198: "*Qu'est-ce que la souveraineté? Les associes mettent-ils en commun et font-ils représenter la totalité de leurs forces et de leurs moyens? Non, assurément. Ainsi la souveraineté prise pour un pouvoir suprême qui dominerait et embrasserait tout n'existe pas. Il n'est point déposé dans la masse prise ensemble de tous les fonctionnaires publics, et si la constitution sépare les pouvoirs, si chacun d'eux borne à sa mission spéciale ne peut en sortir sans usurpation et sans crime, ou placer l'idée gigantesque de souveraineté? Il est clair qu'on ne peut entendre par les mots autorité suprême ou souveraine que la décision finale de plusieurs autorités spéciales dont le jugement est en dernier ressort.*"

in particular Yet, in the case of Sieyès, the highest power is *not* ascribed to the nation even as an abstract and fictional subject.

In explaining the principle of national sovereignty, Carré de Malberg transforms Sieyès' idea of representation into the idea of the personification of the nation by the state. The personhood of the state, as Carré de Malberg emphasizes, is not a fiction, not a metaphor, nor a comparison. It is a juridical reality which is prerequisite to the conception of the unity of the legal space within the state and the legitimate existence of other associations.[34] "The personality of any association or establishment which will be formed within the state . . . depends on the superior will of the state to grant permission or not to exist to groups that claim to be created within it and exercise their rights under it."[35] Together with the exclusive power to authorize the existence of other associations, the idea of the state *qua* legal person permits the imagination of the continuity of the existence of the state across time.

In order to distance his theory of the personification from its German influences, specifically through Georg Jellinek's theory of state, Carré de Malberg emphasizes that the state is neither a person capable of legitimizing itself nor is it bound together though and by the person of the monarch. Rather, the state acquires its legitimacy through being the personification of the nation:

> The state is nothing else but the nation itself. The nation has no powers, it is not a subject of law, it does not appear as sovereign unless it is legally organized and follows the laws of its organization. In other words, the nation becomes a person only by the fact of its state organization, that is to say by the fact of being constituted as a state.[36]

The double-bind of the state and the nation is a way, on the one hand, to rule out any prior, non-instituted manifestation of the people (an ultimate rejection of constituent power) and, on the other hand, to legitimize

[34] Carré de Malberg, *Contribution à La Théorie Générale de l'Etat*, I, 40.

[35] *Ibid.*, 42: *Que la personnalité des associations ou établissements quelconques qui viennent a se former a l'intérieur de l'État, ne puisse se concevoir sans une loi qui lui serve de base, cela s'explique tout naturellement par ce motif qu'il dépend de la volonté supérieure de l'État d'accorder ou non l'autorisation de vivre aux groupes qui prétendent se créer au dedans de lui et y exercer la capacité de sujets de droits.*

[36] Carré de Malberg, *Contribution à La Théorie Générale de l'Etat*, I, 15: *L'État n'est autre que la nation elle-même.* < . . . > *La nation n'a de pouvoirs, elle n'est un sujet de droit, elle n'apparaît comme souveraine qu'en tant qu'elle est juridiquement organisée et qu'elle agit suivant les lois de son organisation. En d'autres termes, la nation ne devient une personne que par le fait de son organisation étatique, c'est-a-dire par le fait qu'elle est constituée en État.*

the actions of state organs by the claim that they are made in the name of the nation.

To understand why, at root, Carré de Malberg thinks that nothing else except national identity works as a legitimation of the state, one must look at his criticisms of the various legal theories of his time. Both Otto von Gierke's anti-individualist theory of social associations, developed in his *Das deutsche Genossenschaftsrecht*, and Maurice Hauriou's theory of institutions are criticized by Carré de Malberg for privileging other social and political identities which keep people together over national allegiance. Those identities can only be "a tendency to unification," but never a properly consolidating force. Léon Duguit is criticized for rejecting grand notions of sovereignty, the personality of the state, and national will, in the name of the rule of law. For Duguit, in a system of checks and balances where every power is limited by another power, there is no room for sovereignty as absolute power and national will as a unitary entity.[37] Against Duguit's suggestion to understand the state as the collection of currently functioning public offices, Carré de Malberg insists on the necessity of preserving grand narratives of the state and national will for the sake of the congruence of various governmental powers:

> the personality of the state results from a second fact, its continuity. . . . The state collectivity is a continuous unity, as, by the very effect of its legal organization, it maintains itself across time identical to itself and independent of its transient members.[38]

A native of Strasbourg, Carré de Malberg, to a large extent incorporated his national feelings into his theory. The Franco-Prussian war, "a great trauma"[39] of Carré de Malberg's childhood, left the mark of rivalry and competition on his reception of German legal thought and on his conception of the unique character of the French constitutional state. Carré de Malberg developed his political and legal views under the influence of

[37] Duguit's argument is echoed today by Pavlos Eleftheriadis, who maintains that sovereignty and the rule of law are incompatible, see P. Eleftheriadis, "Law and Sovereignty," *Law and Philosophy*, 29, 5 (2010), 535–69.

[38] Carré de Malberg, *Contribution à La Théorie Générale de l'Etat*, I, 48: "*La personnalité de l'État résulte d'un second fait, qui est sa continuité . . . La collectivité étatique est une unité continue, en tant que, par l'effet même de son organisation juridique, elle se maintient, a travers le temps, identique a elle-même et indépendante de ses membres passagers.*"

[39] O. Beaud, "Carré de Malberg, Juriste Alsacien. La Biographie Comme Élément d'explication d'une Doctrine Constitutionnelle," in O. Beaud and P. Wachsmann (eds) *La Science Juridique Française et La Science Juridique Allemande de 1870 à 1918*, (Strasbourg: Presses universitaires de Strasbourg, 1997), 222.

discussion of the Alsace-Lorraine region.[40] From his earlier articles, devoted to the status of Alsace-Lorraine under the German Empire and to the legal basis of the reparation payments, until his later programmatic work on the state, he depicted Germany as an imperialist aggressor enforcing domination and causing unrest on the continent. He juxtaposed the French state built around "the national sentiment" to the German state constructed around the *Herrscher,* the figure of the monarch – the one uniting the many.

While Carré de Malberg's intention is to demonstrate how the French state is deeply rooted in the revolutionary tradition and finds its legitimacy in the French nation, at the same time he attempts to pass between the Scylla and Charybdis of French post-revolutionary politics: the threats of Jacobinism and the excesses of Napoleonian dictatorship. Consequently, while, on the one hand, devising an alternative theory to the German monarchic state, on the other hand, Carré de Malberg distances himself from exaggerated resort to democratic method, or from the positing of sovereignty in the people. To this end, he counterposes the concepts of the people and the nation and establishes a distinction between popular and national sovereignty on the basis of their ability to constitute a lasting and stable state. In other words, even though Carré de Malberg criticizes the German domination model of the state, the alternative that he wants to see in the French state needs to be equally strong in order to stand as an equal adversary to Germany. This agenda leads to Carré de Malberg's conception of the state as the personification of the nation and his substitution of the allegedly excessively democratic concept of the sovereign people with a more unitary and consolidated concept of the nation.

Grappling with the instability of the French state both externally – facing the threat of the German expansion – and internally – facing the challenge of democratization and contested representative claims, Carré de Malberg is challenged by the idea of popular sovereignty. Unwilling to accommodate democratic conflict, Carré de Malberg rejects Rousseau's theory for being too democratic and presupposing the existence of the people prior to or independently of the state. Today regarded as a canonical element of French constitutional thought, Carré de Malberg's theory had momentous impact when it was first published in the aftermath of World War I. It acquired a renewed significance, however, when it was rediscovered in the 1960s during the presidency of Charles de Gaulle. Presidential power had been consolidated by de

[40] *Ibid.*, 232–33.

Gaulle's initiative of a constitutional amendment, in the early years of the Fifth Republic, to allow the president to be directly elected by the people for the first time since Louis Napoleon in 1848. The amendment was approved by a referendum in 1962 despite the strong opposition of Parliament. This is the context in which Carré de Malberg's national sovereignty doctrine was reanimated by the liberal opposition as ballast for the claim that presidential power should not be invigorated by means of a plebiscite, with its direct appeal to the constituent power of the people. Popular sovereignty once again played the role of a scapegoat for epitomizing two perennial enemies of French liberalism – Bonapartism and uncontrolled popular power.

4 The People's Super-Ego

Carré de Malberg believed that we cannot dispense with grand narratives of states, nations, and sovereignty. Those serve to provide symbols of unity that bring people together and organize their collective life. Without sovereignty being grounded in the narrative of the nation it allegedly loses its legitimacy and the ability to sustain the collective myth over time. Written after the outbreak of World War I, Carré de Malberg's tale about sovereignty and its subject resonates with our contemporary situation. While some believe that nation-states provide the only ground for meaningful political life and sentiment of collective belonging,[41] nations primarily bring about divisions, to which the prominence of far-right movements and the current migrant crisis vividly attest. National identity, on which Carré de Malberg insisted a century ago, today again serves as a form of identity that is used effectively both to consolidate against internal divisions and to construct external threats. In the name of protecting their national democracies and the rule of law, states are turning fundamental human rights into the rights of nation-state citizens.[42] Contemporary liberal projects, disillusioned with the cosmopolitan utopia, are attempting to incorporate the concepts of sovereignty and nation into their discourse while attempting to distinguish themselves from the exclusionary versions of those concepts used by illiberal ideologies. Carré de Malberg's theory is a reminder that, notwithstanding

[41] P. Manent, *A World Beyond Politics? A Defense of the Nation-State*, (Princeton: Princeton University Press, 2006).

[42] H. Arendt, *The Origins of Totalitarianism* (Harcourt Brace & Company, 1976).

these efforts, the concepts of sovereignty and nation employed with liberal intentions bear unavoidable oppressive and discriminatory traits.

The double role of a constitutional nation-state as a shared project of responsible citizenry and an oppressive institution of control and domination is reflected in Carré de Malberg's distinction of the political and legal meaning of the state. At the end of World War I, he wonders what kind of a future state can be envisioned as adequate to the new world order. He places the future of the state at the borderline between "collaboration" and "domination." Politically speaking, he says, the state is a form of collective participation in the common cause where people contribute to the common project of their collective life – what he calls "*collaboration.*"[43] This is the same idea that appears in contemporary theory under guises such as "collective self-actualization," "people's self-determination," "self-constitution," etc. For Carré de Malberg, collective cooperation is exercised by citizens in the form of their electoral activity, "the power of public opinion," and partaking in the "national sentiment." This is a conflict-free understanding of the political, something that was extensively criticized by Carl Schmitt[44] and was later attempted to be amended by post-Marxist theory in France. Yet, conflict is introduced by Carré de Malberg not in the political but in the legal dimension of the state.

For him, collective cooperation is not given but needs to be produced. Although it is the people who are supposed to be cooperating, it is only the nation that can embody the ideal of cooperation. The stability of the state, much desired by state theorists of the nineteenth century, and, equally, the continuity of the constitutional project, much sought after by contemporary theorists such as Habermas, can only be guaranteed, according to Carré de Malberg, if connected with the idea of state domination grounded in transgenerational community bound by "national sentiment."

> neither the state nor the nation should be confused with the passing generation of the present-day nationals; it may well form a unity in the present, but it has but an ephemeral existence, while the nation, personified by the State, has a character of permanence and constitutes a unit over the course of time.[45]

[43] Carré de Malberg, *Contribution à La Théorie Générale de l'Etat*, vi.

[44] Schmitt, *The Concept of the Political*.

[45] *Ibid.*, II, 332: "*Ni l'État, ni la nation, ne doivent être confondus avec la génération passagère des nationaux actuellement en vie: celle-ci peut bien former une unité dans le présent, mais elle n'a qu'une existence éphémère, tandis que la nation, personnifiée par l'État, a un caractère de permanence et constitue une unité dans le cours des temps.*"

What Carré de Malberg calls "ephemeral existence" usually embraces the most "real" – as in concrete and vivid – political moments, yet he ascribes genuine reality only to the imagined community. The nation appears an indispensable idea to represent the unity of the cooperative project and at the same time serves as a subject exercising control and coercion. When collective cooperation is under threat, the state employs its domination power "to reduce individual resistances"[46] "in the name and on behalf of the nation."[47] Where contemporary theorists say that sovereignty "symbolizes a unity of ordering,"[48] Carré de Malberg provides a reminder that sovereignty of the nation-state is not just a symbol, it is a real practice of domination. By refusing sovereignty to the people due to their revolutionary potential and ascribing it to the nation, Carré de Malberg turns the nation against the people. The nation in its legal dimension acts as a censor manifesting itself in "extreme cases," in "extraordinary possibilities."[49] Since unanimous cooperation is impossible, the oppressive power of that nation is used against those who refuse to cooperate along the lines determined by state institutions.[50]

The nation as a legal argument and the foundation of the constitutional order as suggested by Carré de Malberg, as was explained earlier, was used in the 1960s against the populist power of Charles de Gaulle. A similar argument lies behind the law and order discourse introduced in the 1960s by neoliberal conservatives like Ronald Raegan and Richard Nixon. Used against the civil rights movement, it aimed to criminalize resistance and increase punishment for non-normalized forms of behavior. Liberal theories in subsequent decades tried to rescue the plurality of popular subject from the unifying pretense of the nation. They did so in a variety of ways, including reimagining the state as the neutral platform for contestation and popular claims or seeing the rule of law as a neutral framework of national and international cooperation. Now the law and order discourse is back again and nations are turning against the people, demonstrating the failure of the neutral project. Carré de Malberg's national oppression of the people needs to be revisited and debunked anew.

[46] *Ibid.*, xiv.
[47] *Ibid.*, xii.
[48] Loughlin, "Why Sovereignty?," 48.
[49] Carré de Malberg, *Contribution à La Théorie Générale de l'Etat,* xiii.
[50] *Ibid.*, xiv.

8

A Positive or Negative Conception of Sovereignty? Marcel Gauchet, Benjamin Constant and Liberal Democracy

NORA TIMMERMANS

> La philosophie politique restaurée ne semble guère pousser sa réflexion au-delà de ce que les gestionnaires de l'État peuvent arguer sur la démocratie et la loi, sur le droit et l'État de droit. En bref, elle semble surtout assurer la communication entre les grandes doctrines classiques et les formes de légitimation ordinaires des États dits de démocratie libérale.[1]
>
> Jacques Rancière, *La Mésentente*, 1995.

In what follows I present a critical analysis of the conception of popular sovereignty that underpins Marcel Gauchet's innovative interpretation of Benjamin Constant. Gauchet's interpretation is a key instance of the liberal democratic turn that first occurred around 1980 and that continues to set the tone within Constant-scholarship today. Even though the liberal democratic idiom is thus well established now, it was not self-evident that it would come about. For a long time, the nineteenth-century Swiss-French thinker, journalist, politician and writer seemed destined to go down in history as the ultimate spokesperson for modern French 'liberalism'. Benjamin Constant (1767–1830) himself hardly ever used the term 'democracy' and certainly did not think of himself as its advocate. According to his own, oft-quoted introduction to the *Melanges de littérature et de politique*, he was above all a defender of liberty:

[1] 'The revived political philosophy nowhere seems to push its reflection beyond what administrators of the state would argue about democracy and law, about rights and the rule of law. In short, above all it seems to guarantee the correspondence between what the great classical doctrines and the ordinary forms of state legitimation posit about liberal democracy'. Unless indicated otherwise, all translations are my own.

> For forty years I have defended the same principle, liberty in everything, in religion, in philosophy, in literature, in industry, in politics: and by liberty I mean the triumph of individuality over both an authority wishing to rule despotically and the masses demanding the right to make a minority subject to a majority.[2]

The collection of texts published in 1829 was meant to assemble Constant's intellectual testament and support his application to the *Académie Française*. Constant eventually did not succeed in obtaining one of the prestigious seats in the *Académie*, but his self-appreciation and self-presentation as a 'defender of liberty in everything' did achieve a tremendous resonance.

An early case in point was his state funeral service on 12 December 1830, where reportedly a massive crowd had shown up and waved the flags of the Liberal Party as a tribute.[3] In the century and a half that followed his death, the political philosophical reception of Constant's work was distinctively marked by its purportedly 'liberal' character. His thought was always discussed – approvingly or critically – for its promotion of individual liberty and private interests, for its plea for minimal state interference and limited governmental power, for its acceptance of commerce and the free market or for any given combination of the former characteristics. Already in 1852, Karl Marx mockingly listed Constant among the 'true spokesmen and interpreters of bourgeois society', a society that was 'entirely absorbed in the production of wealth and in peaceful competitive struggle'.[4] Carl Schmitt even cast Constant in the role of 'the initiator of the whole liberal spirit in the nineteenth century'[5] and read his political theory as a paragon of the 'bourgeois liberalism'[6] that he himself so vehemently detested. That 'bourgeois' liberalism is defined, according to Schmitt, by its protection of 'personal freedom, private property, contractual liberty, and freedom of commerce and profession'[7] and its downgrading of the state to a 'strictly regulated

[2] B. Constant, *Mélanges de littérature et de politique* (Paris: Pichon et Didier, 1829), p. vi. The translation is taken from G. A. Kelly, *The Humane Comedy* (Cambridge University Press, 1992), p. 2.

[3] J. Powell, *The Triumph of Liberty: A 2,000-Year History, told through the Lives of Freedom's Greatest Champions* (New York: Free Press, 2000), p. 99.

[4] K. Marx, The Eighteenth Brumaire of Louis Bonaparte, www.marxists.org/archive/marx/works/1852/18th-brumaire/, p. 5.

[5] C. Schmitt, *The Concept of the Political* (The University of Chicago Press, 1996), p. 74.

[6] C. Schmitt, *Constitutional Theory* (Durham and London: Duke University Press, 2008), pp. 318–319.

[7] *Ibid.*, p. 169.

servant of society'.[8] From a radically opposite political position, but based on the very same aspects of Constant's work, Isaiah Berlin in his famous 1958 Oxford inaugural lecture nominated Constant as 'the most eloquent of all defenders of freedom and privacy',[9] and (together with John Stuart Mill) as 'one of the fathers of liberalism' who advocated 'a maximum degree of non-interference compatible with the minimum demands of social life'.[10] Berlin insisted that Constant had understood that 'the real cause of oppression' lies 'in the mere fact of the accumulation of power'.[11] Later on, none other than the neoliberal economist and Nobel laureate F. A. Hayek approvingly mentioned Constant as one of the 'intellectual leaders of 19th century liberalism',[12] who despite his nationality belonged to the superior British tradition of liberalism that understood liberty in terms of 'spontaneity and the absence of coercion' rather than as 'the pursuit and attainment of an absolute collective purpose'. According to Hayek, the latter – distinctively French – understanding of liberty was at the source of 'totalitarian democracy'.[13]

The 'liberal' reception of Constant's work was predominant until the late 1970s, when a discernible shift took place in the appreciation of his thought. Not only has it become a far more popular object of study over the past four decades; the way its general political orientation and implications are understood has also changed remarkably. More contemporary interpreters have moved away from the uncomplicated understanding of Constant as a credulous defender of individual liberty and minimal government. Instead, they started to read Constant as a more nuanced and complex political thinker by emphasizing the 'democratic' elements of his thought.[14] Today, scholars in intellectual history, constitutional theory and political philosophy study Constant's political theory

[8] *Ibid.*

[9] I. Berlin, 'Two concepts of liberty' in *Four Essays on Liberty* (Oxford University Press, 1969), p. 126. Helena Rosenblatt classifies Berlin's account as 'anti-Rousseauian and essentially anti-democratic'. H. Rosenblatt, 'Eclipses and revivals: Constant's reception in France and America, 1830–2007' in H. Rosenblatt (ed.), *The Cambridge Companion to Constant* (Cambridge University Press, 2009), p. 370.

[10] *Ibid.*, p. 24.

[11] *Ibid.*, p. 26.

[12] F. A. Hayek, *The Constitution of Liberty* (The University of Chicago Press, 2011), pp. 129–130.

[13] *Ibid.*, pp. 110–111. Hayek refers to and quotes from J. L. Talmon, *The Origins of Totalitarian Democracy* (London: Secker and Warburg, 1952).

[14] Helena Rosenblatt has developed a similar, but more nuanced argument within the context of a more complete overview of the reception of Constant's work. Because of the comprehensiveness and sophistication of her overview, Rosenblatt is less attuned to

first and foremost for its supposedly visionary synthesis of liberalism and democracy. While doing so, they either implicitly assume or explicitly argue that Constant's work has lost little or none of its relevance for theory and practice today and that it can (and should) serve as a template for contemporary Western constitutionalism.

Within the Anglo-American literature, Stephen Holmes has been one of the first to take issue with what he calls the 'conventional' reading of Constant as an 'antidemocratic liberal'.[15] Instead, he has urged other contemporary liberal democratic theorists to follow his lead and read Constant's constitutional theory for its successful *combination* of 'liberal freedom' and democratic 'self-rule'.[16] Constant is especially commended for the way in which he 'favoured popular sovereignty so long as it was organized within the framework of a liberal constitution'.[17] Many projects akin to Holmes's have since been pursued by Constant scholars,[18] some of them even expressly claiming that Constant's work was one of the primary sources of western liberal democratic theory.[19] More recent contributions have certainly kept the ball rolling. Helena Rosenblatt, for instance, has insisted that we should pay attention to Constant's 'promotion of profoundly democratic values and his deeply moral vision'.[20] Similarly, Thierry Chopin has argued that 'Constant provides the elements that allow us to go beyond the limitations of modern individualism and conceive of the indispensable synthesis of the liberal vindication of

the significant features that are shared by the 'liberal democratic turn', of which I argue she is also a part. Rosenblatt, 'Eclipses and revivals', pp. 351–377.

15 S. Holmes, *Benjamin Constant and the Making of Modern Liberty* (Yale University Press, 1980), p. 2.

16 *Ibid.*, p. 78. Emphasis in the original.

17 *Ibid.*, p. 10.

18 E.g. Kelly, *The Humane Comedy*; G. A. Kelly, 'Constant commotions: avatars of a pure Liberal', *The Journal of Modern History*, 54 (1982), 497–518; B. Fontana, *Benjamin Constant and the Post-revolutionary Mind* (Yale University Press, 1991); P. Delbouille, 'Aux sources de la démocratie libérale: Benjamin Constant', *Revue d'Histoire littéraire de la France*, 2 (2006), 259–207; L. Jaume, *L'individu effacé ou le paradoxe du libéralisme français* (Paris: Fayard, 1997); K. S. Vincent, *Benjamin Constant and the Birth of French Liberalism* (New York: Palgrave Macmillan, 2011); A. Jainchill, *The Republican Origins of French Liberalism* (New York: Cornell University Press, 2008); H. Grange, *Benjamin Constant amoureux et républicain 1795–1799* (Paris: Les Belles Lettres, 2004); T. Chopin, *Benjamin Constant: Le libéralisme inquiet* (Paris: Editions Michalon, 2002); T. Todorov, *Benjamin Constant: la passion démocratique* (Paris: Hachette, 1997).

19 Holmes, *The Making of Modern Liberty*; Todorov, *Benjamin Constant: la passion démocratique*; Delbouille, 'Aux sources de la démocratie libérale'.

20 H. Rosenblatt, 'Re-evaluating Benjamin Constant's liberalism: Industrialism, Saint-Simonianism and the Restoration years', *History of European Ideas*, 30 (2004), 37.

individual liberty and the democratic aspiration to equality: Constant aims to prove that it is feasible to hope for a real liberal democracy'.[21] Even the 'fresh account of modern liberalism's beginnings and evolution'[22] provided by Andreas Kalyvas and Ira Katznelson aligns itself smoothly with the tried-and-true recipes of Constant-scholarship when it concludes that Constant's mature thought culminated 'in a more synthetic hybrid' of 'immanent liberalism . . . encompassing three apparently opposing principles of legitimacy: democratic, liberal and traditional'.[23]

Even without going into the details of each of these particular accounts, this brief anthology shows that indeed a proper 'liberal democratic turn' has taken place in Constant-scholarship, even if it may not have been explicitly labelled as such. This turn insists on having discovered in Constant's political writings the prototype of a liberal democratic theory that is able to merge individual liberty and limited government with popular sovereignty and that is hence of crucial relevance for the present. This is, of course, a weighty claim. Because despite the fact that liberal democracy is a familiar element of our political imaginary in day-to-day practice, formulating its exact definition remains a complex and much-contested theoretical puzzle. And the concept of popular sovereignty is one of the pieces that is notoriously difficult (and crucial) to put into place. Recently, this has been illustrated once again by the upsurge of literature generated by the 'populist challenge'. The fact that populism is considered to be 'a threat not to democracy per se but rather to the dominant liberal variant of democracy'[24] explicitly attests to the cumbersome incorporation of the concept of popular sovereignty into liberal democratic theory.

In this chapter, I aim to contribute to the ongoing efforts to theorize the concept of popular sovereignty within a liberal democratic framework, as well as to suggest a fresh avenue for research within Constant-scholarship. My contribution takes the form of a critical analysis of the interpretation of Benjamin Constant put forward by the famous contemporary French philosopher Marcel Gauchet. This interpretation, distinctively shaped by the theoretical framework of the Lefortian circle, has

21 Chopin, *Le libéralisme inquiet*, p. 117.

22 A. Kalyvas and I. Katznelson, 'We are "modern men": Benjamin Constant and the discovery of an immanent liberalism', *Constellations*, 6 (1999), 513.

23 Kalyvas and Katznelson, 'We are modern men', 514.

24 W. Galston, 'The populist challenge to liberal democracy', *Journal of Democracy*, 2 (2018), 11.

become a prominent point of reference, both within the literature on Constant and within the broader philosophical debate on democracy. I will single out the 'positive' conception of popular sovereignty that underpins Gauchet's reading and is exemplary for the liberal democratic turn in Constant-scholarship. The alternative reading of Constant that I will point to starts from the assumption that Constant developed a 'negative' conception of popular sovereignty.[25]

Gauchet made one of his earliest theoretical contributions in the form of a lengthy and dense introduction to a collection of Constant's political writings edited by Gauchet himself.[26] 'L'illusion lucide du libéralisme', first published in 1980, remains a standard reference in the literature on Constant, and it has been a key source for the liberal democratic turn that Constant-scholarship has taken since. It is no coincidence that Gauchet's account has been credited with helping 'to propel the Constant revival',[27] as it is grounded in a solid theoretical reflection on the principle of popular sovereignty. In the ensuing liberal democratic contributions to the literature on Constant, the conception of popular sovereignty remains much more implicit or underdeveloped. As an unfortunate consequence of its theoretical depth, Gauchet's study of Constant is a perfect example of the complexity of thought and style for which he is known. This may very well be one of the reasons why, after forty years, Gauchet's 'brilliant and absorbing exposition and defence of Benjamin Constant's thought' has not yet been critically assessed, at least not in terms of its philosophical content.[28]

[25] Gauchet published a complementary text entitled 'Constant: Le libéralisme entre le droit et l'histoire' in 1986, see M. Gauchet, 'Constant: Le libéralisme entre le droit et l'histoire', in F. Châtelet, O. Duhamel and E. Pisier (eds.), *Dictionnaire des œuvres politiques* (Paris: Presses Universitaires Français, 1986). This text was reprinted in M. Gauchet, *La condition politique* (Paris: Gallimard, 2005), pp. 275–304. I will refer to the reprint of 2005. Gauchet also devoted the last chapter of his *La révolution des pouvoirs* to Constant's conception of a neutral power, M. Gauchet, *La révolution des pouvoirs: La souveraineté, le peuple et la représentation 1789–1799* (Paris: Gallimard, 1995), pp. 237–255.

[26] M. Gauchet, 'L'illusion lucide du libéralisme' in Gauchet (ed.), *De la liberté chez les modernes: Ecrits Politiques* (Paris: Librairie General Française, 1980), pp. 11–91. I have made use of the former original version here, even though in the literature on Constant, references are usually based on the slightly updated version of 1997, M. Gauchet, 'L'illusion lucide du libéralisme' in Gauchet (ed.), *Ecrits politiques* (Paris: Gallimard, 1997), pp. 12–110.

[27] H. Rosenblatt, 'Preface' in H. Rosenblatt (ed.), *The Cambridge Companion to Constant* (Cambridge University Press, 2009), p. xi.

[28] A notable exception is the brilliant article by Samuel Moyn from which this quote is taken. S. Moyn, 'Savage and modern liberty. Marcel Gauchet and the origins of New French Thought', *European Journal of Political Theory*, 4 (2005), 172.

The structure of my analysis is three-pronged. First, I will demonstrate the historical embeddedness and particularity of the liberal democratic rendition of Constant by means of an overview of the historical research that covers the intellectual and ideological transformations that characterized the 1970s and 1980s. This research shows that Gauchet's work on Constant was part of a larger trend in Western philosophy that was particularly evident in France. It might seem redundant to insist on the fact that interpretive accounts of historical sources (such as Gauchet's interpretation of Constant) are themselves also historically laden, but due to the contemporary predominance of the liberal democratic idiom in Western political theory and practice, this historical particularity often tends to go unnoticed.

Following this historical contextualization, I will present my conceptual reflections on Gauchet's interpretation of Constant. My aim in this respect is not primarily to assess the soundness of this interpretation but rather to lay bare its philosophical presuppositions and implications. In order to do so, Gauchet's position first needs to be situated within the theoretical framework of the Lefortian circle of which he was a part. This framework – which Gauchet helped to develop in the late 1970s and early 1980s – is still an important source of inspiration for contemporary continental political philosophy and democratic theory. And it had an obvious influence on Gauchet's analysis of Constant. The theoretical core of that analysis consists of a distinction between the republican and the liberal democratic conception of popular sovereignty, the latter of which Gauchet acclaims and attributes to Constant. By teasing out the different theoretical elements of these conceptions, I show that they both boil down to what I will call a *positive* conception of popular sovereignty, meaning that their elementary structure has the form of a positive or a constitutive relationship. The liberal democratic conception of popular sovereignty that Gauchet formulates refines the understanding of this relationship, but remains within that *positive* structure.

In the third and final section of the chapter, some arguments and suggestions are offered for an alternative interpretation of Constant's political thought that is based on a *negative* conception of sovereignty. The contextualization established in the first section suggests, indeed, that Gauchet's liberal democratic rendition of Constant's work is only one possible and historically specific interpretation. I believe that Constant-scholarship could benefit from a fresh perspective in order to reassert its contemporary relevance. The *negative* conception of sovereignty starts from the idea that Constant's theoretical considerations about the limited nature of popular sovereignty do not aim to posit a relation between the collective subject and the constitutional system but, on the contrary, to undo this relation altogether. To put it even more strongly, I believe Constant's notion of popular sovereignty does not posit the existence of a collective subject at all.

1 The French Liberal Moment and the Third Wave of Democracy: The Liberal Democratic Turn in Historical Context

The French intellectual climate of the late 1970s and early 1980s has long since fascinated intellectual historians of both continental and Anglo-American signature.[29] Research ongoing since the 1990s has shown that, under the sway of a particular coalescence of historical circumstances, French political thought underwent a 'perceptible turn in intellectual orientation'[30] that resulted in 'something akin to an ideological revolution'.[31] The existence of this turn, also labelled in the literature as the 'French liberal moment', is now taken as fact.[32] Within the span of roughly a decade, the dominant thread in critical and progressive political thinking shifted from Marxism to a strongly anti-totalitarian and distinctly liberal outlook. The effects of this shift include a wide range of approaches and political perspectives, ranging from the 'liberalization' of radical left-wing thought (e.g. Cornelius Castoriadis), to the popularization of the more conservative centrist liberalism (e.g. Raymond Aaron) to the polemical anti-philosophy (e.g. Bernard-Henri Levy and other 'nouveaux philosophes').

The causes, interpretation and effects of the shift are, however, still heavily debated. The earlier 1990s approach, mostly pursued by American scholars,[33] tends to single out the slow (but felicitous) process

[29] For the most prominent examples, see the references below.

[30] M. Lilla, 'The other velvet revolution: Continental liberalism and its discontents', *Daedalus*, 2 (1994), 148.

[31] I. Stewart, 'France's anti-68 liberal revival' in E. Chabal (ed.), *France since the 1970s: History, Politics and Memory in an Age of Uncertainty* (London: Bloomsbury Publishing, 2014), p. 199.

[32] See e.g. the title of a collection of essays by I. Stewart and S. Sawyer (ed.), *In Search of the Liberal Moment: Democracy, Anti-totalitarianism, and Intellectual Politics in France since 1950* (New York: Palgrave Macmillan, 2016).

[33] Lilla, 'The other velvet revolution' and M. Lilla (ed.), *New French Thought: Political Philosophy* (Princeton University Press, 1994). Other well-known contributions are T. Judt, *Past Imperfect: French Intellectuals 1944–1956* (University of California Press, 1992); S. Khilnani, *Arguing Revolution: The Intellectual Left in Postwar France* (Yale University

of 'progressive embourgeoisement' of post-war society, according to which France and other Western European countries had gradually come to embrace 'a limited constitutional government, an independent judiciary, multiparty elections, universal suffrage, civilian control of the military and police, rights to free assembly and worship, a large middle class, and a developed consumer economy'.[34] According to the 1990s narrative, this so-called 'third wave of democracy' deepened the gulf between everyday social practices and the political theories defended by European left-wing intellectuals, who stubbornly persevered with their 'endless theorizing about Marxism'.[35] The gap was purportedly bridged very abruptly in the early 1970s, when 'world events that elicited little immediate response elsewhere in Western Europe – the translation of Alexander Solzhenitsyn's Gulag Archipelago, the butcheries in Cambodia, the flight of the boat people, the rise of Solidarity in Poland – suddenly set off a profound *crise de conscience* among the French'.[36]

More recent contributions to the literature are less univocally enthusiastic about the French liberal turn. The change in appreciation seems to coincide with the turn of the millennium when the success of right-wing parties in France as well as in other European countries was perceptibly rising.[37] French scholars in particular have been ruthless in their criticism of the purported conservatism on the 1980s 'neo-reactionary' liberals, arguing that their rejection of the Marxists ideals and their acclamation of the status quo (i.e. their advocacy of human rights, representative democracy and social unity) had provided a second wind to nationalist and xenophobic tendencies.[38] Contemporary research also focuses more on developments specific and internal to France, rather than on the general flow of world

Press, 1993); T. Judt, *The Burden of Responsibility: Blum, Camus, Aron, and the French Twentieth Century* (The University of Chicago Press, 1998).

34 Lilla, 'The other velvet revolution', 130.

35 *Ibid.*, 148.

36 *Ibid.*, 149.

37 A useful overview of the success of right-wing parties in Europe was published in *The Guardian*. 'Special report: Europe's far right', www.theguardian.com/gall/0,711990,00.html. Among French left-wing intellectuals something akin to a collective trauma exists with regard to the unexpected success of Jean-Marie Le Penn, then-president of the French extreme-right party *Le Front National*, in the presidential elections of 2002.

38 E.g. D. Lindenberg, *Le rappel à l'ordre : Enquête sur les nouveaux réactionnaires* (Paris: Editions du Seuil, 2002); D. Eribon, *D'une révolution conservatrice et de ses effets sur la gauche française* (Paris: Editions Léo Scheer, 2007); S. Audier, *La pensée anti-68: Essai sur les origines d'une restauration intellectuelle* (Paris: La Découverte, 2008); C. Fauré, *Les néoconservateurs à la française* (Paris: Chryséis Editions, 2012). For earlier criticism, see e.g. P. Anderson, *In the Tracks of Historical Materialism* (London: Verso, 1983).

history as an external trigger. It points to particular catalysts for the 1970s and 1980s 'liberal moment' that were present both in the French intellectual community and in the broader public sphere. These factors include the strong dissatisfaction with the nationalist and statist politics that the early Fifth Republic pursued under the sway of president De Gaulle,[39] the initial enthusiasm for and the subsequent disappointment with the uprisings of May 1968, which were particularly intense in France,[40] and the aversion to the centralist strategies of the *Parti Communist français* and its 1973 *Union de la gauche* with the *Parti socialist.*[41]

Over and above their differences, both the older and the more recent intellectual historical approach show that the late 1970s and early 1980s constituted the closing chapter of the transitional period that followed the end of the Second World War. More concretely, they both demonstrate that in France, the philosophical processing of these altered social and political conditions amounted to a deliberate endeavour to renew social and political philosophy.[42] The prevailing theoretical frameworks – orthodox Marxism (associated with the ideal of an all-sweeping and potentially violent proletarian revolution) and classical liberalism (associated with elitism and conservatism) – were no longer considered adequate to conceptualize contemporary society. This was a society that longed for peace, prosperity and technological progress, but where at the same time a vibrant anti-authoritarian and anti-bureaucratic ambience was present, combined with resilient demands for individual freedom, social emancipation and political participation, as well as an inclination to collective action.[43]

[39] E. Chabal, *A Divided Republic: State, Nation and Citizenship in Contemporary France* (Cambridge University Press, 2005), pp. 17, 59.

[40] For an in-depth analysis of the events, see e.g. J.-P. Le Goff, 'Mai 68: La France entre deux mondes', *Le Débat*, 2 (2008), 83–100.

[41] M. S. Christofferson, *French Intellectuals against the Left: The Anti-Totalitarian Moment of the 1970s* (Oxford: Berghahn Books, 2004); Stewart, 'France's anti-68 liberal revival', pp. 212–213.

[42] F. Berthot, 'Textures et Libre (1971–1980): Une tentative de renouvellement de la philosophie politique en France' in F. Hourmant and J. Baudouin (eds.), *Les revues et la dynamique des ruptures*, p. 2.

[43] M. Gauchet, J. Lambinet, C. Lefort, R. Legros, M. Loreau, and M. Richir, 'Editorial', *Textures*, 2–3 (1971), 4; C. Lefort and M. Gauchet, 'Sur la démocratie : le politique et l'institution du social', *Textures*, 2–3 (1971), 7–8. The latter text is said to be a summary by Gauchet of the course that Lefort had taught at the University of Caen in 1966–1967. It has a somewhat notorious status, because the disagreement over its original intellectual ownership eventually caused a rift between Lefort and Gauchet.

Even though this project of renewal was not in and of itself historically oriented, it is not surprising that it was deemed necessary to connect it to a larger historical tradition. The 'liberal moment' therefore also amounted to a 'liberal revival', in the sense of 'the recovery of canonical French liberal thinkers by recent French thinkers with an interest in traditional liberal themes'.[44] The contemporaneous work of the famous intellectual historian François Furet (1927–1997), whose *Penser la Revolution Française* (1978) defended a view of the French Revolution as an essentially anti-democratic and totalitarian event, paved much of the way for these semi-historical undertakings. In particular, the theories of nineteenth-century French post-revolutionary thinkers, such as Benjamin Constant, Alexis de Tocqueville and François Guizot, were reclaimed as an important source of inspiration for the philosophical reflections triggered by the contemporary social and political conditions.

This is precisely where and when the theoretical interest in liberal democracy came to the fore. In fact, I think it is fair to say that 'the third wave of democracy' and 'the liberal moment' in France amounted to the emergence of a distinct branch of *liberal democratic* theory,[45] aspiring to analyse the conditions of possibility of social and political change *from within* the contemporaneous legal, political, social and economic setting (rather than changing the setting altogether). This comes down to an aspiration to give liberal democracy as a distinct political regime a proper theoretical foundation. Such a theoretical/political ambition was indeed difficult to accommodate within the framework of either Marxism or liberalism. Marxism was deemed too radical both in terms of its revolutionary purposes and its historical determinism: it seemed to discard the idea of change within the existent institutional system from the outset. The position of classical liberalism and its bourgeois ruling class was deemed too conservative, too exclusionary and not politicized enough. Both paradigms treated political power as a side-effect of other, more elementary, economic forces.[46] As an

[44] N. Rosenblum, 'Rethinking the French liberal moment: Some thoughts on the heterogeneous origins of Lefort and Gauchet's social philosophy', in Stewart and Sawyer, *In Search of the Liberal Moment*, p. 62. Many other commentators have noted that these historical reflections always had contemporary intentions.

[45] Gauchet would later specify that the aim of 'detrivialising the idea of liberal democracy' was an important intellectual project for him. M. Gauchet, *L'avènement de la démocratie*, 4 vols. (Paris: Gallimard, 2007), *La révolution modern*, vol. I, p. 15. The reference is taken from B. Bachofen, 'Detrivialising democracy. Marcel Gauchet between enchantment and disenchantment', *La vie des idées.fr*, 30 April 2008, https://booksandideas.net/Detrivialising-democracy-Marcel.html.

[46] Lefort and Gauchet, 'Sur la démocratie', 8.

alternative to both approaches, the 'Lefortian' circle of French intellectuals developed a specific conception of liberal democracy which put the notion of political power at its very centre. Their theoretical approach, discussed in the section below, has greatly influenced contemporary, radical democratic thought,[47] to the point that the validity of the Lefortian paradigm often seems to be taken for granted. Yet as I have shown, this approach also has a specific historical background, from which its content cannot be disentangled.

2 Lucid Liberal Democracy. Gauchet's Positive Conception of Popular Sovereignty

Political Modernity and Popular Sovereignty: The Constructivist Framework of the Lefortian Circle

As mentioned above, Marcel Gauchet was part of a small but influential group of intellectuals that in the post-1968 era gathered around the person of Claude Lefort.[48] Lefort, at the time teaching sociology at the University of Caen, was a former student of Merleau-Ponty and well known for his participation in *Socialisme ou Barbarie*, the anti-Stalinist 'revolutionary' group and journal that he had cofounded with Cornelius Castoriadis in 1949 and left in 1958.[49] The intellectuals associated with this Lefortian circle (Lefort, Castoriadis and Gauchet, but also Miguel Abensour, Pierre Rosanvallon and Pierre Manent) all had their distinct philosophical ambitions and later pursued their careers in very different directions. But their initial theoretical projects did have as a strong common denominator the objective to reflect on the conditions of possibility of social and political subjectivity from the point of view of the present. And these reflections produced resonant theoretical positions about modern society and its particular political forms (i.e. totalitarianism on the one hand and liberal

[47] See the references in P. Minkinnen, 'The tragic politics of public law', in M. A. Wilkinson and M. W. Dowdle (eds.), *Questioning the Foundations of Public Law* (New York: Hart Publishing, 2018), p. 54, footnotes 22–23.

[48] M. Behrent, 'Religion, republicanism and depoliticization: Two intellectual itineraries, Régis Debray and Marcel Gauchet' in J. Bourg (ed.), *After the Deluge: New Perspective on the Intellectual and Cultural History of Post-war France* (Oxford: Lextington Books, 2004), pp. 329–330.

[49] Moyn, 'Savage and Modern Liberty', 166; Berthot, 'Textures et Libre', pp. 5–6. *Socialisme ou Barbarie* originated as a dissident subdivision of the *Parti Communiste Internationalist* and the journal was originally meant to disseminate the group's political views among their adherents.

democracy on the other).[50] In their more anthropologically oriented works, Lefort and Gauchet even hinted at the discovery of an 'elementary form and general reason' of political power, i.e., a universal logic of power that is not confined to the specific historical conditions of modernity.[51]

In its most basic configuration, this 'elementary form and general reason' of political power refers to the philosophical assumption – shared by Lefort, Gauchet and other 'Lefortians' – that the *institution* of society is an inherently political fact. According to this reasoning, the validity of concrete laws, norms and customs within a society, and thus social order as such, depends upon a more original founding principle. This principle endows society (as a whole) with a particular meaning or identity, or, more precisely, with an understanding of itself as a collective entity.[52] There is hence a form of reflexivity at play in this collective understanding: society perceives itself as a unity with a certain meaning, through its founding principle. Lefort and Gauchet emphasize that the institution of this collective meaning or identity requires the manifestation of power, and that this power needs to be understood as both symbolic and political in character.[53] In other words, they understand the nature of political power to be inherently symbolical and the function of symbolic power to be inherently political. This claim is fundamental because it implies that not only the meaning but the very existence of society relies on the manifestation of (political) power. As a second, equally fundamental pillar of their theoretical framework, both Lefort and Gauchet posit pluralism and conflict as the basic ontological condition of society.[54] This ontological position in fact implies that the collective identity upon

[50] Lefort and Gauchet, 'Sur la démocratie', 11.

[51] See e.g. C. Lefort, 'L'échange et la lutte des hommes', in *Les formes de l'histoire* (Paris: Gallimard, 1978), pp. 21–77; C. Lefort, 'Permanence du theologico-politique?' in *Essais sur le politique* (Paris: Seuil, 1986), pp. 251–300; M. Gauchet, 'La dette du sens et les racines de l'état : politique de la religion primitive', *Libre*, 2 (1977), 5–43. Reprinted in M. Gauchet, *La condition politique* (Paris: Gallimard, 2005), pp. 277–304. In the following footnotes, I refer to the reprint of 2005.

[52] Gauchet, 'La dette du sens', pp. 45–46.

[53] The work of the Lefortian circle is known for reinterpreting the heterogeneous French 'phenomenological' tradition (including thinkers as divergent as Levinas, Merleau Ponty, Mauss, Levi-Strauss and Lacan) that emphasized the overarching symbolic dimension and structure of collective life, in a distinctively political manner. For an excellent analysis, see G. Labelle, '"Institution symbolique", "Loi", et "Décision sans sujet" ? Y a-t-il deux philosophies de l'histoire chez Marcel Gauchet?', *Studies in Religion/Sciences Religieuses*, 3–4 (2004), 469–493.

[54] Lefort and Gauchet, 'Sur la démocratie', 10.

which social order is necessarily based is merely a representation of unity, rather than a unity that is actually present within society. It has a necessary but purely virtual, i.e., constructed, character.[55] Society cannot exist without a representation of unity, but it can never be objectively 'one'.[56]

In a more detailed rendering, the 'elementary form and general reason' of political power points to the fact that the manifestation of power/the organization of society follows a specific *structure*. In his early works, Gauchet was particularly insistent on the claim that political power is situated in and exercised from a 'transcendent' position that is distant and hence distinct from society: not only does society need a locus of political power in order for it to see and understand itself as a whole (and thus to exist), this locus also needs to be separated from society.[57] For Gauchet 'transcendence' thus implies a form of 'original dispossession' that society inflicts on itself, but of which it is not necessarily aware.[58] Hence, there are a number of ways in which a society can relate to this foundational dispossession. Within Gauchet's theory, the 'elementary form and general reason of political power' therefore also points to the assumption that a society's political *form* (i.e. its concrete political organization or regime) determines and expresses the way in which society understands and copes with this original 'dispossession'.

The latter assumption determines the stakes of Lefort's and Gauchet's analyses of the democratic regime. Their aim is to examine and explain how democracy – as the contemporary form of political power – simultaneously shapes and discloses the relationship between the social and the political and, in other words, how it determines the possibilities for social and political change. The Lefortian approach to democracy is considered to be an important source of inspiration for contemporary continental political philosophers who are working on 'open-ended, post-foundational, radically democratic political theory'.[59] It is evident why the normative implications of the fundamental theoretical principles that this circle defended are evidently still appealing to critical thinkers: not only did they consider diversity and conflict to be the ontological

[55] *Ibid.*, 17–18.
[56] *Ibid.*, 16.
[57] Gauchet, 'La dette du sens', p. 64.
[58] *Ibid.*, p. 48.
[59] J. D. Ingram, 'The politics of Claude Lefort's political: Between liberalism and radical democracy', *Thesis Eleven*, 8 (2006), 133. Ingrams names Laclau and Mouffe, and Nancy and Lacoue-Labarthe as the most prominent examples.

condition of society but they also emphasized that the sense of collective identity that determines social order is inherently subject to contestation and to change. And it must be noted that, despite the fact that Gauchet's political position is nowadays considered to be controversially conservative,[60] at the very beginning of his academic career, he was deemed to be 'the most brilliant member of Lefort's circle'.[61]

Both Lefort and Gauchet define democracy as a distinctively modern form of political power, as they assume that it is based on the principle of popular sovereignty, which came to the fore in the revolutions of the seventeenth and eighteenth centuries.[62] In Gauchet's terminology, the principle of popular sovereignty gave political power an explicitly 'representative character', meaning that 'its purpose is no longer to guarantee the submission to an external norm, but to assure that the social body corresponds to itself'.[63] This implies that the locus of political power became expressly situated within society (rather than in an unattainable outside).[64] Yet Gauchet also emphasizes that this representative character did not mark the advent of a radically new form and reason of political power, but that it merely entailed a transformation, albeit a profound one, of the 'elementary form and general reason' that was discussed above. In modern society, political power remains constitutive of and distinct from society because it is allocated to a separate and distinct sphere of human existence, i.e., the sphere of 'the political'. Or as Michael Behrent has succinctly put it: 'The political, in short, is the "other" through which society becomes its "own"'.[65] Yet at the same time, for Gauchet, democracy, or liberal democracy to be more precise, is the regime that makes it possible for society not so much to overcome its original dispossession but to become aware of it and gain control over it.[66]

60 In 2014, two left-wing public intellectuals, Edouard Louis and Geoffroy de Lagasnerie, launched a boycott and a petition against Gauchet in the newspaper *Libération*, because the latter was selected to give the inaugural lecture at the prestigious yearly forum *Rendez-vous de l'histoire*. In the end, the petition was signed by 229 intellectuals. See www.liberation.fr/debats/2014/08/06/pourquoi-il-faut-boycotter-les-rendez-vous-de-l-histoire-un-appel-collectif_1076316.

61 Behrent, 'Religion, republicanism and depoliticization', p. 330.

62 N. Doyle, 'Democracy as socio-cultural project of individual and collective sovereignty. Claude Lefort, Marcel Gauchet and the French debate on modern autonomy', *Thesis Eleven*, 75 (2003), 77. Doyle points to the difference with Castoriadis's understanding of democracy, which is based on the ancient Greek model.

63 Gauchet, 'Le libéralisme entre le droit et l'histoire', p. 289.

64 Doyle, 'Democracy as socio-cultural project', 77.

65 Behrent, 'Religion, republicanism, and depoliticization', p. 330.

66 Doyle, 'Democracy as socio-cultural project', 88–89.

As discussed below, Gauchet's analysis starts from eighteenth-century social contract theory (as exemplified by the work of Rousseau). It was there and then that the purest and most absolute philosophical expression of popular sovereignty was formulated, thereby providing the *intellectual* resources for the modern democratic revolution. While Gauchet spends a considerable amount of time on his discussion of the republican conception of popular sovereignty, he never conceals his critical position towards it. Gauchet claims more precisely, as I explain, that the republican ideal of 'radical' democracy has an inherently 'holistic' element to it, as a result of which its conception of popular sovereignty generates a conservative logic.[67] Ultimately, Gauchet's argument thus attests to the normative supremacy of 'liberal' democracy, as it differentiated itself from 'radical' republicanism. More precisely, Gauchet insists that the ideal view of a modern democratic society theorized by republicanism could not have started to 'materialize' before the theoretical and practical structures of liberal democracy were put into place.[68] And the work of Benjamin Constant takes pride of place in the development of these structures:

> The entire development of our political reality is the result of the confrontation and ensuing modification – for better or for worse – of these two interpretations of the exercise of democratic sovereignty. Rousseau remains the one who has designed the *end* to which it responds. Constant remains the one who has named the *means* by which it is concretized. Our entire truth is constituted by the subtle intertwinement of a double recognition with a double disapproval.[69]

Gauchet is interested in Constant's work because he assumes that, rather than a 'radical' version of democracy, it theorizes a 'liberal' approach that adheres to the principle of popular sovereignty.[70]

[67] Gauchet, 'Le libéralisme entre le droit et l'histoire', pp. 290–291.

[68] Gauchet, *La révolution des pouvoirs*, p. 8.

[69] Gauchet, 'Le libéralisme entre le droit et l'histoire', p. 284: 'Le développement entier de notre réalité politique sort de la confrontation et de l'ajustement trouvé tant bien que mal entre ces deux interprétations de l'exercice de la souveraineté démocratique. Rousseau demeure celui qui a désigné la fin à laquelle il répond Constant reste celui qui a nommé le moyen par lequel il s'est concrétisé. Voilà de quoi notre vérité s'est faite de l'entrecroisement subtil d'une double reconnaissance avec une double méprise'.

[70] Gauchet, 'Le libéralisme entre le droit et l'histoire', pp. 282–283.

La faute à Rousseau: The Republican Conception of Popular Sovereignty

Gauchet's analysis of democracy thus starts from his interpretation of the republican conception of popular sovereignty. From its unrefined interpretation and hasty dismissal of revolutionary republicanism, it is clear that 'L'illusion lucide du libéralisme' (1980) predated the thorough analysis of Rousseau's work that Gauchet would complete a few years later. Already in 'Le libéralisme entre le droit et l'histoire' (1986), Gauchet had taken a much more nuanced and positive stance towards the issue, and his second monograph *La révolution des droits de l'homme* (1989) offered 'a complete re-evaluation of Rousseau's thought and its Jacobin posterity, which highlights the radical novelty of Rousseau's political philosophy'.[71] Yet the aim here is neither to recount Gauchet's narrative on the merits of revolutionary republicanism nor the evolution of his views on the matter. Instead, it is to analyse the conceptual structure that underlies his interpretation of the republican conception of popular sovereignty.[72] The essence of this structure was already in place in 1980 and it has remained largely unchanged in his subsequent writings. I argue that it contains three fundamental components, each of them introducing a different theoretical element of Gauchet's understanding of the republican conception of popular sovereignty:

(i) According to Gauchet, republican theory locates the *source of popular sovereignty* in the fundamental right to freedom and equality that it attributes to each individual member of society. Gauchet stresses that eighteenth-century social contract theory was revolutionary in the sense that it advocated a 'radical theoretical individualism'. This means that, ontologically speaking, it conceives of society as a collection of autonomous, independent and self-sufficient individuals, without assuming any inherent form of social cohesion. As a consequence, each form of social and political association needs to be instituted and maintained on a strictly voluntary

[71] Doyle, 'Democracy as socio-cultural project', 70.

[72] Needless to say, Rousseau's views on popular sovereignty, being notoriously controversial and difficult to grasp, are hotly debated in political philosophy. Present purposes allow me to sidestep this interpretive quandary because what interests me here is only Gauchet's interpretation – even if it is inaccurate or prejudiced – as a first stepping stone towards a proper insight into the latter's own (liberal democratic) conception of popular sovereignty.

basis. And each individual has a right to free and equal participation in this institution and maintenance.[73]

(ii) While the individual is the theoretical source of republican sovereignty, Gauchet emphasizes that the republican conception of sovereignty requires a *collective subject* that is capable of a unified will and agency. Republican sovereignty refers to the political community as its subject, an entity that is in theory perfectly unified and homogeneous, and that wills and acts as a single body. As a consequence, the 'representative character', i.e., the correspondence that the principle of popular sovereignty presupposes between the subject and the object of sovereignty, takes the form of a complete identification in republican theory. According to Gauchet, modern republicanism assumes the complete identity of the *subject* of popular sovereignty (i.e. the political community as a unified whole, capable of a collective will as well as collective agency) and its *object* (i.e. society at large, as a diverse and fragmented collection of individuals).[74] Republicanism allows neither reserve nor any form of demarcation or separation between the collective subject of sovereignty and society. For Gauchet, this means that the republican conception of popular sovereignty aims to articulate an understanding of political power that is purely and absolutely 'immanent'.[75]

(iii) Finally, Gauchet assumes that the republican conception of popular sovereignty posits an immediate and undistorted relation between the collective subject of sovereignty and its *product*, the legal and political institutions that are deemed to be the direct translation of that collective subject's (collective) will, without any restrictions in terms of content or extension. Consequently, republican popular sovereignty denotes not only an immanent but also an absolute form of political power: 'because it is the people itself that can decide, it can decide on everything; and those who oppose its decision, exclude themselves from the people'.[76]

When these separate theoretical elements that Gauchet traces in the positions of Rousseau and other modern republicans are put together into one comprehensive scheme, it becomes clear why this scheme

[73] Gauchet, 'L'illusion lucide du libéralisme', pp. 46–47.
[74] *Ibid.*, pp. 38, 48.
[75] *Ibid.*, p. 47.
[76] *Ibid.*, p. 45: '[P]uisque c'est le peuple même qui décide, il peut décider sur tout ; et qui s'oppose à ses décisions s'exclut du people'.

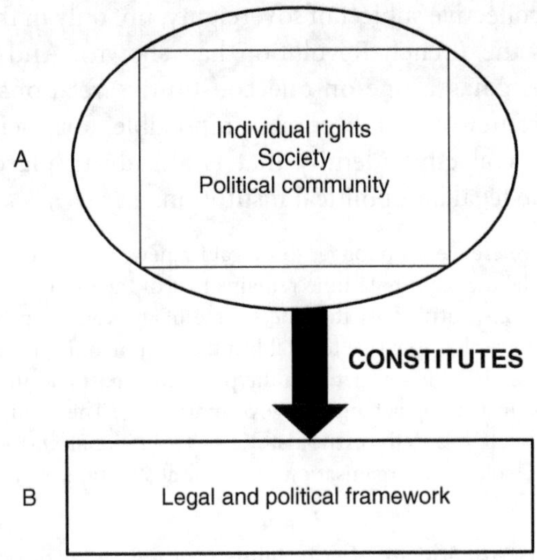

Figure 8.1 The traditional republican *positive* conception of sovereignty (a)

depicts a *positive* conception of sovereignty. My use of 'positive' here points to the fact that this conception posits a constitutive or positive relationship between two elements. In a very simplified rendering, this relationship takes the form of 'A constitutes B'. 'A' is in this case the collective subject of republican popular sovereignty, considering that it has – according to Gauchet's reading of republicanism – completely absorbed society as a collection of individuals.[77] 'B' is the legal and political framework that is produced by the will of collective subject of sovereignty (Figure 8.1).

As noted, Gauchet's critique of the republican conception of popular sovereignty concerns its 'holistic' tendencies.[78] He argues that in spite of its strong theoretical foundation in individual freedom and equality, the identity that republican theory assumes between the subject and the object of popular sovereignty ultimately requires the full assimilation of the individual (and hence of society as the collection of individuals) to the collective, unified dimension of the political structure.[79] Social diversity and pluralism need to be suppressed because of the demand for a strongly

[77] Gauchet, 'Le libéralisme entre le droit et l'histoire', p. 289.
[78] *Ibid.*, p. 289.
[79] *Ibid.*, p. 289: 'Si référence n'est plus faite à une loi antérieure à la volonté des hommes, le temps légitime demeure celui de l'origine ; c'est dans le passé fondateur, toujours, que la règle a sa source ; c'est à réaliser (éventuellement à recouvrir contre l' oubli) la

homogenized collective subject of sovereignty, not only in theory but also in practice (as the French Revolution had shown). And because that collective subject has a one-on-one constitutive relationship with the institutional framework, it becomes impossible for society to break away from the collective identity that is already in place and that is expressed in the legal and political institutions:

> Even if the reference is no longer to a legal framework preceding the will of the people, the legitimate time remains that of the origin; it is always within the constitutive past that the source of the rule is to be found. Sovereign power has to strive to establish the conjunction (or perhaps to protect it against oblivion) between the primordial past and the present; between the instituting act and the governing norm. The horizon that is defined as such is strictly extra-historical. The rational and legitimate principle of collective organisation exists in abstraction, since and for ever.[80]

The republican conception of sovereignty failed to understand that the identity of the political community is merely a constructed unity, and supposed instead its actual realization within society. It does not consider the possibility of social diversity or social change. In other words, Gauchet's critique implies that the holistic tendencies of the republican view on popular sovereignty amount to an inherently conservative political structure. This conservative structure – and hence Gauchet's critique – concerns precisely what I have defined as the *positive* aspect of the republican conception of sovereignty: it is because the republican understanding of popular sovereignty, at least in Gauchet's reading, posits a constitutive relation between its unified collective subject and its legal and political institutions, that society remains trapped within the framework of the existent collective identity.

La rupture libérale: The Liberal Democratic Conception of Popular Sovereignty

Gauchet claims that Constant's 'limited' conception of popular sovereignty is able to make a 'rupture' with the republican conception precisely with regard to its holistic and conservative tendencies.[81] However, as I argue below, the liberal democratic interpretation of popular sovereignty

conjonction entre ce passé primordial et le présent, entre l'acte instituant et la norme régnante que la puissance souveraine doit œuvrer'.

80 *Ibid.*, p. 290.

81 *Ibid.*, p. 293.

that Gauchet approvingly ascribes to Constant remains within the same frame of a *positive* conception of popular sovereignty and can, therefore, be subjected to the same criticism. For the sake of simplicity and clarity, I will hereafter refer to Gauchet's interpretation of Constant simply as 'the liberal democratic conception of popular sovereignty'. The most important elements of that liberal democratic conception are contained *in nuce* in a passage that Gauchet calls 'the centrepiece' of Constant's 1806 unpublished manuscript, *Principes de politique applicables à tous les gouvernements:*[82]

> There is a part of human existence which remains, by necessity, individual and independent and which is, by right, outside of any social competence. Sovereignty does not exist except in a limited and relative manner. At the point where the independence of individual existence starts, the jurisdiction of this sovereignty ends.[83]

In order to show that the liberal democratic conception of popular sovereignty indeed amounts to a more sophisticated but still essentially *positive* conception of popular sovereignty, I will disentangle its different theoretical elements according to the same scheme applied earlier to the republican conception:

(i) The liberal democratic conception of popular sovereignty does not locate the *source* of popular sovereignty in the rights of the individual. On the contrary, it posits the fundamental anteriority and irreducible exteriority of individual rights vis-à-vis political power: 'The rights of individuals – personal liberty or "liberty of action", religious liberty, liberty of opinion, "including its publicity" and the judicial guarantee against any form of arbitrariness – are anterior to and should remain exterior from the formation of political authority'.[84] These rights are deemed to have a particular semi-natural and pre-political status, as a consequence of which they can never be

[82] Gauchet, 'L'illusion lucide du libéralisme', p. 68.

[83] B. Constant, *Principes de politique applicable à tous les gouvernements*, E. Hoffman (ed.) (Paris: Hachette, 1997 [1806]), p. 49: 'Il y a une partie de l'existence humaine qui, de nécessité, reste individuelle et indépendante et qui est de droit, hors de toute compétence sociale. La souveraineté n'existe que d'une manière limitée et relative. Au point où commence l'indépendance de l'existence individuelle, s'arrête la juridiction de cette souveraineté'. The passage is cited in Gauchet, 'L'illusion lucide du libéralisme', p. 45 and 68 and in Gauchet, 'Le libéralisme entre le droit et l'histoire', p. 286.

[84] Gauchet, 'Le libéralisme entre le droit et l'histoire', pp. 286–287: 'Les droits des individus – liberté personnelle ou 'liberté d'action', liberté d'opinion 'dans laquelle est comprise sa publicité', garantie judiciaire contre tout arbitraire – sont antérieurs et ont à rester extérieurs à la formation de l'autorité politique'.

legitimately reduced or abolished by or in the name of the collective subject of popular sovereignty. Instead, the liberal democratic conception sees popular sovereignty as 'emanating' from society as such.[85] While pluralism and diversity within society are irrevocably accepted, the liberal democratic conception also takes it as a given that a certain form of 'sociability', i.e., elementary social cohesion always already exists. As Gauchet explains: 'No individualism, in other words, without a certain "sociologism", one could almost say, if one is careful to define the content of that term: without a minimal recognition of the distinctive consistency of the social bond and without taking into account, at least implicitly, the autonomous character of its process of creation with regard to the consciousness and willingness of human beings'.[86]

(ii) Even though the liberal democratic conception acknowledges that popular sovereignty 'emanates' from society, it also posits a conceptual distinction between society (as the source from which political power emanates, and the object on which political power is exercised) and the *collective subject* of popular sovereignty.[87] The liberal democratic conception hence does not conceive of the correspondence between the subject and the object of sovereignty as a complete coincidence, as the republican conception does. The key to the distinction lies in the principle of political representation: the collective subject of sovereignty is understood to be a representation rather than an instantiation of society.[88] The representative distance that consequently emerges between the collective subject and society makes it possible to see society as a plural and diverse entity where differences and conflict can flourish instead of having to be suppressed in order to create a unified collective subject.

(iii) For the more naïvely liberal theorists who were Constant's contemporaries (Gauchet mentions Thomas Paine as the most obvious example) the distance between society and political power was a

[85] Gauchet, 'L'illusion lucide du libéralisme', p. 59: 'Le libéralisme entre le droit et l'histoire', p. 283.

[86] *Ibid.*, p. 52: 'Pas d'individualisme, en d'autres termes, sans un certain 'sociologisme', oserait-on presque dire, en prenant soin de bien préciser le contenu du terme : sans une reconnaissance minimale de la consistance propre du lien de société et une prise en compte au moins tacite du caractère autonome de son processus de création par rapport à la conscience et à la volonté des hommes'.

[87] Gauchet, 'Le libéralisme entre le droit et l'histoire', p. 287.

[88] *Ibid.*, pp. 296–297.

consequence of the view that society was a fully autonomous, self-sufficient entity and the sphere of political power a purely secondary instrument. If they did not consider political power to be completely redundant, it was at most a necessary evil that should be strictly limited and confined within the sphere of its predetermined tasks.[89] The liberal democratic conception of popular sovereignty is, however, more 'lucid' (and less naive) because it sees through this 'illusion' of the autonomy of society. It grasps that the political sphere always plays a constitutive symbolic function vis-à-vis the social order.[90] Society cannot conceive of itself as a meaningful collective entity (and hence cannot exist, let alone have any political agency) without the transcendent perspective that the political sphere provides. This means that the collective subject of sovereignty is the product of the legal and political framework, rather than the other way around as the republican conception assumed.

To put it more succintly, Gauchet reads a prototypical version of his own fundamental insight into Constant's conception of political power:

> But even if it has withdrawn itself from the position of the sensitive seat of identity, of the visible incarnation of an ultimate will, and even it has liberated the autonomous affirmation of society, power has not stopped, however, in the last instance, and under completely different conditions, fulfilling the function of symbolic institution, of producing collective identity and cohesion, by means of which individuals are able to feel like they are living in a world which answers to a meaningful order and on which they have a grip.[91]

More precisely, Gauchet argues that this distinctive insight is incorporated in Constant's argument for the necessity of a 'neutral power' within the institutional framework, which purportedly translates and concretizes the more philosophical insight that the primordial function of political power is the symbolic constitution of a collective identity and that it is, as such, the condition of possibility

[89] Gauchet, 'L'illusion lucide du libéralisme', pp. 50–51.

[90] *Ibid.*, p. 72.

[91] *Ibid.*, pp. 75–76: 'Mais pour s'être ainsi retire de la position de foyer sensible d'identité, d'incarnation visible d'un ultime volonté, et pour avoir ce faisant libéré l'affirmation autonome de la société, le pouvoir n'a aucunement cessé, ailleurs, en dernier ressort, et selon des modalités complètement différentes, de remplir la fonction d'instituant symbolique, d'instance productrice de l'identité et le la cohésion collectives, par l'action de laquelle les individus accèdent au sentiment de vivre dans un monde qui répond à un ordre sensé et sur lequel ils ont prise'.

for society to exist.[92] Constant first formulated his proposal for a *pouvoir preservateur*, as Gauchet indicates, in his unpublished manuscript *Fragments d'un ouvrage abandonné,* then assigning the function to a collective organ in a republican framework,[93] and he reiterated his thoughts on the subject in the 1815 version of *Principes de politiques*, then integrating it into his defence of constitutional monarchy, where the *pouvoir neutre* would be exercised by the (hereditary) monarch.[94] On both occasions, Constant argued that it is necessary to create a specific 'neutral power' within the constitutional system, whose only function would be to watch over and guarantee the stability of the constitutional order as a whole. Constant did not conceive of the neutral power as an 'active' governing power, although it was an independent and inviolable position to which a number of special privileges or competences were attached that would allow it to restore the balance between the active powers. Because it should be placed over and above the other powers, the neutral power could not be placed in the hands of an elected organ (because it should not be under popular control), nor could it be appointed by the legislative, executive or judiciary power (because it should not be under governmental control either).[95]

On the basis of Constant's constitutional recommendations, Gauchet concluded that his proposal for a 'neutral power' intended to create a specific institution that would allow society to 'see' the independent locus of power that makes it possible for society to exist as a collective entity, i. e., as a collective subject of popular sovereignty:

[92] Gauchet discusses the details and the evolution of Constant's constitutional suggestions in Gauchet, *La révolution des pouvoirs*, pp. 237–255. As Gauchet explains, the idea of a fourth power, over and the above the legislative, executive and judiciary power, to mediate between them and guarantee the stability of the constitutional system in its entirety, was not an original invention of Constant. This suggestion was in line with a steady yet minoritarian and often disregarded tradition within French revolutionary theory and practice. It was precisely the objective of Gauchet's *La révolution des pouvoirs* to trace and reinvigorate this tradition, see Gauchet, *La révolution des pouvoirs*, p. 13.

[93] B. Constant, *Fragments d'un ouvrage abandonné sur la possibilité d'une constitution républicaine dans un grand pays*, H. Grange (ed.) (Paris: Aubier, 1991).

[94] B. Constant, 'Principles of politics applicable to all representative governments', in B. Fontana (trans. and ed.), *Constant: Political Writings* (Cambridge University Press, 2002 [1815]), pp. 183–193.

[95] Constant, *Fragments*, p. 373; Constant, *Principles of Politics*, p. 185. Patrice Rolland is one of the few scholars who have established an excellent and in-depth examination of Constant's theory of the *pouvoir neutre*. See P. Rolland, 'Comment préserver les institutions politiques? La théorie du pouvoir neutre chez B. Constant', *Revue Française d'Histoire des Idées Politiques*, 27 (2008), 43–73.

> Constant has understood, with his unique capacity of perspicacity, that next to or on top of the power that is produced by human beings and that is recognized as such, it is necessary to give form and substance to a place of power exterior to human volition, in reference to which society produces itself, constitutes itself as a collective that is capable of correspondence with itself. [...] In other words, a viable democratic system is not conceivable without reconciling the mechanism that makes power emanate from society on the one hand, with, on the other, a system that makes room for the always already separation between power and society, for the independence of the origins of power vis-à-vis society, and for its generating precedence.[96]

For Gauchet and other 'Lefortians', the primordial symbolic and constitutive function of political power is a 'fact', i.e., it exists prior to and independent from the way in which society actually participates in the exercise of political power and regardless of the way in which society understands its own participation in political power. But liberal democracy is deemed to be a particular, normatively superior political regime because it allows society to become aware of that constitutive, transcendent dimension (even though it cannot be overcome) and consolidates that awareness in a concrete and apprehensible institutional framework. Or, as Gauchet explains elsewhere, liberal democracy is the regime in which the representative relation between the society and the collective subject of popular sovereignty is itself given a 'permanent representation' within the institutional framework.[97] Constant's suggestion for a neutral power makes an important addition to this framework, because it embodies precisely the independent or transcendent aspect of that constitutive structure. Moreover, Gauchet takes Constant's conception of the neutral power to be a case in point of his argument that there exist an 'elementary form and general reason' of political power that transcends the modern/democratic modalities. Gauchet emphasizes that by means of his 'neutral power', Constant introduces a 'monarchical element' into his system, in order to 'safeguard the dimensions of eminence, permanence, and independence that were attached to the person of the

[96] Gauchet, 'L'illusion lucide du libéralisme', p. 86: 'Ce que Constant a compris, avec une faculté unique de pénétration, c'est qu'à côté ou en sus du pouvoir produit par les hommes et reconnu pour tel, il est nécessaire de donner figure et corps à un lieu de pouvoir extérieur à la volonté des hommes, par référence auquel la société se produit, se constitue comme un ensemble capable de correspondance avec lui-même. [...]

Point de régime démocratique viable, pour le dire autrement, sans concilier le mécanisme faisant sortir le pouvoir de la société, avec un système faisant place à la séparation toujours déjà réalisée du pouvoir d'avec la société, à son indépendances d'origine vis-à-vis d'elle, à son antériorité génératrice'.

[97] Gauchet, *La révolution des pouvoirs*, p. 12.

monarch'.[98] As such, Constant's reasoning attests to the 'paradoxical continuity that secretly unites monarchical absolutism with modern democratic power'.[99]

Admittedly the liberal democratic conception of popular sovereignty that Gauchet describes has a far more complex and sophisticated structure than its republican counterpart. Individual rights are altogether dissociated from the scheme and are considered to be independent from the structure of popular sovereignty. And whereas in the republican conception, society is completely absorbed within the collective subject of popular sovereignty, the liberal democratic conception posits a distinction between society and the collective subject. Taken together, the existent legal and political institutions make up the political sphere that constructs the unity (i.e. collective subjectivity) that endows existence and meaning upon society. The political sphere thus has a constitutive relation with regard to society, from which popular sovereignty emanates and on which it is exercised.

All in all, therefore, the liberal democratic view that Gauchet argues to find in Constant's work, like the republican view, adheres to a *positive* conception of popular sovereignty. In the liberal democratic conception this positive relation just takes the inverted form 'B constitutes A' instead of 'A constitutes B', given that A was defined as the collective subject of sovereignty, and B as the legal and political framework (Figure 8.2). The way in which power is concretely organized in liberal democracy has an impact on the way in which a liberal democratic society understands its own diversity: the unity of the collective subject posited by the legal and political framework is recognized as a political construction, rather than as a social reality. Gauchet favors the liberal democratic set-up because the constructed nature of the unity also implies its temporary and contestable character. This means that within liberal democracy, the representation of society as a collective entity will always be up for discussion and open to change.

Contrary to Gauchet's normative assessment of liberal democracy as a regime that stimulates diversity and contestation, I believe that its *positive* structure in fact entails that the liberal democratic conception of popular sovereignty is trapped in the same 'holistic', and hence conservative, logic that Gauchet traces and criticizes in the republican position. In the liberal democratic conception, the institutional dimension takes priority because

[98] Gauchet, 'L'illusion lucide du libéralisme', p. 29.
[99] *Ibid.*, p. 30.

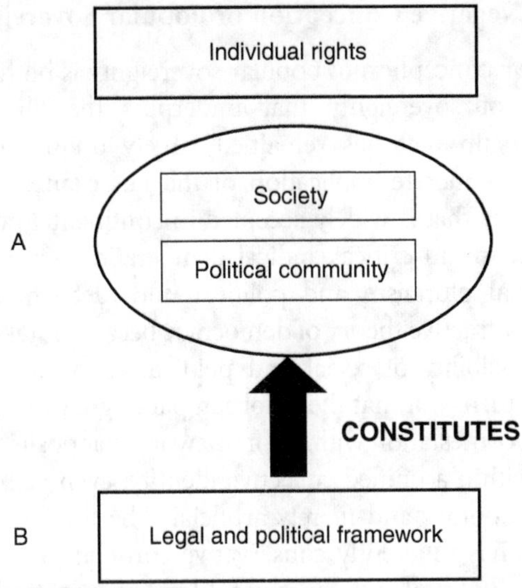

Figure 8.2 Gauchet's liberal democratic *positive* conception of sovereignty (b)

it is the constitutive dimension. Society is understood to be irreducibly plural and diverse, yet ultimately that diversity has to be overcome – temporarily and virtually, but nonetheless necessarily – in a collective unity in order for society to exist.[100] This conservative logic is also present in Gauchet's interpretation of Constant's neutral power, which, as he insists entails the incorporation of a monarchical element in the heart of a modern political system, in order to create and preserve 'an element of eminence, permanence and independence'.[101] As discussed above, the transcendence that Gauchet takes to be indispensable for the institution of social order has the function of (momentarily) creating a sense of (virtual) unity in the social diversity. It can only 'democratically' perform that function if it has no 'content' of its own. Yet upon closer consideration, the neutral power does have a very real content of its own: it has to maintain the stability of the already existing legal and political framework. The neutral power is therefore not strictly speaking 'neutral' and it cannot fulfill the purely reflexive role vis-à-vis society that Gauchet attributes to it, without confirming the conservative, holistic predisposition of liberal democracy.

[100] See Ingram, 'The politics of Claude Lefort', 42, for a similar argument with regard to Claude Lefort's conception of political power.
[101] Gauchet, 'L'illusion lucide du libéralisme', p. 29.

3 A Negative Conception of Popular Sovereignty?

Gauchet's *positive* conception of popular sovereignty is both an example of the conception of sovereignty that underpins the liberal democratic Constant-scholarship that has remained largely unquestioned for forty years now and a concrete application of the Lefortian understanding of modern democracy that is widely accepted in continental political philosophy, and particularly in critical, radical democratic theory. The Lefortian ontology of social pluralism and political underdetermination certainly appears to be an attractive theory of democracy because it takes into account the incessant possibility of social and political change. Yet upon closer consideration, it turns out that the Lefortian paradigm can only make sense of pluralism and contestation within a framework that posits the necessity of their synthesis within a unified collective identity, even if the latter is considered to be temporary and merely artificial. The theoretical necessity of such a synthesis has inherently conservative consequences for the overall framework: if the 'political', i.e., the existent legal and political framework, is constitutive for social order, then social pluralism and social conflict will, in the end, always run into the political status quo. To put it differently, the liberal democratic conception of popular sovereignty is not a theory of radical social and political change; it is a theory of liberal democratic social and political change. The concrete historical background discussed in the first section confirms that this is indeed what Gauchet and other Lefortians were aiming at: to develop a political theory that would make room for social struggle while at the same time ensuring political stability.

The historical contextualization and the conceptual analysis that I have elaborated in this chapter are therefore indispensable theoretical steps in the development of a full-fledged critique of the liberal democratic paradigm and an alternative perspective to it. The sheer fact that this paradigm has been uncritically accepted for almost half a century in itself already warrants the endeavour to look for a fresh perspective. It is needless to add that contemporary society is something altogether different than the post-1968 conjuncture that these philosophers sought to theorize. As a container concept, globalization subsumes many of the profound political, social, cultural, and economic transformations that have been and still are taking place. And indeed these transformations are so closely intertwined that it has become impossible to uphold any clear-cut distinction between them. As a consequence, the priority and independence of the political that is a fundamental part of the Lefort's and Gauchet's framework has become problematic as a theoretical position.

Admittedly, from this perspective, it may seem far-fetched to argue that nineteenth-century political theory would have a more suitable conception of popular sovereignty to offer. Nevertheless, I believe that Benjamin Constant's thought can provide a number of valuable suggestions for further reflection, on the condition that is taken to formulate a *negative*, rather than a *positive* conception of popular sovereignty. A negative conception of popular sovereignty does not posit a constitutive relationship between the collective subject of popular sovereignty and the legal and political framework, or vice versa. In fact, as I discuss below, Constant's conception of popular sovereignty does not posit a collective subject at all. As a consequence, a negative conception of popular sovereignty exhibits an understanding of political power that is less institution-oriented: if political power is understood to be detached from its causal relation to the legal and political framework, it becomes possible to conceive of political power much more broadly, including actions and discourses that would not have an immediate reflection in the collective identity of the political community. Hence, even though a negative conception of sovereignty would not presuppose the priority of the political (because it would not assume a clear distinction between the social and the political), it would not amount to a more instrumental notion of political power.

Obviously, both Constant's contribution to a negative understanding of popular sovereignty and the normative implications of such an understanding need to be examined and discussed more carefully than is possible in the conclusion of this chapter. This is a project that I will take up in future research. Here, I will simply point the reader to one striking indication of Constant's alternative approach towards political power and popular sovereignty, which can be found in the additional comments to his *Principes de politique applicable à tous les gouvernements* (1806). Throughout this text, Constant makes several, very casual and seemingly endorsing references to the idea of the 'the general will'[102]. Yet in a remarkable passage, he explicitly qualifies his understanding of this idea:

> The laws have been defined as the expression of the general will. This is a very false definition. The laws are the declaration of men's relations between themselves. From the moment society exists, it establishes certain relations

[102] See e.g. 'Toute autorité qui n'émane pas de la volonté générale est incontestablement illégitime' in Constant, *Principes de politique applicable à tous les gouvernements* [1806], p. 22 and quoted in Gauchet, 'Le libéralisme entre le droit et l'histoire', p. 283 or 'En un mot il n'existe au monde que deux pouvoirs, l'un illégitime, c'est la force; l'autre légitime, c'est la volonté générale'. in Constant, *Principes de politique applicable à tous les gouvernements* [1806], p. 24.

> between men. These relations are true to their nature, for if they were not true to their nature, they would not become established. These laws are nothing other than these relationships observed and voiced. They are not the cause of these relationships, which on the contrary are anterior to them; on the contrary, they declare that these relationships exist. They are the declaration of a fact. They create, determine, and institute nothing, except forms and procedures such as to guarantee that which existed before their institution. It follows that no man, no fraction of society, nor even the whole society can, properly speaking and in an absolute sense, attribute to itself the right to make laws. The laws being only the expression of relations which exist between men and these relations being determined by their nature, to make a new law is only a new declaration of what existed previously.[103]

This passage suggests that Constant's conception of popular sovereignty did not posit a collective subject at its centre, nor was he interested in the constitution of such a subject. On the contrary, Constant tried to pre-empt as much as possible the need for the constitution of a more comprehensive collective identity in between the individual members of society and the legal and political framework. Instead, Constant was exclusively concerned with the immediate relations between human beings, which he conceived as detached from their institutional implications. Surprisingly, Gauchet quotes this very same passage in his 'L'illusion lucide du libéralisme'.[104] Indeed, a number of scholars, including Gauchet himself,[105] have hinted towards what I have called a negative conception of popular sovereignty, but hitherto no one has defended the position that Constant developed a conception of popular sovereignty that has a different conceptual structure altogether.[106] Yet drawing out the conclusions of Constant's conception of popular sovereignty would open up a new avenue for Constant-scholarship and provide a much-needed fresh perspective to the theoretical debate about popular sovereignty within liberal democracy.

[103] B. Constant, *Principles of Politics Applicable to All Governments*, E. Hoffman (ed.), D. O'Keeffe (trans.) (Indianapolis: Liberty Fund, 2003 [1806]), p. 442.

[104] Gauchet, 'L'illusion lucide du libéralisme', pp. 57–58.

[105] See Gauchet, *La révolution des pouvoirs*, p. 243, for a position that comes strikingly close to my understanding of a 'negative' conception of popular sovereignty.

[106] See L. Jaume, 'Le problème de l'intérêt général dans la pensée de Benjamin Constant' in F. Tilkin (ed.), Le groupe de Coppet et le monde moderne: Conceptions, images, débats (Genève: Librairie Droz, 1998), pp. 159–176; A. Craiutu, 'The battle for legitimacy. Guizot and Constant on sovereignty', *Historical Reflections*, 3 (2002), 471–491; B. Garsten, 'From popular sovereignty to civil society in post-revolutionary France' in R. Bourke and Q. Skinner (eds.), *Popular Sovereignty in Historical Perspective* (Cambridge University Press, 2016), pp. 239–269.

9

Political Idolatry

The Relation of Schmitt's Two Claims in *Political Theology*

STEPHANIE FRANK

Elsewhere I have published a series of articles describing a register in which a version of Carl Schmitt's claim that "all the concepts of the modern theory of the state are secularized theological concepts" was coherent, and perhaps even true in some cases.[1] In those articles, I argued that what was, perhaps, the theoretical turning point of the French Revolution – the Abbé Sieyès' argument for the mode of representation of the National Assembly in the *mandat imperatif* debates of 1789 – was an uncanny echo of the theologian Nicolas Malebranche's argument from a century earlier regarding the mode of representation of the church.

But of course the question of sovereignty runs alongside the question of representation, more and less explicitly. Returning to the Malebranche-Siey ès case, in the present contribution I turn my attention from models of representation to models of sovereignty. In *Political Theology*, Schmitt makes two claims that have become famous: first, what I will call the intellectual historical claim, mentioned above ("all the concepts of the modern theory of the state are secularized theological concepts"), and what I will call the definitional claim ("Sovereign is he who decides the exception").[2] Looking at the case of sovereignty, I want to consider how the Malebranche–Sieyès case ramifies for the relationship between Schmitt's two claims. I am unaware of any consideration of this problem in the literature about Schmitt. More generally, I want to consider the sort of model of sovereignty required

[1] S. Frank, "The General Will Beyond Rousseau: Sieyès' Theological Arguments for the National Assembly," *History of European Ideas* 37 (2011), 337–343; S. Frank, "Permutations of the Theological-Political Analogy: Political Voluntarism, 'Transfer,' and Secularization," in S. Perovic (ed.), *Fragments of Religion: Sacred and Secular Agency in Early Modern France* (London: Continuum, 2011), pp. 104–124. See also my "Re-imagining the Public Sphere: Malebranche, Schmitt's Hamlet, and the Lost Theater of Sovereignty," *Telos* 153 (2010), 70–93.

[2] C. Schmitt, *Political Theology: Four Chapters on the Concept of Sovereignty*, trans. G. Schwab (University of Chicago, 1985), 36, 5.

by the configuration of politics and theology that Schmitt advances in *Political Theology*. Counterintuitively, I find that the model is ultimately necessarily atheological and, indeed, idolatrous.

1 The Case for Schmitt's Intellectual-Historical Claim: Malebranche and Sieyès on Representation

In seventeenth-century France, there was a rift in the church between the Jansenists and the orthodox. One of the important flashpoints of the controversy was the interpretation of 1 Timothy 2:3–4, "God wills all men be saved." The basic problem here will no doubt already be familiar: if God is omnipotent, and God wills to save all men, how can it so obviously be the case (at least if we're seventeenth-century French theologians) that all men are not saved? The Jansenist solution, most forcefully articulated by Antoine Arnauld, was to say that the passage from Timothy meant only that God had a *volonté générale* for human salvation: God's salvific will was not limited to any particular class of people but extended over all human divisions.

The orthodox theologian Nicolas Malebranche appropriated Arnauld's term of *volonté générale* but gave it a different import.[3] He suggested that it would be unbefitting of the majesty of God for God to trifle with willing individual human salvations; that would be too much like human willing, based on partial perspectives and limited power. Rather, in keeping with the greatness of his power and intellect, God must govern the world in a few elegant strokes. Thus, God wills the salvation of all, but he must do so in a way that befits his nature, through a general willing, which, lamentably, leaves by the wayside those who do not heed God's general willing, which, as it happens, is ensconced in the Church.

So why is it that, for Malebranche, the Church represents God's *volonté générale*? In his *Entretiens sur la Métaphysique et sur la Religion* (1688), Malebranche provides two different arguments on the point.[4] First, he makes an instrumental argument: the masses, with their limited energy and education, cannot discern God's will unassisted, so God, in all his providence, provided the Church for them. But he also makes what we might call a metaphysical argument: he claims that there is no *volonté générale* apart from its institutional articulation, because God – perfectly

[3] The history of the term *volonté générale is* covered illuminatingly in P. Riley, *The General Will Before Rousseau* (Princeton, NJ: Princeton University Press, 1980).

[4] N. Malebranche, *Entretiens sur la Métaphysique et sur la Religion* (Rotterdam: Reinier Leers, 1688).

simple being that he is – has no will apart from its execution. The means just *are* the ends, and so the Church just *is* the *volonté générale*.

A century later, at the start of the French Revolution, the question of the *mandat impératif* arose on the floor of the National Assembly: were representatives bound by the wills of their constituents, whose *cahiers* they had borne to Paris, or were representatives the ultimate authorities in discerning the general will of France? The question of the *mandat impératif* was, in other words, a question about the nature of representation, and the Abbé Sieyès' argument against the *mandat impératif* – and for the sovereignty of the National Assembly – ultimately carried the day. Critically, his argument was structured precisely the same way as Malebranche's was. Like Malebranche, Sieyès reasoned that a representative body was the only hope for the enlightenment of the masses. But this instrumental justification was combined with the more robust metaphysical claim that the *volonté générale* was indistinguishable from the relevant institution. Sieyès said, during the debate:

> The national will has come to be considered as if it could be something other than the will of the representatives of the nation, as if the nation could speak in any other way than through its representatives. Here, false principles become extremely dangerous.[5]

Note the strength of Sieyès' claim here: it is not only that if there were no National Assembly, there would be no articulation of the general will; it is also that there would be no general will.

Moreover, there are aspects of Sieyès' argument that only make sense insofar as they derive from Malebranche's argument. For instance, Sieyès postulates that the great majority of his fellow citizens are incapable of discerning the general will. Yet he also simultaneously assumes that they somehow will be self-conscious enough to realize their inadequacy to the task, so that they appoint representatives. I would suggest that this peculiarity derives from Sieyès' deployment of a theological argument without a divine referent. The legitimacy of Malebranche's representative body comes from God. Sieyès' *volonté générale*, on the other hand, cannot make recourse to God for its legitimacy. And so, on Sieyès' analysis, though the people are unable to discern the general will, they are charged with selecting representatives to fill that role.

Rather than belaboring rhetorical parallels I have developed elsewhere, let me summarize: the homologous arguments of Malebranche and

[5] *Archives parlementaires de 1787 à 1860* (Paris, 1875), 8: 593.

Sieyès about representation suggest a construction of Schmitt's claim that the concepts of the modern theory of the state are secularized theological concepts that holds up against the persuasive critique of Hans Blumenberg.[6] When Schmitt says that political-theoretical concepts are "secularized" theological concepts, he is of course evoking the Westphalian roots of "secularization," which signified the process by which church lands were transferred to state control; let's call this sort of secularization "transfer secularization."

Blumenberg's claim is that (unlike land) concepts simply are not the sort of things that can be secularized in this sense – they do not possess the right sort of quiddity to register continuity over time. By changing our focus from continuities between "concepts" to affinities between the argumentative logics in Malebranche's defense of the Church as representing God's *volonté générale* and Sieyès' defense of the National Assembly as representing France's *volonté générale*, we can, I think, elude this problem. Indeed, we can even give a plausible account of how this "transfer" happens: the Malebranche–Sieyès homology suggests that the sorts of arguments that are viewed as "persuasive" in a given situation are historically structured. One's sense of what sorts of arguments are persuasive comes from the sorts of arguments that have been made in the past; and one's sense of what sorts of arguments are persuasive shapes the arguments one advances in the present, which then in turn are among the factors structuring arguments made in the future. In this case, the logics of arguments about representation in the ecclesiological disputes of the seventeenth century shaped the arguments about representation offered on the floor of the National Assembly a century later.

All of this is important insofar as it provides a register in which "transfer secularization" claims might take on some historical heft – that is, become more than mere assertions of affinity or resemblance.[7] But understanding the mechanism by which theological argumentative logics resurface in politics makes clear that this sort of secularization is not an inevitable, unidirectional process whereby theology slowly leaches into politics. For surely originally political arguments could reemerge in

[6] H. Blumenberg, *The Legitimacy of the Modern Age*, trans. R. Wallace (Boston: MIT Press, 1985).

[7] Schmitt vacillated on the question of whether his "all the concepts of the modern theory of the state are secularized theological concepts" dictum was meant to express historical derivation or structural analogy, apparently backing off the former claim in his much-later *Political Theology II*. I suspect that this disavowal has not been taken seriously because "secularization" is so clearly normatively laden for Schmitt.

theology just as well. That is to say, this sort of understanding of "transfer secularization" claims allows us to entertain possible historical derivations without signing on to Schmitt's normative political agenda, which is significantly shaped by the notion that modern political theory is just a poor man's theology. For these reasons, I continue to find compelling the continuities between Malebranche's arguments legitimizing the representation of the Church and Sieyès' legitimizing the representation of the National Assembly.

2 Malebranche on Sovereignty: The "Order of Perfections" and God's Will

Since for Schmitt the claims about the nature of sovereignty and the "secularization" of theological concepts seem to stand in relationship – and since he particularly cites the discourse of the *volonté générale* in *Political Theology* – we might expect a similar intellectual-historical relationship to obtain between Malebranche's and Sieyès' arguments around sovereignty. But in fact the picture becomes more complicated when we turn to that issue. Malebranche's argument about the *volonté générale* rested on the idea that there were constraints on God's will, owing to the sort of being that he was: God was so great that particular willings (that is to say, intervening in individuals' salvations) were beneath him. But though Sieyès' arguments for the representation of the National Assembly track Malebranche's arguments for the representation of the Church quite precisely, we cannot say the same for Malebranche's and Sieyès' arguments around sovereignty. Indeed, sovereignty is a category that Sieyès refuses. In other words, we might, speaking loosely, call Sieyès' theory of representation a "secularization" of Malebranche's, but there is not a corresponding case to make vis-à-vis their theories of sovereignty.

As we have seen, Malebranche's position was that it would not befit God's majesty for him to will the particular salvations of all people individually. So instead, God "willed all men be saved," in the sense of 1 Timothy 2, by ensconcing his general will for human salvation in the Church. For Malebranche, the way we knew that the will was legitimately God's was just that it operated differently than human willing – that is to say, with elegant economy. Humans, with their imperfect foreknowledge and limited power, were confined to a series of stopgap solutions of particular willings, but God, being omniscient and omnipotent, could do his work with a few grand strokes – general willings.

Arnauld's immediate and repeated rejoinder, in the decades-long polemic that followed, was that Malebranche's conception of the *volonté générale* degraded God by suggesting that he was confined by his own nature (i.e., his own greatness) to will in certain ways. Arnauld claimed anyone who truly appreciated God's majesty should have understood that God's will was completely unconstrained. This is, of course, just a version of a much older metaethical controversy – the "Euthyphro dilemma" of whether God commands the good because it is good, or whether the good is good because God commands it. In contrast to Malebranche, Arnauld follows the Cartesian voluntarist line (Descartes, of course, argued that God could will even that his own creatures should hate him).[8] Arnauld argued that Malebranche's exaltation of God's general willing at the price of particular willings tended to denigrate miracles – God's interventions in history in particular situations – as beneath God. As against Malebranche, Arnauld maintained that miracles were the guarantee that the hand pulling the strings of the universe was indeed God's hand. Particular willings – by which Arnauld intended specific interventions in the unfolding of human history – were not a denigration of divine sovereignty, as Malebranche contended, but in fact the proof that there was a sovereign will that transcended mere human understanding.

Over the next two decades of the controversy, without surrendering the crux of the matter Malebranche refined his way of talking about the modality of God's willing. First, though he never surrendered it entirely, he retreated from the language of the general will, preferring instead to speak of God's designs (*desseins*). God's omniscience and omnipotence together meant that he couldn't will something without simultaneously accomplishing it; so far as God's actions in the world were concerned, means and ends were inseparable. This buttressed Malebranche's claim that the Church was one and the same with God's will. (This then gave rise to the analogous argument in Sieyès that the National Assembly was one and the same with France's will.)

More interestingly for the question of the model of sovereignty implicit in the ecclesiology that eventually became the theory of representation for the French Revolution, however, over the same two decades Malebranche reconceptualized the constraints on God's action. Rather than talking about the way in which God's nature constrained God, he began talking about the way in which an order of perfections constrained

[8] On the relation between Jansenists and Cartesians, see T. Schmaltz, "What has Cartesianism to do With Jansenism?" *Journal of the History of Ideas* 60 (1999), 37–56.

God. In his "clarifications" to the *Treatise on Nature and Grace*, published four years after the original text, he explained his position this way:

> A general cause [i.e., like God] ought not act by particular willings. The conduct of God ought to bear the character of his attributes, if the immutable and necessary order of justice obligates him to change it. For order, to God, is an inviolable law: he loves it invincibly, and he always prefers it to arbitrary laws through which he could execute his designs.[9]

Malebranche continues to claim that God is constrained in his willings, but now he conceptualizes God as constrained not by the fact of his nature but instead by "the immutable and necessary order of justice."

This may seem like a distinction without a difference – it did to Arnauld. In Malebranche's new articulation, God is still being constrained to act in certain ways and not others, and thus he is not possessed of the completely unconstrained will so important to Arnauld's understanding of sovereignty. But in fact there is an important difference here. For when Malebranche coined the notion of the *volonté générale* as an entailment of God's nature – God being too majestic to trifle with particular willings – this only had consequences for God's actions. Now that he was conceiving the *volonté générale* as in keeping with what he called sometimes "the order of perfections" and other times "the order of justice," what was binding on God's nature was an immutable order equally binding on "all intelligent beings." Malebranche wrote, "In contemplating the substance of the Word . . . I am able to discover, at least dimly, the relations of perfection which exist between these same ideas; and these relations are the immutable order that God consults when he acts: *the order which also ought to regulate the esteem and love of all intelligent beings.*"[10]

Malebranche's new articulation of the *volonté générale* theodicy has important ramifications for the relationship between divine and human sovereignty. Consider at the beginning of the polemic about the *volonté générale*, both Malebranche and Arnauld trafficked in a certain political-theological analogy: namely, they used earthly sovereignty to help their readers imagine divine sovereignty. Thus, for instance, Malebranche had explained, in his 1683 *Meditations*, that God's general willing was roughly akin to the sort of delegation undertaken by earthly princes.

[9] N. Malebranche, *Traité de Morale* (Rotterdam: Reinier Leers, 1684), 536.
[10] *Ibid.*, 5.

> When you hear it said that God permits some natural disorders . . . [it is in] the same fashion that a Prince lets his ministers act and permits the disorders that he is not able to prevent. It is God who does all, the good and the evils . . . but God *does* the good and *permits* the evils, in the sense that he wills positively and directly the good and he does not so will the evil.[11]

Malebranche assumes we understand how human sovereignty works through delegation to princes and asks his reader to imagine God's sovereignty (which operates through delegation to general rules) in analogous fashion.

Though of course completely disagreeing with Malebranche's interpretation of the *volonté générale*, Arnauld operates from the same premise, conceptualizing divine sovereignty on the basis of human sovereignty. To illuminate the theological distinction between God's will for Adam and Eve antecedent and consequent to the fall from Eden, Arnauld compares it to the will of a human sovereign before and after one of his subjects has committed a crime.

> There is no contradiction whatever [in the fact] that God wills by a *volonté absolue et particulière* the contrary of what he wills *en général*, just as a good king wills by an antecedent will that all his subjects live contentedly, though by a consequent will he executes those who disturb public tranquility by murders and violence.[12]

All of this is to say: their very real theological differences notwithstanding, at the beginning of the *volonté générale* controversy, human sovereignty was assumed as a fixed point by both Malebranche and Arnauld and used as a model for the comparatively unintelligible divine sovereignty. Ironically, the enterprise of modeling divine sovereignty on human sovereignty assumes exactly the premise for which Arnauld and Malebranche criticized each other – the idea that God was recognizably like humans.

But when Malebranche shifted from talking about God's *volonté générale* as a necessary entailment of God's nature to talking about God's *volonté générale* as a manifestation of the order of perfections, so too did the directionality of the analogy between human and divine sovereignty change. In Malebranche's new way of thinking about the relation between God and the good, rather than using inevitably flawed

[11] N. Malebranche, *Méditations Chrétiennes et Métaphysiques* (Lyon: Leonard Plaignard, 1707), 139–140.

[12] Quoted in Riley, *General Will*, 48.

examples of human sovereignty to try to conceptualize divine sovereignty, Malebranche began insisting that we should use the necessary perfection of divine sovereignty as our benchmark for assessing human sovereignty. Thus, Malebranche writes in the *Traité de Morale* (1684):

> No less than the pope, the prince holds his authority over other men by God alone, and the one and the other ought to use it as God himself, by relation to the immutable order, universal reason, the inviolable law of all intelligences and of God himself.[13]

Both the pope and the prince, then, are bound to the "inviolable law of all intelligences and of God himself," which is also associated with "immutable order" and "universal reason." Here, rather than making inferences from the behavior of human sovereigns to what divine sovereignty must look like, as he had a decade earlier, Malebranche is holding out the existence of an immutable order that is binding even on God – and the obligation of earthly authorities to discern and abide by it.

Similarly, in the roughly contemporaneous clarifications to the *Treatise on Nature and Grace*, Malebranche strongly criticizes human leaders who fail to abide by the order of justice. First, he explains why God's actions must be in conformity with standards that transcend God himself.

> I do not say that God chooses and abandons [his plans] simply because he wills it, because I fear making God seem like a man, who conducts himself by caprice and lacks regard for his work. It will not suffice to understand that God is powerful, and that he does what he wants with his creatures. . . . It is necessary to render him worthy of love and adoration at least as much as to render him formidable. . . . [T]he principle of the predestination of the Saints . . . is not a blind, bizarre, imperious will, of the sort that is often noted among the great powers [*les Grands*] of the Earth.[14]

Malebranche here makes the point that if God's will is arbitrary, he is no better than mercurial human beings – but of course (the argument runs) God must be better than mercurial human beings, and therefore his will cannot be a blind command but rather must be in keeping with God's essential worthiness of "love and adoration." That Malebranche is not merely talking about fickleness but (more importantly) adherence to norms that exist independently of God is driven home by his discussion of the predestination of the saints – God does not choose men for

[13] Malebranche, *Traité de Morale*, 122.
[14] *Ibid.*, 306.

elevation arbitrarily, as do the great earthly powers. He chooses them for their conformity to the good.

3 A Reverse in the Direction of the Homology: Malebranche's Mature Theory of Sovereignty

Thus, Malebranche's initial figuring of the analogy between human and divine sovereignty – where princes model for us what God might be like – changed to an analogy whereby God provides the standard by which earthly princes are measured. Of course, by the end of the seventeenth century, the most important articulations of voluntarism circulating were not theological but rather political: that is to say, theories of royal absolutism. It is probably no accident that the shift in Malebranche's strategy coincided roughly with the dramatic centralization of power of Louis XIV through the 1680s – the era of his Gallican reforms and the consolidation of the court at Versailles.

Indeed, in his work Malebranche seems to have specifically targeted his exact contemporary Louis XIV, the great expositor (indeed, the great instantiation) of the theory of royal absolutism. That Malebranche uses "les Grands" to refer to human sovereigns in the passage above is perhaps telling by itself, in the era of "Louis le Grand." Even more suggestive is the name of one of the characters of his *Entretiens sur la Métaphysique et sur la Réligion*. Louis XIV was called Louis Dieudonné ("given by God"). The character that serves as Malebranche's mouthpiece in the *Entretiens* is called Theodore – a Greek translation of the same name. Thus, Malebranche makes Dieudonné's namesake a forceful critic of the sort of voluntarism that Louis so staunchly defended. Perhaps so as not to be too obvious about the critique of the sitting monarch, most commonly Theodore directs himself against the theological version of voluntarism, as articulated by Arnauld. But he does not refrain entirely from drawing out the implications of his critique for politics. Take, for instance, this passage from the twelfth dialogue:

> THEODORE. God forms all societies and governs all nations – the Jewish people, the present Church, the future Church – by the general laws of the union of the spirit with eternal Wisdom. It is through the help of this wisdom that sovereigns reign happily and that they establish excellent laws: "Per me reges regnant, et legum conditores iusta decernunt."[15] It is

[15] "Through me kings rule and discern what is just" (Prov. 8:15). This same verse of Proverbs appears as an epigram on the frontispiece of the original edition of Hobbes'

> even in consulting it that the villainous kings succeed in their pernicious designs; because one can also make the light of reason serve injustice, in consequence of its general laws.[16]

The goodness of good sovereigns, then, inheres in their conformity to "eternal Wisdom."

But Malebranche's primary goal is not to critique the absolutism of his day so much as to continue his long-running theological polemic. Ever the adept rhetorician, Malebranche leverages his political critique against his theological opponents. He articulates an indictment of theology that anticipates some of the major modern critics of religion – namely, that we should understand the labors of the likes of Arnauld as essentially projection, fueled by a fantasy of the theologian's own potency.

> . . . [M]en make God such as they would like to be themselves; and since they prefer power to wisdom, God will always be just enough and wise enough for them, so long as he is powerful and sovereign. People love independence: to them it is a species of slavery to submit to reason . . . they fear making [God] powerless by making him wise.[17]

For Malebranche, thinkers like Arnauld fail to understand what makes God godly – his necessary conformity to universal reason. This is not a detriment to his greatness but an enhancement of it, in Malebranche's view. God properly understood is inextricably bound up with universal standards of reason and justice – not sheer power.

> These people will never understand that the Word of God is sovereign and universal reason; that this reason is coeternal and consubstantial with God himself; that he loves it necessarily, invincibly, inviolably; and that although he is obligated to follow it, he remains independent: and thus that all that God wills is just, wise, and constant, because God is only able to act according to his lights, because he is only able to love according to his order, because he is not able to misunderstand his wisdom and deny himself.[18]

Note Malebranche's very targeted rhetoric here: it is not just that those who would disagree with Malebranche (most importantly, of course,

De Cive (1642). This is interesting insofar as Hobbes is the theorist Malebranche most often targets in his critique of political voluntarism. That is to say, to target Hobbes, Malebranche pulls a similar sleight-of-hand to the one he uses to target Louis XIV through "Theodore."

16 Malebranche, *Entretiens*, 481.

17 Malebranche, *Traité*, 306.

18 *Ibid.*

Arnauld) misunderstand the nature of God's willing. They are further likened to despots and discredited thus. Like unjust sovereigns, Arnauld and his ilk "prefer power to wisdom" and are willing to sacrifice every other value to secure the fantasy of the completely unconstrained will.

Though Arnauld died in 1694, Malebranche lived another 20 years. Over that time span, he used the doctrine of the *volonté générale* as emanating from "the order of justice" ever more vociferously to critique human sovereignty.[19] But Arnauld's viewpoint did not die with him. Taking up the flag for unconstrained divine sovereignty was Laurent-François Boursier, who wrote a treatise on "the action of God over creatures" in 1713, in which he claimed that for anyone to suggest (as Malebranche did) that God was confined by anything like reason, goodness, or justice – let alone *necessarily* so confined – was to render him "impotent."[20]

Malebranche responded to this charge by explaining to say that God is "confined" by his nature is actually to misspeak – God is simply acting in accord with his nature and his love for all of his attributes and perfections, which are also the foundation of all knowledge. The real denigration of God's power, contended Malebranche, was to detach it from his goodness and justice, for – note here, again, the political angle – that was to assimilate him to a certain unfortunate sort of earthly prince. This is most explicit in Malebranche's last work, *Reflexions sur la Prémotion Physique*, published in 1715, the year of his death.

> If God were only omnipotent, without wisdom, justice, goodness, and if his attributes did not have any order or relation among them, . . . if he was similar to princes who glory more in their power than in their nature: then . . . Hobbes . . . would have discovered the true foundation of morality: authority and power giving the right to do anything one wants, quite outside of reason, when one has nothing to fear.[21]

Malebranche considers it self-evident that Hobbes has in fact not discovered the true foundation of morality: thus it must not be the case that God is like these deficient earthly princes – or indeed, like these power-hungry Jansenist philosophers. Elegantly reminding us of the roots of this whole debate, Malebranche returns to the question of the appropriate

19 We might speculate that Malebranche was emboldened to do so more explicitly because of the relative shift in Louis' power after French setbacks in the War of the League of Augsburg.

20 L.-F. Boursier, *De l'action de Dieu sur les créatures* (Paris: Babuty, 1713), 70.

21 Malebranche, *Réflexions*, 186–187.

understanding of "God wills all men be saved" that had begun the controversy some forty years earlier.

> The choice of the elect is not the effect of will of God that is absolute and random, or a will that has no reason other than the will itself, such as certain people are pleased to attribute to God; [these people] apparently prefer force, the law of brutes, that which has given the Lion empire over the animals, to reason. Preferring power to wisdom and to justice, they make God as they would like to be themselves.[22]

Again, Malebranche repeats his critique that the voluntarists are really only indulging in a self-aggrandizing fantasy of their own power.

4 Sieyès on Sovereignty

I began by recounting an argument for the homology between Malebranche's ecclesiology and Sieyès' theory of representation. I suggested that Schmitt's claim about the theological precedents of the concepts of the modern theory of the state were coherent – and indeed, true – in the case of the theory of representation that carried the day in the French Revolutionary debates about the *mandat impératif* and the royal veto. But what we have seen of Malebranche's position with regard to sovereignty suggests that it is quite different from the position on sovereignty that has typically been associated with Sieyès. In other words, if one can see Sieyès' arguments regarding the modality of representation of the National Assembly as a "transfer-secularization" of Malebranche's arguments regarding the modality of the representation of the Church, one cannot say the same of the models of sovereignty in each instance.

At the same time, it is not clear that the conventional understanding of Sieyès' understanding of sovereignty is correct. Lucia Rubinelli has persuasively argued that political theory has misunderstood Sieyès' position on sovereignty.[23] In fact, she argues, Sieyès used the category of *souveraineté* only in order to criticize other positions that he regarded as wrongheaded – in particular, as merely inadequately revising *ancien régime* political theory. In Rubinelli's estimation, readings of the political theory of the French Revolution have distinguished between radical models (which assigned sovereignty to the people) and moderate models (which assigned sovereignty to a construction called the nation). With his

[22] *Ibid.*, 177–178.

[23] L. Rubinelli, "How to think beyond sovereignty: On Sieyès and constituent power," *European Journal of Political Theory* (2016), 1–21.

strong arguments against the *mandat impératif*, Sieyès has been read as a member of the latter group. And indeed, there is no question but that Sieyès was perceived as an enemy of the Jacobin cause – indeed, he ended up fleeing France to escape Jacobin persecution during the Terror.

But Rubinelli argues persuasively that Sieyès' signature contribution of the notion of *pouvoir constituant* ("constituting power") is not a gloss on the idea of the sovereignty of the nation but rather an alternative to it. She cites Sieyès' own writing on the groundlessness of the idea of sovereignty:

> And lastly, let's dare to say it: what is sovereignty?. . . sovereignty understood as a supreme power which dominates/embraces everything does not exist. It cannot be found in the united mass of all public officers, and if the constitution separates the public powers, if each of them is limited to its special mission and cannot abandon it without usurpation and crime, where can this gigantic idea of sovereignty be placed?[24]

Rubinelli advances the view that the orienting value of Sieyès' political theory is his twofold conception of liberty: on the one hand, liberty as the freedom from domination, the lack of impediments vis-à-vis acting according to one's own will, and, on the other, liberty as the possession of sufficient time and resources to pursue one's aims.[25] ("Man needs to be free not to be fruitlessly free, but to exercise or employ his power and to progressively increase it.")[26] For Sieyès, this latter form of liberty was intrinsically bound up with the division of labor.

Sieyès shared the moderates' concerns about the potential excesses of popular sovereignty. He did not, however, agree with their solutions to this problem, which consisted in checks and balances, including a bicameral legislature and a royal veto. For Sieyès, such measures had the undesirable consequence of dividing society once more and thus contravened another of his orienting values: the equality of every citizen. Sieyès instead advocated for a system whereby the people used their *pouvoir constituant* to elect representatives to create ground rules for a system of government that the people would then ratify. Those charged with governing per the terms of the new constitution would only be able to exercise their power (*pouvoir commettant*) in the confines of the constituted order; any changes to the constituted order could only be

[24] Quoted in Rubinelli, "Beyond Sovereignty," 11.

[25] Here Rubinelli's analysis reminds us the extent to which Sieyès' political theory is rooted in his political economy – most particularly considerations about the division of labor. See also W. Sewell, *A Rhetoric of Bourgeois Revolution: The Abbé Sieyès and What is the Third Estate?* (Durham, NC: Duke University Press, 1994).

[26] Quoted in Rubinelli, "Beyond Sovereignty," 6.

undertaken with the approval of the people, which retained in all instances *pouvoir constituant*. By Sieyès' lights, this system avoided the perils of popular sovereignty while still maintaining the equality of all citizens and the indivisibility of the national will.

Though Sieyès' justification of the legitimacy of representation eventually carried the day, Sieyès' reconceptualization of sovereignty under the rubric of *pouvoir constituant* was not similarly successful. Nevertheless, Sieyès refused to revert to the idiom of sovereignty. Indeed, writing in 1795, he diagnosed the excesses of the Terror as deriving from the Jacobins' conceptual confusion of constituting power and constituted power. Where the idea of popular sovereignty prevails, he wrote, "passions are too present ... votes are not confined to a small sphere, through a limited task, the constituent power is confused with the constituted power."[27]

Since Sieyès' position on the problematic nature of the notion of sovereignty remained constant throughout his long career, we might wonder why Sieyès has often been taken as one of its champions. Presumably, the answer to this question has several vectors. There is little doubt, though, that one of them is the interpretation of Carl Schmitt, whose attention to Sieyès contributed to the renaissance of interest in him in the twentieth century.

In the third essay of *Political Theology* – the one that begins with "all the major concepts of the modern theory of the state are secularized theological concepts" – Schmitt offers a characteristically elliptical account of the development of the idea of sovereignty in order to link it to a theological heritage.[28] He begins with Rousseau's adage, "Imitate the immutable decrees of the divinity."[29] Schmitt clearly intends to refer to the discourse of the necessarily general nature of God's willing – in the next paragraph, he quotes Descartes in a letter to Mersenne: "It is God who established these laws in nature just as a king establishes laws in his kingdom." This is meant to be an exercise in what Schmitt calls a "sociology of concepts": "the historical-political status of the monarchy," Schmitt suggests, can be "shown to correspond to the general state of consciousness that was characteristic of western Europeans at that time."[30] Writes Schmitt, "the presupposition of this kind of sociology of juristic concepts is ... a consistent thinking that is pushed into metaphysics and theology."[31]

27 *Ibid.*, 14.
28 This topic is treated in more detailed and historical fashion in Riley, *General Will.*
29 Quoted in Schmitt, *Political Theology*, 46.
30 Schmitt, *Political Theology*, 45.
31 *Ibid.*, 46.

Schmitt writes of the changes in political theory wrought by the influence of the "consistency of exclusively scientific thinking":

> The general validity of a legal prescription has become identified with the lawfulness of nature, which applies without exception. The sovereign, who in the deistic view of the world, even if conceived as residing outside the world, had remained the engineer of the great machine, has been radically pushed aside. The machine now runs by itself. The metaphysical proposition that God enunciates only general and not particular declarations of will governed the metaphysics of Leibniz and Nicolas Malebranche. The general will of Rousseau became identical with the will of the sovereign, but simultaneously the concept of the general also contained a quantitative determination with regard to its subject, which means that the people became the sovereign. The decisionistic and personalistic element in the concept of sovereignty was thus lost. The will of the people is always good. "The people are always virtuous." Said Emmanuel Sieyès, "In whatever manner a nation expresses its wishes, it is enough that it wishes; all forms are good but its will is always the supreme law."[32]

Schmitt here identifies the *malebranchiste* position on the *volonté générale* as bringing about the *deus absconditus* of deism. In Schmitt's narrative, Rousseau's general will marks the entry of a "quantitative decision with regard to its subject." That is to say, because "the people became the sovereign," the general will was no longer unitary and "personalistic."[33]

This seems not to be fair. Though it is unclear what exactly Schmitt means by "personalistic," Rousseau – borrowing the rhetoric of the original controversy between Malebranche and the Jansenists – in several different places writes that when the general will degenerates into multiplicity, it is no longer either the general will or sovereign.[34] Such a position would be more justly associated with Sieyès, who explicitly denied the idea that there could be "unitary" general will – there was just

[32] *Ibid.*, 48.

[33] Schmitt never clarifies why he thinks the sovereign must be "unitary" and "personalistic" – indeed, it is never wholly clear exactly how he defines either of these terms. The obvious explanation, considering his other positions, is that for him the locus of sovereignty properly conceived is in a single decision maker simply because the paradigm of sovereignty is God.

[34] For instance: "When the people of Athens, for instance, elected or deposed their chiefs, decreed honours to one, imposed penalties on another, and by multitudes of particular decrees exercised indiscriminately all the functions of government, the people no longer had any general will properly so called; they no longer acted as a sovereign power, but as magistrates." J.-J. Rousseau, *Du Contrat Social, ou Principes du Droit Politique* (Lyon: J. B. Delamollière, 1790), 52.

the aggregate of singular wills. One of his manuscripts arguing against the Jacobins reads, "Those who conceive [the aim of the political order] as an abstract thing, as public happiness belonging to no one, are wrong . . . the common 'wealth' is for them an abstract being, a superstitious idol to which they offer sacrificial victims."[35]

Schmitt seems to suggest that with this shift away from the unitary, personalistic sovereign (in which a "quantitative determination" was involved) was associated, in Sieyès, with a shift to voluntarism, such that "In whatever manner a nation expresses its wishes, it is enough that it wishes." This is, as we have seen, not true to Sieyès' thinking. Indeed, Sieyès' concept of constituent power was designed precisely to avoid the vagaries implied by this position.

This is not the only place at which Schmitt twists his sources toward a voluntarist understanding of sovereignty. At the very beginning of his account of the history of sovereignty – just after he quotes Rousseau's "Imitate the immutable decrees of the divinity" – he quotes Émile Boutmy: "Rousseau applies to the sovereign the idea that the philosophes hold of God: He may do anything that he wills but he may not will evil."[36] This appears, as Schmitt quotes it, to be an ambiguous pronouncement: does Boutmy read Rousseau to hold that the general will cannot will evil because whatever the general will holds is, by definition, good? Or does he rather hold that the general will – whatever exactly it is – holds unerringly to the good? But in the original, Boutmy is not ambiguous at all: his sentence ends, " . . . he may not will evil because evil is contrary to his nature."[37] This is, of course, in keeping with the *malebranchiste* position on the way God was constrained by his nature.

That is to say, Schmitt truncates Boutmy to (in the context of his history of the development of the notion of sovereignty) give an impression that Boutmy had no intention of giving: that the "secularization" of the idea of sovereignty – which was apparently, for Schmitt, the banner case of an idea of the "modern theory of the state" that was merely a "secularized" theological idea – was bound up with a voluntarist model of sovereignty. In other words, Schmitt misreads his sources – both his primary sources, like

[35] Quoted in Rubinelli, "Beyond Sovereignty," 14.

[36] Quoted in Schmitt, *Political Theology*, 46.

[37] "Rousseau applique au souverain l'idée que les philosophes se font de Dieu: il peut tout ce qu'il veut; mais il ne peut vouloir le mal parce que le mal est contraire à sa nature." E. Boutmy, "La déclaration des droits de l'homme et du citoyen et M. Jellinek," *Annales des sciences politique* 4 (1902), 418.

Sieyès and Rousseau, and his secondary sources, like Boutmy – to find his preferred model of sovereignty in them.

5 Conclusion: Schmitt, Sovereignty, and Secularization

It is not terribly surprising that Schmitt was not always the most faithful of readers – he hardly kept his normative commitments under wraps. But the particular contours of Schmitt's failures of reading cast light on the question I began by posing: how Schmitt's intellectual-historical claim, in *Political Theology* ("All the major concepts of the modern theory of the state are secularized theological concepts"), is related to the book's other oft-cited claim – what I called the definitional claim, "Sovereign is he who decides the exception." For in order for Schmitt's intellectual-historical claim to hold, politics must run parallel to theology and the king must be conceived on analogy with god. Immediately after he writes, "All significant concepts of the modern theory of the state are secularized theological concepts," he continues,

> Not only because of their historical development – in which they were transferred from theology to the theory of the state, whereby, for example, the omnipotent God became the omnipotent lawgiver – but also because of their systematic structure . . . The exception in jurisprudence is analogous to the miracle in theology. Only by being aware of this analogy can we appreciate the manner in which the philosophical ideas of the state developed in the last centuries.[38]

And later in the essay, when Schmitt explains in some detail what he means in saying that political theology amounts to a "sociology of juristic concepts," he explains, "The metaphysical image that a definite epoch forges of the world has the same structure as what the world immediately understands to be appropriate as a form of its political organization."[39] Schmitt's model, whereby what he calls "concepts" are transferred from theology to political theory, depends on theology and political theory running as structurally analogous and parallel – which is to say non-intersecting – systems of thought.

What is interesting is that, though sovereignty seems to be the concept that most interests Schmitt, vis-à-vis the "sociology of juristic concepts," it is also a concept for which his fundamental claim seems to be untenable. As we have already seen, a careful reading of either Malebranche or

[38] Schmitt, *Political Theology*, 36.
[39] *Ibid.*, 45–46.

Sieyès will not sustain the geometry required by Schmitt's notion of "secularization." Malebranche's model of sovereignty enfolds both divine and human sovereignty into the order of perfections that inevitably determine God's will and ought to determine humans' will. Divine and human sovereignty alike are organized under the abstraction of what Malebranche calls "the order of perfections"; they are not analogous to each other so much as two exemplifications of the same excellences. And Sieyès' demarcation of constituting and constituted power is in fact meant to protect against a human sovereignty that too closely parallels divine sovereignty.

Considering that Schmitt systematically misreads his sources, it is tempting to construct the definitional claim of *Political Theology* as conceptually "downstream" from the intellectual historical claim. Schmitt misinterprets Sieyès as espousing a voluntarist model of political sovereignty so that he maintains the conceptual homology between theology and politics – and casts politics as a kind of pale shadow of theology. For if what I have had to say about the structure of the sort of "transfer" Schmitt envisions between theology and political theory is correct, his preferred model of sovereignty would seem to be a necessary entailment. The sovereign who transcends the system and can suspend it at will, completely unconstrained, would seem to be the only theological model of sovereignty that can be detached completely from theology and rearticulated in political theory. As we have seen, Malebranche's theologically inflected politics (whereby human sovereignty is held to standards associated with divine sovereignty) is actually opposed to what Schmitt calls political theology. What model of human sovereignty could be analogous to the sort of divine sovereignty that is necessarily determined by the perfections that constitute God's very nature?

We have already discussed the Westphalian sense of secularization that Schmitt invokes in the beginning of *Political Theology* as pertaining to a transfer of lands from the control of the church to the control of the state; I have made the case that we can use the concept of "transfer secularization" more broadly, so long as we are careful to specify what is being transferred and how – and recognize that (Schmitt's language notwithstanding) the sort of transfer that is being described is neither unidirectional nor inevitable but rather a function of the way that discursive patterns in one field can shape discursive patterns in others.

But of course the Westphalian sense of secularization is not the only sense in which the term "secularization" is deployed. Schmitt wrote *Political Theology* as a contribution for Max Weber's *Festschrift*; so it is,

I think, no accident that in *Political Theology* Schmitt provides a narration of developments in early modern thought that reads as a tangle of Weberian secularization narratives. An articulation of Weber's disenchantment makes quite an explicit appearance in the essay. Schmitt writes,

> To the conception of God in the seventeenth and eighteenth centuries belongs the idea of his transcendence vis-à-vis the world, just as to that period's philosophy of state belongs the notion of the transcendence of the sovereign vis-à-vis the state. Everything in the nineteenth century was increasingly governed by conceptions of immanence.[40]

In the mode of the classic predictive secularization hypothesis *avant la lettre*, he concludes this line of thought, "The main line of development will undoubtedly unfold as follows: Conceptions of transcendence will no longer be credible to most educated people." Schmitt – presumably because he considers the voluntarist model of sovereignty amorphously "theological" – correlates a decline in the plausibility of religious systems and a decline in the plausibility of his preferred form of sovereignty.

But the Weberian modernization narrative that I am more interested in is that associated with "functional differentiation" – the increasing separation of various "spheres" of social life, often applied vis-à-vis the separation of "religion" from "politics." For it would seem that the coherence of a particular case of transfer-secularization is dependent on some form of functional differentiation obtaining: in order for the topography of the concept of human sovereignty to correspond exactly to that of divine sovereignty, human and divine sovereignty must be completely distinct from each other. Or again: the role that the divine sovereign plays in the one system of thought, the human sovereign occupies in the other, such that a conception of "sovereignty" (at least theoretically) could be transferred between them. For the human sovereign to be as a god in political theory, though, God proper has to be absent from political theory. From this perspective, Schmitt's thinking on the subject would be better termed not political theology but rather political atheology – or better, political *idolatry*. Schmitt's sovereign is nothing if not an image of the sovereign he considers the true sovereign.

[40] *Ibid.*, 49.

INDEX

For EU product safety concerns, contact us at Calle de José Abascal, 56–1°,
28003 Madrid, Spain or eugpsr@cambridge.org.

www.ingramcontent.com/pod-product-compliance
Lightning Source LLC
LaVergne TN
LVHW011812200926
848484LV00005B/1166